Literary Allusion in *Harry Potter*

Literary Allusion in Harry Potter builds on the world-wide enthusiasm for J. K. Rowling's series in order to introduce its readers to some of the great works of literature on which Rowling draws. *Harry Potter*'s narrative techniques are rooted in the western literary tradition and its allusiveness provides insight into Rowling's fictional world. Each chapter of *Literary Allusion in Harry Potter* consists of an in-depth discussion of the intersection between *Harry Potter* and a canonical literary work, such as the plays of Shakespeare, the poetry of Homer, Ovid, the *Gawain*-poet, Chaucer, Milton and Tennyson, and the novels of Austen, Hardy and Dickens. This approach aims to transform the reader's understanding of Rowling's literary achievement as well as to encourage the discovery of works with which they may be less familiar. The aim of this book is to delight *Potter* fans with a new perspective on their favourite series while harnessing that enthusiasm to increase their wider appreciation of literature.

Beatrice Groves is a Research Lecturer and tutor at Trinity College, Oxford. In addition to teaching at Oxford University, she has published two books on allusion in Renaissance literature and numerous articles in peer-reviewed journals on the process of literary allusion (including a prize-winning essay in 2013).

Literary Allusion in *Harry Potter*

Beatrice Groves

Routledge
Taylor & Francis Group

LONDON AND NEW YORK

First published 2017
by Routledge
2 Park Square, Milton Park, Abingdon, Oxon OX14 4RN

and by Routledge
711 Third Avenue, New York, NY 10017

Routledge is an imprint of the Taylor & Francis Group, an informa business

British Library Cataloguing-in-Publication Data
A catalogue record for this book is available from the British Library

Library of Congress Cataloging-in-Publication Data
Names: Groves, Beatrice, 1978- author.
Title: Literary allusion in Harry Potter / Beatrice Groves.
Description: Abingdon, Oxon : New York : Routledge, 2017. | Includes
    bibliographical references and index.
Identifiers: LCCN 2016056454| ISBN 9781138284661
    (hardback : alk. paper) | ISBN 9781138284678 (pbk. : alk. paper) |
    ISBN 9781351978729 (epub) | ISBN 9781351978712
    (mobi/kindle)
Subjects: LCSH: Rowling, J. K.—Criticism and interpretation. |
    Children—Books and reading—English-speaking countries. |
    Children's stories, English—History and criticism. | Fantasy fiction,
    English—History and criticism. | Rowling, J. K.—Characters—
    Harry Potter. | Potter, Harry (Fictitious character) | Allusions in
    literature. | Wizards in literature. | Magic in literature.
Classification: LCC PR6068.O93 Z6785 2017 | DDC 823/.914—dc23
LC record available at https://lccn.loc.gov/2016056454

ISBN: 978-1-138-28466-1 (hbk)
ISBN: 978-1-138-28467-8 (pbk)
ISBN: 978-1-315-26933-7 (ebk)

Typeset in Bembo
by Swales & Willis, Exeter, Devon, UK

For Michael and Edward

Contents

Acknowledgements

This book began when Caoimhe Treanor gave me the *Harry Potter* books and it has been supported along the way by the friendship and erudition of many: Odette Christie de Rivas, Maud Hurley, Felicity James, Timothy Knapman, Helen Lavy, Arabella Milbank, Jolyon Mitchell, Esme Neale, Pratibha Rai, Rachel Wade and, in particular, William Sartain, whose encyclopaedic knowledge of *Harry Potter* first illustrated to me the enduring enthusiasm of the next generation.

Many thanks are due to those – Peter Kemp, Cathy Groves, Jessica Reid, Barnaby Taylor and Brian Davies – who so kindly read and commented on the manuscript. My gratitude is due likewise to its anonymous readers: both their enthusiasm and their corrections were much appreciated. I am also grateful to my editors at Routledge – Polly Dodson and Zoe Meyer – with whom it has been a pleasure to work.

Particular thanks are due to Jessica Reid, to whom I owe much besides, but who has been so generous with her time and expertise during this project.

My greatest debt of gratitude is to my family: Peter, Michael, Edward, Jane, Peter and James. This book is dedicated to my sons, with love.

Note on texts used

This book references the British editions of *Harry Potter*, published by Bloomsbury. American readers will notice, therefore, that the first book is referred to as *Philosopher's Stone* (rather than *Sorcerer's Stone*) in keeping with Rowling's first conception. The page numbers refer to the Bloomsbury editions but chapter numbers (in addition to page numbers) are included for each citation, so readers should be able to locate quotations in whatever edition they are using.

In *Harry Potter* fandom 'canon' is a term that covers not only the content of the original novels but also all Rowling's related works – *Tales of Beedle the Bard*, *Quidditch Through the Ages* and *Fantastic Beasts and Where to Find Them* (both the book and the film screenplays) – as well as her interviews, Twitter account, *Pottermore* and *Harry Potter and the Cursed Child* (a play-script written by Jack Thorne with Rowling's input and authorisation). In literary studies, however, it is only the text itself – in this case the seven *Harry Potter* novels – that has 'canonical' authority. This book will keep that distinction. Rowling's commentary, however, forms an illuminating context for her work and *Literary Allusion in Harry Potter* quotes extensively from her interviews (and includes relevant material from the other sources listed above).

Rowling's Twitter account, which is cited by date of entry, can be found at https://twitter.com/jk_rowling

All biblical references are to the King James translation (1611), as this is the translation used for biblical quotation within *Harry Potter*.

All classical references are to the Loeb editions (widely available, and also visible on Rowling's desk on her new website, http://www.jkrowling.com/opinion/); all other translations are my own.

All dictionary references are to the second edition of the *Oxford English Dictionary* (20 vols, Oxford, 1989).

Introduction

If it is the case that people are moving from Harry to other books then nothing could make me prouder.

(Rowling, 2005d)

The portals of *Harry Potter*, such as Platform 9¾, take the hero from the mundane to the magical world, and they also function as metaphors for the way in which literature itself transports its readers. Rowling has spoken of the Wood between Worlds (in C. S. Lewis's *The Magician's Nephew*) as a place where 'you can jump into the different pools to access the different worlds. And that, for me, was always a metaphor for a *library* . . . that, for me, is what literature should be' (2005g). Rowling believes in the bewitching power of reading: 'there is a kind of magic that happens when you pick up a wonderful book and it lives with you for the rest of your life' (1999f). This transportive pleasure – the world-creating, paradigm-shifting nature of great literature – means that *Harry Potter* (a way into reading for so many people) is itself a portal. It is not simply a path into the world of Hogwarts but, like Rowling's 'library' of pools in the Wood between Worlds, a gateway into the world of literature itself.

Harry Potter is rooted in the Western literary tradition and its allusions to classic texts deepen its treatment of the 'eternal human predicaments of love, death and the pursuit of happiness' (Rowling, 2007j). Intertextuality and magic are ideas that complement each other for, as Sarah Annes Brown has argued, allusive patterning can 'mirror and reinforce . . . magical subject matter' (2012, p.2). *Harry Potter* imagines two different types of reality existing alongside each other as it creates a Wizarding realm parallel to, and sometimes intertwined with, the Muggle world. For the reader of a fiction, the awareness of an allusion brings a momentary incursion of the 'real' world into the fictional. As Brown notes, such a shift in perspective is particularly effective for a book about magic, for just as such magical worlds 'take their place in the complex, ever-branching multiverse, so, in our real world, do books depend upon each other in an intertextual web . . . an allusion is effected by a similar transgression of the barrier separating the enclosed world of the text' (2012, p.2). This book listens to *Harry Potter*'s allusions. It argues for the enriched understanding of the text that is created by listening to its 'conversation' with writers from Homer, Aeschylus and Ovid to Jane Austen and Victorian novelists.

Rowling has spoken of reading as a 'sort of conversation' – a meeting of minds between author and reader:

> My readers have to work with me to create the experience. They have to bring their imaginations to the story . . . together, as author and reader, we have both created the story. Reading is not like watching a film or television, because we both see the same images and that's a very passive experience. Reading is an active experience because you bring your imagination to it. When you do that, the reader and the author are having sort of a conversation. In a good story, the reader is very aware of what's in the author's mind. That's what makes reading magical.
>
> (1999g)

This readerly awareness of 'what's in the author's mind' is never closer than on finding an allusion. Recognising an allusion is like eavesdropping on a conversation; it is a moment when a reader identifies with the writer as a reader like themselves.

Rowling has pointed her readers towards Thomas Hardy's *The Mayor of Casterbridge*, by explaining that this book is the source of Dumbledore's name (2000n). But if you go and read the sentence in which dumbledores are mentioned, you will find that it also contains the name of another of *Harry Potter*'s favourite characters. In *The Mayor of Casterbridge* Elizabeth-Jane has to 'unlearn' her native dialect in order to please her new father and appear more genteel. She learns not to call bumblebees by their country name of 'dumbledores', and 'when she had not slept she did not quaintly tell the servants next morning that she had been "hag-rid", but that she had "suffered from indigestion"' (1985 [1886], p.200).[1] It feels like a little gift left unmentioned by Rowling for those who choose to retrace her steps.

Harry Potter's playful use of allusion is pleasurable for the reader – spotting allusions is fun, it makes the reader think, and rewards that thought – and it is clear that Rowling also enjoys putting her work in dialogue with other texts. She started reading the classics when she was young (2000n) and has spoken of the way that 'it was through reading that I realised I wasn't alone on all sorts of levels' (2005g). This companionship within the written word is something that Rowling loves to share with her readers: 'I'm never bored by meeting people who lived at Hogwarts with me. This is the miracle of literature to which no other medium can compare – that the writer and the reader's imaginations must join together to make the story' (2010c). This book explores this literary companionship within *Harry Potter*. It reveals the way in which exploring allusion can deepen our understanding of and appreciation for the series, but also aims to draw the reader into their own dialogue with great literary texts.

Harry Potter has well-researched links with earlier children's literature. Its names, for example, often recall classics of the genre. Trelawney and 'Captain'

Flint, for instance, can both be found in Robert Louis Stevenson's *Treasure Island* (where Flint is the captain of a pirate ship rather than a Quidditch team) and both the name and fate of Cedric Diggory recall Digory Kirke (from Lewis' *The Magician's Nephew*) who is likewise an upright young man who is tricked into touching a Portkey. *Harry Potter*'s debt to classic children's and fantasy writing, in particular that of C. S. Lewis, J. R. R. Tolkien, Elizabeth Goudge, Ursula Le Guin, Diana Wynne Jones, E. Nesbit and traditional boarding school novels,is well known (see, for example: Lurie, 1999; Nel, 2001; Steege, 2002; Smith, 2003; Carey, 2003; Caselli, 2004; Stouffer, 2007; Andrade, 2008; Villaluz, 2008; Prinzi, 2009; Granger, 2009; Garrett, 2010; Saxena, 2012; Steveker, 2015). Fantasy and children's literature are part of *Harry Potter*'s 'generic mosaic' (Alton, 2003, p.159) but this book explores its less obvious debts to canonical, adult literature. This is an under-explored critical area, with only two in-depth studies – John Granger's *Harry Potter's Bookshelf* (2009) and Richard A. Spencer's *Harry Potter and the Classical World* (2015) – even though, as Spencer argues, 'much of the richness, distinctiveness, and attraction of the novels derive from the force and uniqueness of the preceding tradition and [Rowling's] variations on it' (p.8). Allusions 'establish a special kind of rapport between author and reader' (Machacek, 2007, p.531) and *Harry Potter* builds on the rapport created through its generic connections with the common culture of childhood reading – of fairy tales, Lewis, Tolkien, Enid Blyton and Roald Dahl – to take its readers forward into its more subtle connections with the great works of the Western literary tradition.

Rowling plays Dumbledore to our Hermione: she leaves us books to read, willing us to read them carefully with the implicit promise that they will teach us more than we might at first have thought they could. Dumbledore (who shares much with his creator[2]) favours the Socratic method of teaching (Spencer, 2015, p.64); he wants his students to find things out for themselves. By explaining the Mirror of Erised and returning the invisibility cloak he provides the trio with all the tools they need to face their first adventure. Dumbledore takes study seriously – Rowling has described him as 'an academic' (Twitter, 27 Oct 2015) – and he leaves Hermione a book to ponder, just as Rowling does for her readers. The internal patterning of self-referencing within the series as a whole trains its readers in an attentive, literary mode of reading that is nourishing in and of itself (see Chapters 1 and 8); but it also leads *Harry Potter*'s readers out into some of the greatest works of the Western canon.

Allusion comes naturally to Rowling. It began early in life (one of her teachers has noted the creative use she made of Golding's *Lord of the Flies* in a school composition [Smith, 2002, p.56]) and has continued post-*Potter*. (Her novel *Silkworm*, for example, has a quotation from an often heroically obscure early modern play at the start of each chapter.) Rowling uses literary quotation extensively in interview and on Twitter. She has referenced Graham Greene on the nature of writers and the nature of faith (2006b; 2007g). She has quoted Dorothy L. Sayers on detective fiction, Maya Angelou on feminism and F. Scott Fitzgerald on class (2005b; Twitter, 17 Sept 2015; 2012d). She has quoted Austen to describe her emotions and Stella Gibbons to describe her emotions about Austen (1999b; 2000c). And she has quoted Virginia Woolf on how well Austen writes (2014b). As Marjorie Garber notes, 'quotation creates authority by its very nature and form. It instates an authority elsewhere, and, at the same time, it imparts that authority, temporarily, to the speaker or the writer' (2003, p.2). Quotation is an interesting rhetorical device: at once self-effacing and authoritative, simultaneously displaying one's own knowledge and deference to the knowledge of another. It is one of Rowling's most characteristic devices in her public discourse and, in *Deathly Hallows*, it also finally appears within *Harry Potter* itself (both in the novel's epigraphs and in the biblical quotations on the tombstones in Godric's Hollow).

Deathly Hallows has two epigraphs: the first quotation is from Aeschylus' *Libation Bearers* and the second from William Penn's *More Fruits of Solitude* (for more on these see Chapters 1 and 4). The publication of *Deathly Hallows* finally allowed Rowling to be open about things she had spent seventeen years keeping under wraps; and these quotations are the first explicit acknowledgement of the literary underpinning of *Harry Potter*. Rowling has been cautious about revealing this side of her work in general – she wants her readers to find it out for themselves – but when asked if such literary devices might be a little complicated for young readers she came close to admitting that, for her, allusion is a fundamental part of the pleasure of reading: 'if they love them enough, they'll reread them. And then it will be like finding another sweet in the bag' (cited in Nel, 2001, p.52).

Although Rowling is generally chary of acknowledging or claiming influence, she has noted Homer, Chaucer, Shakespeare and Austen as writers whose texts have left traces in her own. *Harry Potter* also has some fairly explicit references to classic works of literature. The clearest instance is the naming of Filch's deeply unpleasant cat after Austen's superbly villainous Mrs Norris (in *Mansfield Park*). But there are many others: McGonagall is named after a 'very, very, very bad Scottish poet' (Rowling, 1999e); the Wizarding band The Weird Sisters share their name with the witches in *Macbeth* and Durmstrang (the school that is a little over-keen on the dark arts) puns on Germanic *Sturm und Drang* novels (Colbert, 2007, pp.83–6). Most of *Harry Potter*'s allusions, however, are not verbal parallels. Rowling's 'passion is story' (2012e) and it is at the level of story – similarities of situation, character and action – that most allusions occur.

One such example is the link between the antagonistic garden conversation between Scrimgeour and Harry in *Half-Blood Prince* and that between Lady Catherine de Burgh and Elizabeth Bennet in Austen's *Pride and Prejudice*. Lady Catherine (who has been listening to rumours) wants to extort from Elizabeth a promise that she will not marry Mr Darcy; and Scrimgeour (acting on rumours that Harry is the Chosen One) wants to extort from Harry a promise that he will behave as Scrimgeour wishes. In both novels a person of high status calls unexpectedly on the protagonist and suggests that they leave the family circle and join them for a walk in the garden. Scrimgeour asks to 'take a turn' with Harry around the Weasleys' 'charming garden' (Chap 16, p.321); Lady Catherine, likewise, requests, "'Miss Bennet, there seemed to be a prettyish kind of a little wilderness on one side of your lawn. I should be glad to take a turn in it, if you will favour me with your company'" (Austen, 1995 [1813], p.284). Both want to take a turn in the garden so that the young protagonist will be alone with them, and will be more likely to submit to their wishes. Lady Catherine and Scrimgeour's bullying tactics, however, meet with unexpected resistance. While the older characters, in both scenes, enjoy a high social status, the rhetorical strength lies with the younger character. Elizabeth has some fabulous ripostes in this scene and her discourtesy to a person of rank (and the view she expresses that she is Mr Darcy's social equal) would have seemed strikingly radical at the time they were written – and she still reads as startlingly, wonderfully, rude today. The scene in *Half-Blood Prince* distils the effect of Austen's and both illustrate the independence, truthfulness and courage of their protagonist.

In another example, Harry – depressed in his isolation at Privet Drive early in *Chamber of Secrets* and feeling deserted by his friends after Dobby has stolen his letters – has a dream that he is displayed, starving, like an animal in a cage. This dream is based on the caged, starving protagonist of Kafka's 'A Hunger Artist' (1922).[3] Kafka's protagonist has turned self-starvation into an art-form in which his once enthusiastic audience have lost interest. Harry's dream reflects his fear of abandonment and draws on Kafka's caged hunger artist, the epitome of such isolation. *Harry Potter* may even be responding to the loneliness of the hunger artist in a deeper way. The starving artist can be read as Kafka's comment on the isolation of authorship; a brutal portrayal of an author's uneasy dependence on their audience. Christopher Ricks has written of the way that allusion embodies 'the comfort of company . . . and solidarity' (2002, pp.196–7) for an author. Allusion provides proof that a text has been read and remembered; *Harry Potter*'s allusion to Kafka, therefore, provides proof of an audience for a text that appears to cry out for companionship.

Allusion is a companionable idiom, and it is a companionableness that Rowling relishes. *Harry Potter*'s Porlocks, for example (magical creatures that turn up in both *Order of the Phoenix* and the 2001 spin-off book *Fabulous Beasts and Where to Find Them*) reference Samuel Taylor Coleridge's explanation of his failure to complete his visionary poem 'Kubla Kahn'. Coleridge claimed that he was interrupted by 'a person from Porlock'. The poet Stevie Smith has suggested that in all likelihood Coleridge's excuse was an invention to explain away his writer's block and 'Porlock' has become short-hand for this phenomenon. (Douglas Adams, who suffered titanic struggles with writer's block, made 'a person from Porlock' a central plot-device in his novel *Dirk Gently's Detective Agency*.) Rowling has taken a spirited approach to writer's block on Twitter: 'I haven't had it since 1998. I wrote through it. That showed it who was boss' (8 Feb 2015). Her Porlocks, likewise, create a companionable allusion to Coleridge's writer's block and perform a service to other writers by transforming it into a cute, furry animal, incapable of menace.

Harry Potter follows in Coleridge's footsteps in more ways than one here, for Coleridge was himself a deeply allusive and companionable author. Coleridge wrote as part of a circle of friends who composed together and who used allusion to each other's works to carry over their friendship into the written form. One of Coleridge's more famous short poems – 'This Lime-tree bower my prison' (1797) – recounts his imagining of a walk taken by his friends in which he was unable to join. In one verse he refers explicitly to his friend Charles Lamb:

> Yes! they wander on
> In gladness all; but thou, methinks, most glad,
> My gentle-hearted Charles! for thou hast pined
> And hungered after Nature, many a year,
> In the great City pent, winning thy way
> With sad yet patient soul, through evil and pain
> And strange calamity!
>
> (1863, p.243)

Behind these lines lie a reference to one of the most tragic events in Coleridge's friendship circle, and one that bears a striking connection with Dumbledore's own family history. In September 1796 Charles' sister Mary Lamb killed their mother in a manic fit. The court verdict was 'Lunacy', which (as it designated a fit of madness rather than an incurable mental condition) meant that Mary could be cared for within the family rather than imprisoned, as long as her brothers would vouch to look after her for the rest of her life. John Lamb refused to be burdened with caring for Mary, but Charles dedicated his life to looking after her.

Coleridge, and many later critics, treats Charles rather in the way that Elphias Doge treats Dumbledore. They cast his matricidal, mentally ill sister as an encumbrance that stifled his genius: 'the "cross" the Christ-like Charles was burdened with' (James, 2008, p.212). As Felicity James has argued, however, even well-meaning, sympathetic friends can rewrite you in their own image and Lamb seems in reality to have been much more of an Aberforth than an Albus. He loved his sister and saw her not as a burden but as an inspirer and facilitator of his work (James, 2008, p.92). Like Aberforth, Charles was none too impressed with the sweetly sad picture painted by others. He responded to Coleridge's poetic description of him as 'gentle-hearted Charles' by asking him not to 'make me ridiculous any more by terming me gentle-hearted in print . . . please to blot out *gentle hearted*, and substitute drunken dog, ragged-head, seld-shaven, odd-ey'd, stuttering, or any other epithet which truly and properly belongs to the Gentleman in question' (quoted in James, 2008, p.85). Charles' Aberforth-like response to Coleridge's attempt to write him into the role of victim is attractive for its lack of self-pity but also for its implied defence of his sister ('don't think I'm a martyr because I care for her'). The modern critical rehabilitation of Mary Lamb herself echoes the way that when the reader finally meets Ariana at the climax of *Deathly Hallows* she is not the 'burden' of which Doge had spoken, but Harry's guide into Hogwarts and an enabler of the victory against Voldemort.

Ariana's name is a version of the Greek name Ariadne (as in Joseph Haydn's cantata *Arianna a Naxos*). Like the Ariadne of myth who enables Theseus to escape from the labyrinth with her spool of thread, Ariana likewise guides the hero on his way. Ariana's name recalls the sadness of Ariadne's fate (she is abandoned by Theseus on the island of Naxos) but also the way that Ariadne found a simple solution (a spool of thread) to the seemingly impossible puzzle of the Minotaur's labyrinth. The events of Ariana's death split her brothers apart but, in death, she unites them. Shira Wolosky has argued that the portraits of *Harry Potter* 'act as windows between the worlds of death and life . . . above all, as works of art they show the power of the imagination to create and shape reality' (2010, p.21). This is nowhere clearer than with Ariana's portrait, and the passageway down which she takes Harry both literally and metaphorically unites Albus' and Aberforth's worlds.

HARRY POTTER'S INTERNAL REFERENCES

Harry Potter also contains a complex network of internal references (see, for example: Lee, 2011; Granger, 2015; Spencer, 2015, pp.76–7, 275–84) in which spells, characters and events from earlier novels recur later in the series with a deepening significance. Sirius Black, for example, is merely mentioned in passing in *Philosopher's Stone* but he will go on to become one of the most loved and complex of Harry's many father-figures. The surprising number of students who turn up to the dissident gathering at the Hog's Head in *Phoenix* is recalled at the climax of *Deathly Hallows* when unexpected numbers flood back through the same pub to join the Battle of Hogwarts. Harry's invisibility cloak grows from an enjoyable aid to rule-breaking in the early books to a profoundly magical Deathly Hallow by the climax of the series. Seamus' seemingly ghoulish question about the Bloody Baron at the opening of the series – '"How did he get covered in blood?"' (*Philosopher's Stone*, Chap 7, p.93) – turns out by its conclusion to have been highly pertinent.

Through such recapitulations *Harry Potter* creates a densely layered, self-referential world and they cluster, in particular, around Snape. Harry's impression that Snape can read his mind in the early novels is revealed as literally true in *Phoenix* while in his first class Snape mentions the bezoar (which will enable Harry to save Ron's life in *Half-Blood Prince*) and speaks of his ability to stopper death (a crucial clue to his later actions). These revisited moments within Harry and Snape's relationship point to the way that the reader will themselves have to rethink all Harry and Snape's interactions in the light of what is revealed in *Deathly Hallows*. Snape's final action in the series is the same as his first: to look into Harry's eyes. In *Philosopher's Stone* Harry misinterpreted this look, and thought that it triggered the pain in his scar, but in *Deathly Hallows* the reader finally understands who Snape is seeking as he gazes into Harry's eyes.

Many literary texts use this tactic of introducing images or ideas that gain in significance throughout the work. In classical music this is called a 'motif' – a tune that reappears throughout the piece accruing complexity, prescience or nostalgia as it does so. Motifs tie a work together – recalling their birth in their growth and their growth in their ending – but in literature they can also reveal, and deepen, aspects of the plot. In Shakespeare's *Coriolanus*, for example, the frequent fire imagery complements the protagonist's 'choleric' (literally 'fiery') nature, but also prefigures his threat to burn Rome to the ground at the end of the play.

Each *Harry Potter* novel has new spells, characters or concepts that are introduced at the beginning of the book but whose true significance is not revealed until the end. When Doge's obituary at the beginning of *Deathly Hallows*, for example, claims that Dumbledore was always working '*for the greater good*' (Chap 2, p.24), what seems like a banal commendatory cliché will accrue unexpected significance as the novel progresses. There are also structural patterns and frequently recurring events and objects – such as severed heads, underground battles, tiaras and goats – that accumulate meaning across the series. This patterning gives the novels an enjoyable knowingness: in each book, for example, the reader is primed to look out for why the Defence against the Dark Arts teacher will have to leave that year. But it is also a literary technique that can be used to build depth and complexity and in a linked series of texts, such as *Harry Potter*, recurring motifs can develop in significance.

This happens, likewise, in classic examples of linked writing, such as Edmund Spenser's *Faerie Queene* (1596). This poem, like *Harry Potter*, is a seven-part epic set in a magical world.[4] In Spenser evil constantly mirrors good and doppelgängers (such as Una and Duessa and the false and true Florimell) mean that it can be increasingly difficult to tell whose side the reader should be on. Eyes, however, always tell the truth in Spenser's world, as they do in Rowling's: Archimago – the first 'false friend' of the poem – keeps his eyes fixed on the ground when he meets the hero (2001 [1590/6], 1.1.29). From that point on the reader knows to search for the truth in characters' eyes: a great lady, who 'seemd a woman of great bountihead,/ And of rare beautie' gives herself away with her 'wanton eyes' (3.1.41), while a trustworthy woman has eyes that are 'stedfast still' (4.10.49). One character addresses an unknown fisherman as a 'good man' but the reader knows better for he has 'deceiptfull eyes' (3.8.24). Red eyes, as in *Harry Potter*, are not a good sign: Fury has 'burning eyen, whom bloody strakes did staine' (2.4.15) and Wrath has eyes that 'hurle forth sparcles fiery red' (1.4.33). Eyes are windows into the soul in the *Faerie Queene* just as they are in *Harry Potter*, where the green eyes Harry has inherited from his mother, the piercing blue of the Dumbledore brothers' eyes, the occluding black of Snape's and the satanic red of Voldemort's all provide insight for the reader. *Harry Potter*, like the *Faerie Queene*, uses repeated motifs to knit the books together and assist the reader in their interpretative task (see also: Hardy, 2011; Wolosky, 2010).

Shakespeare's Henriad (*Richard II, Henry IV parts 1* and *2*, and *Henry V*) is perhaps the greatest linked writing in English. The relationships between Shakespeare's central characters in the Henriad – in particular between Hal, Falstaff and Henry IV – develop as the series evolves. The Boar's Head Tavern remains the location of comic fooling but the jokes between Hal and Falstaff that take place there in *Henry IV part 1* are replayed in *Henry IV part 2* only to fall flat. These recurrences in the plot reveal the way that the relationship that lies at the heart of the series (the friendship between Hal and Falstaff) is beginning to disintegrate. Likewise, the heroic single combat between Hal and Hotspur at the climax of *Henry IV part I* sets up an (intentionally unrealised) expectation for a chivalric encounter in the battles that close the next two plays. The failure of *Henry IV part 2* and *Henry V* to provide an adequate parallel to Hal and Hotspur's heroic encounter in their climactic battles subtly changes the way that these battles are experienced by the audience. In a similar way, the duel between Voldemort and Harry at the end of *Philosopher's Stone* sets up the expectation for a climactic battle between these two at the end of each novel (and arguably one of *Harry Potter*'s most successful endings comes in *Azkaban* when, as in Shakespeare, this expectation is subverted).

A number of *Harry Potter* critics have wondered whether Shakespeare's Hal – the prince at the heart of this series – is one source for Harry Potter's name. Alison Lurie, for example, notes how Harry's name conjures up 'both English literature and English history: Shakespeare's Prince Hal and Harry Hotspur' (1999, p.6). Between them Hal – 'young Harry' (1.1.85) – and Hotspur – 'young Harry Percy' (1.1.53) – are referred to as 'Harry' thirty-eight times in *Henry IV part 1* alone. (Likewise the setting for much of the comic action of these plays is the Boar's Head Tavern, whose name recalls the Hog's Head pub [Stouffer, 2007, p.121].)

Henry IV part 1 charts Hal's progress from an apparently dissolute young Prince – 'unthought-of Harry' (3.2.141) – to a heroic champion:

> I saw young Harry with his beaver on,
> His cuishes on his thighs, gallantly armed,
> Rise from the ground like feathered Mercury,
> And vaulted with such ease into his seat
> As if an angel dropped down from the clouds
> To turn and wind a fiery Pegasus,
> And witch the world with noble horsemanship.
> (4.1.105–112)

One of the ways in which *Henry IV part 1* achieves Hal's transformation is through matching him with a double: Harry Hotspur. Hotspur is the standard of valour against which Hal is measured and found wanting, but by the end of play Hal has beaten Hotspur in single combat. Shakespeare makes the comparison between these two even clearer by making them the same age, although historically Henry 'Hotspur' Percy was over twenty years older than Prince Henry. Harry Potter is likewise pretty much identical in age with his double, Neville Longbottom. As the prophecy in *Phoenix* makes clear, both were born near the end of July, 1980. The pairing of Harry and Neville in the prophecy in *Phoenix* has been prepared for in *Azkaban* when Harry borrows Neville's name as an alias on Knight Bus and has a nightmare that Neville has replaced him in a Quidditch match. Neville's grandmother wishes that the two might really swap places – 'she'd give anything to have you as a grandson' (*Half-Blood Prince*, Chap 7, p.133) – just as Hal's father does:

> O, that it could be proved
> That some night-tripping fairy had exchanged
> In cradle clothes our children where they lay,
> And called mine Percy, his Plantagenet!
> Then would I have his Harry, and he mine.
> (1.1.85–9)

Hal's continual failure to live up to the chivalric pattern of Hotspur's behaviour leads his father to express the wish that the two Harrys might have been swapped at birth.

Doubles are an important feature of *Harry Potter* (Wolosky, 2010, pp.99–126), as they are in Shakespeare's Henriad. Both the pairing of Hal and Hotspur, and the connections between Harry and Neville, create a more rounded sense of the different facets of heroism. The comparison of these two young men illustrates Hal's ability to marry Hotspur's purely martial heroism with the political acumen needed for government – Hotspur represents only one ideal, while Hal unites the various strands that are needed by a future leader. In *Harry Potter*, likewise, Neville embodies a slightly different type of heroism to Harry. He underscores the importance of bravery that is loyal, steadfast and uncelebrated, as opposed to the central character's more showy triumphs. The reader gradually realises that Neville, in his quiet way, has suffered as much, and responded as bravely to his trials as Harry.

Both *Harry Potter* and the Henriad use a double for their hero to interrogate the heroic ideal. (And, in what may be either an odd coincidence or a subconscious memory, the great historical rivals of Hotspur's family were the Nevilles.) As with Shakespeare's linked plays, the internal references in *Harry Potter*'s novels create structural parallels that add depth and complexity to characters, events and relationships.

OVERVIEW OF CHAPTERS

The chapters of this book follow a chronological path through *Harry Potter*'s literary forbears, from Homer through to Victorian novels and poetry. Each chapter traces both direct allusions, and more general literary influence, between the series and at least one canonical work or writer. Each chapter argues for the ways in which recognising these connections can enrich our understandings of these texts.

The first two chapters look at classical influences on *Harry Potter*. The first chapter argues for *Harry Potter*'s connections with Greek myth and, in particular, with the oral storytelling traditions of Homer. Children's literature is unique among contemporary fiction in that it continues to partake in the ancient, oral nature of storytelling. Rowling studied Homer as an undergraduate and *Harry Potter* contains a number of specific connections to Homeric narrative in the return of Cedric's body, the entrancing Veela and its scarred hero. This chapter argues that, in addition to such specific connections, *Harry Potter* shares a number of aspects of Homer's storytelling techniques, such as his narrative repetitions and flashbacks, which are both key parts of his oral composition.

Rowling loves names. The second chapter argues that those *Harry Potter* characters whose names correspond to their natures (the werewolf named Remus Lupin, for example) draw on a comic naming tradition that derives, ultimately, from Plato. *Harry Potter*'s revealingly named Animagi draw on a classical tradition of shape-shifting most famously embodied in another text Rowling studied at university: Ovid's *Metamorphoses*. This chapter illustrates the literary sources for many of *Harry Potter*'s names (in particular those deriving from Shakespeare and Ovid) but also for the literary meaning encoded in these names. All of Ovid's stories revolve around a literal metamorphosis – in the case of Narcissus the withering of the young man into a flower and of the woman who loves him into an echo – and *Harry Potter* takes this famous story and metamorphoses its meaning.

The central chapters of this book concentrate on the series' medieval and early modern sources – from Chaucer and the Gawain-poet, to Shakespeare and Milton. The third chapter argues for the influence of medieval folklore and poetry on the aesthetic of Hogwarts as a whole, and on the Deathly Hallows in particular. It argues for the importance of the fourteenth-century poem *Gawain and the Green Knight* and Chaucer's 'Pardoner's Tale', as well as fairy tales and medieval folklore, in the creation of *Harry Potter*'s most powerful objects. *Harry Potter*'s rewriting of 'The Pardoner's Tale' as 'The Tale of the Three Brothers' transforms Chaucer's tale about the perils of greed into a meditation on the right response to death.

The influence of *Gawain and the Green Knight*, in particular, also points to the still under-explored Christian aspects of *Harry Potter*'s narrative. The fourth chapter of this book argues for some new connections between *Harry Potter* and biblical narrative. The novels' embodiment of the struggle between good and evil in the persons of 'Harry' and 'Voldemort' draws on the way that Christianity personifies this binary in Jesus and the Devil. In Christian tradition there are two specific moments when these two come face to face: the Temptation in the Desert and the Harrowing of Hell. In both the Temptation and the Harrowing Satan fails to understand who Jesus really is, and this failure to recognise Jesus' divine nature is due to his inability to comprehend the magnitude of God's love for mankind. Voldemort's failure to understand the power of love – which mimics Satan's failure – leads, likewise, to his fatal underestimate of his adversary. This chapter explores the Temptation and the Harrowing in the English literary tradition (in works such as medieval mystery plays, *Piers Plowman* and Milton's epics) and argues for the importance of this tradition to *Harry Potter*.

Harry Potter is a humorous work and comedy is an essential part of how it handles its serious material. The fifth chapter explores the way that Shakespeare – the master of the mixed-mode of tragicomedy – has influenced *Harry Potter's* synthesis of tragedy and comedy. Shakespeare is one of Rowling's favourite authors and she has cited both *The Winter's Tale* and *Macbeth* as influences on her novels. This chapter argues that *Harry Potter* is influenced by Shakespeare's handling of fate in *Macbeth*, the depiction of power relations between magical and mortal worlds in *A Midsummer Night's Dream*, and sexual tension in *Much Ado about Nothing*.

The final three chapters look predominately at the influence of nineteenth-century writers (Austen, Hardy, Dickens and Tennyson) on *Harry Potter*. The sixth chapter discusses the connections with Rowling's 'favourite writer of all time' (2000c): Jane Austen. *Emma* is Rowling's favourite novel and this chapter argues for its influence over *Harry Potter's* narrative style, plotting and exploration of romantic relationships. It also argues that the presentation of the Gothic within *Northanger Abbey* is fundamental to the comic–Gothic of *Harry Potter*. Both Austen's and *Harry Potter's* satiric Gothic novels at once humorously dissect and rationalise Gothic effects while nonetheless partaking in the romance that lies at the heart of the Gothic sublime.

The seventh chapter explores this romance further. It argues that the love potions and romantic love that lie at the heart of the *Half-Blood Prince* draw on Petrarchan sonnets, Shakespearean plays and Thomas Hardy's *Far from the Madding Crowd*. This chapter argues that *Harry Potter* draws the plot-line (and ensuing comic chaos) of Romilda Vane's love potion from *A Midsummer Night's Dream*. However, in *Harry Potter*, as in Shakespeare, there is a thoughtful climax to this comic fooling. The story of Merope – which alludes to the suffering of Fanny Robin in *Far from the Madding Crowd* – contemplates the serious side of enslavement through love. The increasingly sceptical attitude displayed towards love potions in *Half-Blood Prince* reflects the importance of love in *Harry Potter* as a whole and draws on Shakespeare's own interrogation of the differences between true love and infatuation.

Rowling has said that all her characters are defined by their relation to death. The final chapter of this book argues for the way in which *Harry Potter* is shaped by its engagement with mortality. Rowling's mother died as Rowling began *Harry Potter* and she is enshrined within the importance it places on maternal love. Literature – from Homeric epic to Shakespearean sonnets – has championed its ability to confer immortality on the object of its praise; its ability to withstand the obliterating power of death. For an author who loses someone they love this is a peculiarly potent idea and as Rowling has said of the relationship between *Harry Potter* and her mother: 'The books are what they are because she died. . . because I loved her and she died' (2010b). This chapter argues for the crucial importance of mortality to *Harry Potter*, and its links with Tennyson's *In Memoriam*, one of the greatest poetic works of bereavement. Form is central to the way both Tennyson's poetry and *Harry Potter* respond to grief, and this chapter returns to the chiastic form of the series (first discussed in the opening chapter) and argues that this structure, germane to both *In Memoriam* and *Harry Potter*, is linked to a desire to find meaning in mortality.

Notes

1 Rowling has not given a specific source for Hagrid's name in interview, although she has explained its meaning: 'if you were hag-rid – it's a dialect word – you'd had a bad night. Hagrid is a big drinker – he has a lot of bad nights' (1999e). The *Oxford English Dictionary* notes 'hag-rid' as a form of 'hag-ridden': 'ridden by a hag; *esp.* afflicted by nightmares.'

2 '[Dumbledore] would often say things I didn't know I believed, but once I saw that Dumbledore had said them, "Oh yeah, that's right, that's true"' (Rowling, 2012g). Rowling has also called writing Dumbledore a type of 'automatic writing' (2013d) (which is writing believed to have been directed by the subconscious).

3 Nel, 2001, p.35. For another possible Kafka allusion, see Harry Potter Wiki, 2016a.

4 *The Faerie Queene* – which is also comparable in length to Rowling's text – consists of six completed books, plus a concluding section known as 'the Mutability Cantos'.

1 *Harry Potter*, Greek myth and epic storytelling

Children's literature remains uniquely connected with ancient, oral, traditions of storytelling for – unlike most modern writing – children's stories are still spoken aloud. *Harry Potter* has been listened to by millions of children, read aloud by parents, friends, siblings and in audiobook form. Rowling has spoken of how satisfying she finds it that her books are being read aloud: 'there's nothing more gratifying than to listen to people saying that entire families read the books together . . .. They read one chapter together and then they gathered again to read the next one . . .. A lot of families told me they did that and that is gratifying in so many levels. The books have become a social act' (2008b). While Rowling is not a true oral storyteller (she writes down stories that others read out, rather than retelling works from memory) *Harry Potter* connects with the oral storytelling tradition both in the way her stories are consumed and in the ways in which they are constructed.

This chapter argues for the influence on *Harry Potter* of one of the oldest forms of spoken story that we have: the epic poems of Homer. Rowling studied Homer as an undergraduate and has spoken of how deeply moving she found him (2000j). Aspects of *Harry Potter* – such as the Veela who derive from the Sirens in the *Odyssey* (Spencer, 2015, pp.31–2, 201) and the return of Cedric's body – show the influence of Homer upon the series. The clearest influence, however, lies in its hero's scar. Rowling has described how his scar marks Harry out: 'I wanted him to be physically marked by what he has been through. It was an outward expression of what he has been through inside. I gave him a scar in a prominent place so other people would recognise him' (2001b). In the *Odyssey* Odysseus returns home to Ithaca (after ten years fighting at Troy and ten years wandering at sea) and is recognised by his scar. When Harry returns to the Wizarding world – after '"ten dark and difficult years"' (*Phoenix*, Chap 37, p.736) – he is likewise recognised by his scar. This scar plays a regular and prominent part in the narrative, both when it pains Harry and every time that he meets someone new and their eyes perform 'the familiar flick upwards to the scar on Harry's forehead' (*Goblet*, Chap 7, p.81). The scar is crucial to Harry's delineation as a hero, and for many years Rowling intended 'scar' to be the final word of the series (2007e).

Harry Potter is in many ways an ordinary boy with whom children can identify – he gets detentions, frets over homework and endures bullying teachers – but his scar marks him out as a hero in the classical mould. While he remains an Everyman-style hero – 'a normal boy but with those qualities most of us really admire' (Rowling, 1999c) – he is also a descendant of the scarred hero of the classical imagination who returns from a long absence to revenge himself on those who have harmed his family.

Harry's scar allows him to enter Voldemort's mind, and it takes him to different places and times. Such 'flashbacks' are likewise a distinctive part of Homeric narrative (as will be discussed below in the famous example of the description of how Odysseus came by his scar). Homer's abrupt breaks in the dominant time-line are linked to his oral composition, and it is a narrative device of which Rowling is so fond that she has given it a local habitation and a name: the Pensieve. Throughout the series the Pensieve becomes progressively more important. In *Deathly Hallows* Harry finally enters Snape's memory at the height of the Battle of Hogwarts to learn the truth about the past and what that means for his future. At crucial moments of high plot tension both Homer and Rowling use the technique of an embedded story to take the reader back into the past.

'I BOUGHT HIM OFF A GREEK CHAPPIE': THE INFLUENCE OF CLASSICAL LITERATURE ON *HARRY POTTER*

Richard A. Spencer's recent study of Rowling's classical allusions provides evidence for the extensive influence of Greek and Roman myth, languages and literature on *Harry Potter*. The influence of classical languages on Rowling's magical language has also been explored by M. G. Dupree (Dupree, 2011; Spencer, 2015, pp.246–72). Spencer is particularly interesting on the classical names of the series, noting that the goddess Minerva (like Minerva McGonagall) watched over schoolchildren and that the classical Cadmus (like Cadmus Peverell, the brother who asks for the Resurrection Stone) was engaged in a hopeless quest for a lost loved-one (2015, pp.70, 135).

Rowling read French with additional Greek and Roman Studies as an undergraduate at Exeter University in the early 1980s. The classical literature part of her course did not require her to read the texts in the original languages and she responded with immediate enthusiasm to the captivating stories and 'ancient wisdom' (Rowling, 2008d) she discovered: 'tripping ecstatically off to the book shop to buy a stack of stylish black-covered Penguins' (Rowling, 1998d, p.25). Rowling has written of how her undergraduate studies began a life-long enthusiasm for Greek literature: 'a shelf next to me as I tap out these words is dotted with books on Greek mythology, all of which were purchased post-Exeter' (1998d, p.27). Rowling studied Greek drama, Homeric epic and ancient myth as an undergraduate and became quite well informed enough to tell 'a pair of bemused four year olds with whom I watched Disney's latest offering that Heracles *definitely* didn't own Pegasus. That was *Bellerophon*, as any fule kno' (1998d, p.27). A friend who studied with her at Exeter has recalled how 'Jo liked the Classics side of things. She liked those mythological stories' (quoted in Smith, 2002, p.91). Ancient myth, with its fabulous beasts and 'thrilling tale[s] of kidnap' (Rowling, 1998, p.26), fired Rowling's imagination and it is an indebtedness she wittily acknowledges when Hagrid explains that he bought his three-headed dog '"off a Greek Chappie"' (*Philosopher's Stone*, Chap 11, p.141). Fluffy's Greek origins are a nod to the fact that he is a version of the three-headed dog of Greek myth, Cerberus.

Harry Potter contains many creatures – such as Centaurs, Chimaera, the basilisk and the Sphinx – that originate in Greek myth. In the case of the Centaurs, in particular, their actions within *Harry Potter* resonate with their significance in Greek culture. As Spencer has noted, while Centaurs were generally considered as antagonistic to mankind, there was one (Chiron) who was particularly wise, kind and gifted and became a tutor to heroes such as Jason and Achilles – in a way that recalls Firenze (2015, pp.66, 191–2). Centaurs, however, were generally considered to embody an untamed barbarism that stood in contrast to Greek civilisation, most notably in their attempted rape of the Lapith women after they were invited to the Lapith wedding feast (which resulted in the famous mythological Battle of the Lapiths and the Centaurs, depicted on the Parthenon frieze). The importance of sexual violence in the Greek conception of Centaurs forms a disturbing undercurrent to the fate of Umbridge at their hands (McCauley, 2015, pp.135–6).

The influence of ancient Greek thought is also present in *Harry Potter* in quite subtle ways. It was the Greeks who first systematised medical study and, as Dupree has noted, this is probably the reason that the only two purely Greek spells in *Harry Potter* (Anapneo and Episkey) are connected with healing (2011, p.42). There may also be a more deep-seated link between Greek medical thought and another of *Harry Potter*'s spells. Rowling has described how she came up with the idea for the killing curse: '*Avada Kedavra* . . . is an ancient spell in Aramaic, and it is the original of abracadabra,[1] which means "let the thing be destroyed." Originally, it was used to cure illness and the "thing" was the illness, but I decided to make it the "thing" as in the person standing in front of me. I take a lot of liberties with things like that. I twist them round and make them mine' (2004b). Rowling's creative impulse to make a killing curse out of a healing spell may have been inspired by the connections of hurt and healing in ancient Greek. Famously, the Greek word *pharmakon* can be translated either as 'remedy' or 'poison'. (It is a concept that might hold a particular appeal for Rowling as a *pharmakeus*, one who hurts or heals, can also be translated as wizard or sorcerer – pointing to the way that magic can be used for good or ill.)

BEARING LIBATIONS: THE EPIGRAPH OF *DEATHLY HALLOWS*

It is the quotation from Aeschylus' *Libation Bearers* prefacing *Deathly Hallows* that makes the influence of Greek literature on *Harry Potter* explicit. Rowling has stressed the importance of these quotations (the other is from William Penn's *More Fruits of Solitude*) to the series as a whole: 'I'd known it was going to be those two passages since *Chamber* was published. I always knew [that] if I could use them at the beginning of book seven then I'd cued up the ending perfectly. If they were relevant, then I went where I needed to go . . . . They just say it all to me, they really do' (2007g).

The Libation Bearers is the central play of Aeschylus' great dramatic trilogy (the *Oresteia*), which is one of the foundational texts of Western literature. It concerns the ill-fated House of Atreus and follows the cataclysmic results of Agamemnon's decision to sacrifice his daughter, Iphigenia, in order to enable the Greek fleet to sail to Troy. The Trojan War is presented as a conflict that must be fought, and hence the decision to sacrifice Iphigenia is not presented as a free choice. Agamemnon, famously, 'puts on the yoke of necessity'; but this is not an excuse accepted by his wife, Clytemnestra, who murders him in revenge when he returns. In the second play of the trilogy – *The Libation Bearers* – Electra (Agamemnon and Clytemnestra's daughter) waits for her brother, Orestes, to avenge their father's death and kill their mother. *The Libation Bearers* ends with Orestes murdering Clytemnestra, and the final play of the trilogy – *The Eumenides* – tries to unravel the weight of responsibility and guilt that Orestes carries for this deed and to find a way out of perpetuating this cycle of violence.

Harry Potter's epigraph asserts that the sufferings endured by the House of Atreus – 'the torment bred in the race' – can only be solved from within the family itself: 'there is a cure in the house,/and not outside it, no,/ . . . Bless the children, give them triumph now.' It is Orestes, the son of Agamemnon, who must avenge his father's death. The use of this quotation of an epigraph implies that the weight of responsibility for disentangling events will likewise fall on the young hero of *Deathly Hallows*. Dumbledore has died and the children must go it alone. It is Harry who will face Voldemort, Harry who must avenge his parents, as he had somehow always known it would be: 'it was always going to be a quest really to avenge them' (Rowling, 2007l).

As the use of this quotation suggests, *Harry Potter* draws on Greek tragedy's belief in family as destiny. The House of Atreus – the family into which Orestes is born – is cursed because of the ancient sins of its first founder Tantalus. Tantalus curses his successors by sacrificing his son, Pelops, and feeding him to the gods. The gods – horrified by this act – return the boy to life. (Incidentally, they do this by boiling his body parts in a sacred cauldron – a resuscitation that may have inspired Voldemort's odd mode of resurrection at the end of *Goblet*, when he comes back to life by boiling various body parts in a cauldron.) Pelops then fathers Thyestes and Atreus, only for history to repeat itself when Atreus murders Thyestes' son (also, unpropitiously and confusingly, called Tantalus). Atreus is the father of Agamemnon and Agamemnon's decision to sacrifice his daughter is prefigured in his great-grand-father's sin: like Tantalus, Agamemnon sacrifices his child for the gods. The *Oresteia* illustrates the enslaving nature of the system of blood vengeance: Agamemnon kills his daughter, so his wife kills him, so their son kills her.

One reason that *Deathly Hallows* begins with a quotation from the *Oresteia* is that *Harry Potter*, too, is interested in the idea of generations replaying the actions – and sins – of their predecessors. Harry's group of friends, for example, play out the relationship dynamics of his father's circle (Asher-Perrin, 2013;

Bartel, 2015). In *Harry Potter*, as in Aeschylus, your parents are your fate. At the end of *Deathly Hallows*, Harry seems intent on seeing that the bad blood between him and Draco should continue between their children. Strikingly, however, Rowling has chosen to break this cycle in the 2016 play *Harry Potter and the Cursed Child* (written by Jack Thorne, but based on an original idea by Thorne, Rowling and John Tiffany). In this play Albus Potter and Scorpius Malfoy become best friends. Within the *Harry Potter* novels themselves, however, there are also glimmers of hope that the endless cycles of enmity can be broken.

The *Oresteia* concludes with the miraculous ending of violence in which the House of Atreus has become embroiled and there is a hint of such a rapprochement in Hogwarts likewise. On Christmas Day in *Azkaban* Dumbledore pioneers the idea of sitting together without the division of House tables and it is an idea that comes to fruition at the end of *Deathly Hallows*. After the Battle of Hogwarts the traditional enmity between Gryffindor and Slytherin has been broken along with Voldemort's power: 'nobody was sitting according to house any more: all were jumbled together, teachers and pupils, ghosts and parents, centaurs and house-elves' (Chap 6, p.597).

The quotation from *The Libation Bearers* suggests a parallel between the weight of destiny carried by Orestes, and that which is being placed on Harry's shoulders. But there is also another clear link between the two heroes: they both have a scar on their forehead. As John Granger has noted: 'there are no other "young men coming into his own stories" that I know which feature a boy with scar on forehead prophesied and determined to avenge the murder of his father' (2008b). The myth of Orestes states that he has been long absent (sometimes the myth runs that – like Harry – he was sent away as a baby) and so when he returns in *The Libation Bearers* it is difficult for his sister to recognise him. In Aeschylus' *Libation Bearers* Electra knows that her brother has returned because she finds a lock of hair that looks like her own left at their father's tomb and a footprint identical to her own. In Euripides' version of the story, however, Orestes is recognised through the 'scar on his brow.' Euripides is a rather irreverent dramatist and his version of this story, in his *Electra*, parodies Aeschylus' recognition scene in the *Libation Bearers*. Euripides – the only Greek tragedian who finds a place for comedy in his plays – points out some of the inconsistencies in Electra's traditional recognition of her brother. In Euripides' play Electra is brought the news of her brother's return by an old man who, as in the earlier play, suggests that the identical lock of hair and footprint prove that her brother has returned. In this play, however, Electra does not accept this evidence: brothers and sisters do not always have matching hair, still less the same size feet. Instead it is only through the scar, visible on his brow, that Orestes is finally recognised: 'the scar next to his eyebrow: once in your father's house he fell and cut it as you and he chased a fawn' (ll.573–4).

It seems likely that Rowling would have enjoyed the impudence of Euripides' rewriting of Aeschylus' famous scene, and her hero's visibly scarred forehead recalls Euripides' Orestes' scarred brow. Both of these heroes, however, also draw on the most famous scarred hero of ancient epic: Homer's Odysseus. Orestes' scar is intended to recall Odysseus: like Odysseus he returns to a home that has been taken over by hostile powers, like Odysseus he is awaited by a faithful woman and like Odysseus he returns disguised but is recognised by his scar. Odysseus, Orestes and Harry are all recognised by their scars upon their return because a scar is the mark of a hero, evidence of both human vulnerability and heroic power; the mark of an ordeal that has been passed through and survived. The epic nature of Odysseus' scar resonates with the near-fatal genesis of Harry's scar and its subsequent importance for the plot. But the irreverent rewriting of the epic scar tradition in Euripides – where Orestes sustains his injury chasing a fawn with his sister, rather than (Odysseus-like) taking on a wild boar in a coming-of-age hunt – resonates with the comic tone of *Harry Potter*. As in Euripides the 'recognition' of Harry through his scar is frequently a comic moment. When, for example, the language barrier prevents Fudge from introducing Harry to the Bulgarian Minister for Magic, 'the Bulgarian wizard suddenly spotted Harry's scar and started gabbling loudly and excitedly, pointing at it. "Knew we'd get there in the end," said Fudge wearily' (*Goblet*, Chap 8, p.91).

TELLING STORIES: HOMER'S ORAL POETRY AND *HARRY POTTER*

Harry Potter is influenced not only by Homer's subject-matter but also by the way he tells his tales. Since the last century Homer critics have been interested by the way that the oral nature of Homer's storytelling has influenced his style. In the 1930s Milman Parry and Albert Lord studied present-day examples of oral storytelling in the former Yugoslavia to research how oral composition might have influenced Homer's style. They argued, for example, that in oral cultures it is the main events of the story (not its precise wording) that is reproduced when the stories are retold. For example these are the opening lines of the song of 'Marko and Nina of Kostur', sung by the same singer a year apart:

Marko Kralijević is drinking wine	Kralijević Marko arose early
With his old mother,	In Prilip in his white tower,
And with his true love,	And next to him his old mother,
And with his only sister.	And next the mother his true love,
When Marko had drunk his wine,	And next his love his sister Anđelija.
Then Marko brimmed the glass	He toasted them in clear brandy:
To the health of his old mother,	'Yesterday a brief letter arrived
And his love and his only sister.	From the sultan, illustrious czar.
'Expect the sun and the moon,	The sultan summons me to the army,
But me Marko never!'	To serve him for nine years.'
And his old mother asked him:	

'Whither are you going, Marko, my only son?'
Marko Kralijević spoke:
'I am going, mother, to the sultan's army
For a period of nine years.'

(Lord, 2001, pp.71–3)

The plot is stable but the details and the language are not: the hero toasts his companions in each, but in the first example he does so with wine, and in the second, with brandy; the rhetorical flourishes of the first version have been replaced by the careful situating in place and time of the second.

Rowling has commented on the way in which fairy tales are altered by oral transmission (1999f) and *Harry Potter* includes a fictional version of the changing nature of oral stories over time. When Hermione says she has a copy of 'The Tale of the Three Brothers' Xenophilius enquires sharply as to whether it is the original, or merely some later version (*Deathly Hallows*, Chap 21, p.330). Hermione begins to read 'The Tale of the Three Brothers' – '"*There were once three brothers who were travelling along a lonely, winding road at twilight*'" – but Ron interrupts her to say that when his mother tells the story it takes place at midnight. Mrs Weasley – or the oral tradition of which she is a part – has changed the time at which the story is set. Like the later version of 'Marko and Nina of Kostur' (above), which states that the story begins in the morning – presumably because the storyteller feels that this is the right time to start a story about new beginnings –, the Weasley family have changed the setting of their tale to midnight, as that seems the right time to set a story about meeting Death. *Harry Potter* creates an imagined history of oral transmission for its fictional fairy tale.

A number of other aspects of *Harry Potter* demonstrate that Rowling is invested in the idea that she is writing a story that will be spoken aloud and listened to, rather than simply read. Rowling places intense importance on the spoken word within the novels: 'I really love writing dialogue . . . . And when I hear you [Stephen Fry] reading it, it gives me a whole new sense of pleasure' (2005g). Maria Tatar, a Harvard scholar of children's literature, has spoken about how it was only when she listened to the audiobooks of *Harry Potter* that she finally understood their popularity: 'all of a sudden, I *got* it—I could remember it, and I could visualize it. So much of it is dialogue. It's not exploring minds. It's conversations and actions that drive these books' (quoted in Rowling, 2012d).

One example of the way that *Harry Potter* indicates its status as a text that will be read aloud is in its aural puns. It is likely to be a listener, rather than a reader, for example, who will first spot that Grimmauld Place is a grim old place. Or that Diagon Alley lies diagonally (suggesting its magical intersection with reality) and that Knockturn Alley ('nocturnally') might be linked with the Dark Arts. Or to hear the 'cadaver' in *Avada Kedavra*. With a number of these puns the spelling is likely to 'mislead' the reader: 'Prophet' is a good name for a Wizarding newspaper, so it is again likely to be the listener rather than the reader who first spots that the *Daily Prophet* may be more interested in sales ('profit') than truth. Dolores Umbridge has a name that is spelt exactly how 'umbrage' is pronounced ('u-m-br-i-dj') rather than how it is spelt. Rowling has explained how the expression 'to take umbrage' gave her the idea for this name – 'Dolores is offended by any challenge to her limited world-view; I felt her surname conveyed the pettiness and rigidity of her character' (2015d). Older meanings of 'umbrage' ('shade, shadow') also resonate with Dolores' character. It is once again the listener, rather than the reader, who – given their exact aural equivalence – is likely to note the subtle resonances between Umbridge and 'umbrage'. It is the listener, likewise, who may spot the clue that Slytherin's heir makes a 'slithering' sound (*Philosopher's Stone*, Chap 15, p.187) or that a Pensieve creates a 'pensive' pause for thought as well as the more visually obvious 'sieving' of thoughts ('*penses*' in French).

HOMER'S ORAL NARRATIVE FORM

Homer's oral composition is reflected in a number of stylistic aspects, such as his repetitive narrative structures: frequently repeated 'building blocks' of language or story (Kelly, 2011, p.21). Oral literature, such as Homer's, is characterised by its 'economy of language in the words chosen to portray images and ideas' and its structure is likewise often highly formulaic and 'composed of recurring themes' (Niditch, 2010, pp.3–4). Such repetition helped Homer compose his work, but it also assists the listener.

Harry Potter, too, is full of recurring structures. Each book follows the pattern of the school year – there will be the journey from Privet Drive at the beginning of the novel (and a return at the end); there will usually be a Sorting, Halloween and Christmas feasts, Easter and summer holidays and exams. Within this overarching structure, much of the action follows the regular routine of the school day: there are frequently repeated meals, lessons, attempts to catch-up with homework, night-time escapades and dreams. There is also likely to be a shopping expedition to Diagon Alley, a Quidditch match or two, a trip to Hagrid's hut and adventures in the Forbidden Forest and under the invisibility cloak; someone will say that Harry has his mother's eyes and Hermione will berate them for not reading *Hogwarts: A History*. A new method of magical transport will appear, there will be some kind of underground battle/adventure and Snape will do something suspicious. Once the reader has spotted the pattern, they will be primed to wonder why the Defence against the Dark Arts teacher will have to leave this year.

Such patterning draws the attention of *Harry Potter*'s audience towards the formal aspects of the novels. *Half-Blood Prince* plays with the reader's expectations by having the predictable Quidditch match unexpectedly commentated by Luna. Expectations create a jolt when they are subverted: the knowledge that every previous book has ended with Dumbledore's explanation of what has really been going on, makes the end of *Half-Blood Prince* even more of a shock.

RING COMPOSITION/CHIASMUS

These regular repetitions also take place within a more formal ring or 'chiastic' structure, in which events are repeated in an inverse order. Spencer, who looks at ring composition in both *Harry Potter* and its classical sources, illustrates the way events are replayed at the beginning and end of each novel, as well as between the beginning and the end of the series (2015, pp.76–7, 275–84). John Granger (2015) believes that each novel is structured in a chiastic form with a pivot chapter around which the story turns; and this is also enacted in a larger form for, as has been convincingly demonstrated by J. Steve Lee (2011), each novel in the series has its own pair. The first novel is paired with the last, the second with the sixth and the third with the fifth. This chiastic criss-cross form (the name *chiasmus* derives from the Greek letter *chi* ['X'] in which two lines cross at the centre) takes place around the 'pivot' of the fourth novel. The powerful symmetry of chiastic form has a long literary history in part because it confers both solidity and progression. Granger argues that the power of chiasmus is due to its being 'the formal vehicle of the circular hero's journey . . . the completion of a circle is to arrive at its defining point because in the completed circle, the center is revealed' (2015, p.218).

The layered structure of Rowling's chiastic narrative structure enables the development and intensification of her themes as each of the later novels echoes and recalls an earlier one. These paired allusions can be relatively simple and direct: such as the Knight Bus, which appears only in *Azkaban* and *Phoenix*. Sometimes they grow in importance, such as the way that the authentic prophecy Trelawney utters in *Azkaban* paves the way for the revelation of her fateful prophecy in *Phoenix*. Or the way in which, as mentioned in the introduction, the trivial association between Neville and Harry in *Azkaban* (when Harry borrows Neville's name as an alias on Knight Bus and dreams Neville replaces him on the Quidditch field) form a pre-echo of the mirroring of their fates revealed in *Phoenix*. The connections between *Chamber* and *Half-Blood Prince* are particularly striking and Rowling has noted that *Harry Potter and the Half-Blood Prince* was the working title for *Chamber* (2000f). Direct links between the two novels include exams being cancelled in both, rumours of Harry being a great dark wizard being mentioned in both, Hogwarts being threatened with closure, Harry and Draco duelling using Snape's spell, Tom Riddle appearing in Chapter 13 and Polyjuice Potion being used either to transform into, or out of, being Crabbe and Goyle (Granger, 2011, pp.42–7).

The chiastic structure, however, is at its clearest in the relationship between the first and last books of the series. To an unprecedented extent *Deathly Hallows* remembers and reiterates – and even includes direct, italicised quotes from – *Philosopher's Stone* (see: *Deathly Hallows*, Chap 2, p.25, Chap 26, p.427). Rowling has drawn attention to some of these echoes in interview: she has said that she 'wanted to come full circle' (2007h) in making Teddy Lupin an orphan at the end of the series (as Harry was at the beginning); and has noted that Harry is saved by a mother's love for her son at both the start and the end of the series (2012h) (see Chapter 8 for a further discussion of this).

These chiastic connections generally show a deepening of seriousness or significance across the series: the Vanishing Cabinet seen in Borgin and Burkes in *Chamber* becomes fatally important in *Half-Blood Prince* and the duel between Harry and Draco in *Half-Blood Prince* is both more violent and more significant, than that in *Chamber*. While the apparently genial new teacher in *Chamber* has a secret that is both not very serious and not very secret (all the teachers know Lockhart is a fraud), the apparently genial new teacher in *Half-Blood Prince* has a secret that is both harder to penetrate and far more consequential. *Azkaban* and *Phoenix* both revolve around Sirius, but while in the earlier novel Harry saves Sirius' life, in the second he will lead him to his death. Griphook, who had taken the young Harry (then full of innocent wonder) round Gringotts in the first novel, guides him again when he enters Gringotts on his more morally complex and difficult journey in the final novel. Neville's bravery led to victory for Gryffindor in the House Cup at the end of the *Philosopher's Stone*; at the end of *Deathly Hallows* Neville's bravery enables him to draw Gryffindor's sword and destroy the final Horcrux. The tall ghostly woman who wafts past Harry in his night-time wanderings in *Philosopher's Stone* will return as a crucial part of the plot in *Deathly Hallows*. The prediction of Harry's death at Voldemort's hands is mentioned in passing when Harry first enters the Forbidden Forest in *Philosopher's Stone* but becomes reality when Harry meets Voldemort in the Forest again in the final novel. As Dumbledore turns out street lamps in the opening chapter of *Philosopher's Stone* his Deluminator is little more than a party trick, but when it returns at the close of the series it marks Dumbledore's deep knowledge of Ron's character and communicates (through that knowledge) insight and hope to Harry: '*You gave Ron the Deluminator. You understood him . . . you gave him a way back . . . what did you know about me, Dumbledore?*' (*Deathly Hallows*, Chap 24, p.391).

Although such 'ring composition' or chiastic structuring is by no means unique to classical literature, it is 'very widely practiced there' (Spencer, 2015, p.275) and Homer's chiastic structuring is another aspect of his style that has been linked to his oral form. One critic has described how chiasmus – for example in the recognition scene of *The Odyssey* – enables Homer to lead his listener gently towards the expected conclusion. Odysseus orders his nurse to fetch his wife Penelope, then he orders her to fetch the serving women; the serving women arrive and immediately recognise Odysseus, then Penelope arrives and eventually recognises him too. The expectations set up by the chiasmus means that the audience can be confident that – although Penelope's recognition is much more protracted than that of the serving women – she will complete the chiasmus and recognise him also (Kelly, 2011, p.7). The symmetry in *Harry Potter*, likewise, offers its readers and listeners the pleasures of familiarity but also uses these known structures to create surprise as well as recognition. Both Rowling and Homer use symmetry to relate disparate episodes and bring structure to their very long stories. In both repetition – and particularly the structurally satisfying repetition of chiasmus – is an effective tool for holding the listeners' attention.

ODYSSEUS' SCAR

As mentioned above, another aspect of Homer's oral style can be found in his abrupt shifts from the main narrative line. These, often quite startling, long digressions or flashbacks occur frequently in Homer's poems and it has been argued that they directly reflect 'the poet's technique and its origins in the context of performance' (Kelly, 2011, p.12). *Harry Potter* shares such journeys back into the past and its hero's most distinctive feature corresponds with one of Homer's most celebrated flashbacks: the story of how Odysseus came by his scar.

The moment in the *Odyssey* when the hero is recognised by his scar is one of the most famous in Homer. But it is also very odd. Odysseus has returned home to Ithaca in disguise and has not been recognised. Odysseus' old nurse washes his feet – the traditional welcome for a stranger – but upon touching the scar on his thigh, she instantly knows who he is. At this precise moment there is a sudden break in the narrative. Instead of following the main action, and hearing about the recognition of Odysseus, the listener is instead taken back into the past and told the story about how Odysseus came by his scar:

> So she drew near and began to wash her lord; at once she recognized the scar of the wound which long ago a boar had dealt him with his white tusk, when Odysseus had gone to Parnassus to visit Autolycus, his mother's noble father, who excelled all men in thievery and in oaths . . . as soon as early Dawn appeared, the rosy-fingered, they went out to hunt, the dogs and the sons of Autolycus too, and with them went noble Odysseus. Up the steep mountain, Parnassus, clothed with forests, they climbed, and presently reached its windy hollow. The sun was now just striking on the fields, as he rose from softly gliding, deep-flowing Oceanus, when the beaters came to a glade . . . . Now nearby a big wild boar was lying in a thick lair, through which the strength of the wet winds could never blow nor the rays of the bright sun beat, nor could rain pierce through it, so thick it was; and fallen leaves were there in plenty . . . Odysseus rushed forward, raising his long spear in his stout hand, eager to stab him; but the boar was too quick for him and struck him above the knee, charging upon him sideways, and with his tusk tore a long gash in the flesh.
>
> (Book 19, ll.390–451)

The most famous critical discussion of this passage – Erich Auerbach's 'Odysseus' Scar' – argues that this long interpolation is not for reasons of suspense (as a modern reader might expect) but in order to immerse the reader fully in Odysseus' world. Each thing – in the past as much as the present – is given life by Homer's fiction:

> The broadly narrated, charming, and subtly fashioned story of the hunt, with all its elegance and self-sufficiency, its wealth of idyllic pictures, seeks to win the reader over wholly to itself as long as he is hearing it, to make him forget what had just taken place during the foot-washing . . . . [Homer] knows no background. What he narrates is for the time being the only present.
>
> (2003 [1946], pp.4–5)

Auerbach argues that the reason Homer writes like this is that he is intent on creating a delightful physical world, experienced as real by his listeners, so that his creations 'bewitch us and ingratiate themselves to us until we live with them in the reality of their lives; so long as we are reading or hearing the poems, it does not matter whether we know that all this is only legend, "make-believe" . . . his reality is powerful enough in itself; it ensnares us, weaving its web around us, and that suffices him' (2003 [1946], p.13).

Harry Potter, like the *Odyssey*, creates a world in which its listeners are content to be ensnared. Rowling has spoken of how 'the world that I've created is a particularly shining example of a world to which it is very pleasant to escape' and of how she wanted to create a world that could be believed in 'whole-heartedly' (2005g). In an early interview she noted that 'it is an escapist book and by writing it I was escaping into it' (1997b). Ian Rankin has described how unusual is Rowling's relationship with her fictional world. He saw her in an Edinburgh café 'writing longhand, doing this family tree for a character' and commented: 'I can't think of any other author I know who would go into that kind of detail for something that's not going to be there on the page' (quoted in 2012d). The highly detailed information Rowling has revealed in interviews and on *Pottermore* illustrate the way that she has 'complete histories' (2002a) for even minor characters; it is a world she has 'loved and lived in for seventeen years' (2007j). It is, as Joan Acocella has put it, 'the great beauty of the Potter books . . . their wealth of imagination, their sheer, shining fullness' (2000).

Homer's world, likewise, has been celebrated for this 'sheer, shining fullness'. Homer's style 'knows only a foreground, only a uniformly illuminated, uniformly objective present' (Auerbach, 2003 [1946], p.7) and this aspect of his writing is clearest in his abrupt transitions into the past. The listener learns in the passage above not merely the details of Odysseus' fight with the boar but why he was visiting his grandfather, the origins of his grandfather's name, what they had eaten the night before and what the weather was like in this ever-present moment: 'the sun was now just striking the fields.' Homer turns the past into something that the listener experiences as present. It is an effect that *Harry Potter* creates through the Pensieve. In the Pensieve, as in Homer's flashbacks, the past has the same narrative reality as the present (and Harry is often rather slow to realise that he is not, in fact, in the present when he journeys in the Pensieve).

The believability of the narrative past in Homer, as in *Harry Potter*, imbues it with an unquestioned truth-value (it would never occur to a listener to doubt that this relation of the encounter with a wild boar tells the true history of how Odysseus came by his scar). *Harry Potter*, however, uses the audience's belief in what they see in the Pensieve in a tricksy way. While Homer's flash-backs give his listeners unmediated access to the past, *Harry Potter* delights in wrong-footing its audience. The 'uniformly illuminated, uniformly objective present' of the Pensieve – the fact that what we are shown actually happened – is intentionally designed to be misleading. The denouements of *Chamber* and *Goblet*, for example, reveal the way in which the accurately rendered memories of the Pensieve can yet deceive. The Pensieve records 'reality . . . what you remember is accurate in the Pensieve' (2005b) and yet in *Chamber* (in which Riddle's diary functions as a Pensieve) Harry and the reader are tricked by the memory they see into thinking that Hagrid opened the Chamber of Secrets. In *Goblet*, likewise, Harry – like the reader – is misled by Barty Crouch Jnr's accurately rendered protestations of innocence in the Pensieve into believing that he might have been wrongly convicted.

From the fifth book onwards, however, the Pensieve becomes both more important and (apparently) more reliable. In *Phoenix* Harry finds out two crucial facts from a Pensieve: first, that his father was not exactly the paragon he had imagined, and second, the full prophecy of his future. In *Half-Blood Prince* he learns the truth about Voldemort's past in the Pensieve from the memories of Dumbledore, Hokey, Ogden, Morfin and, eventually, Slughorn. In *Deathly Hallows* the Pensieve finally teaches Harry the whole truth about Snape. Even in these examples, however, we are often being tricked by an author who – as she says – 'loves to pull the wool over her readers' eyes' (2005h). The plot of *Half-Blood Prince* revolves around Harry's efforts to acquire Slughorn's recollection of his Horcrux conversation with Tom Riddle. It turns out, however, that the information this memory gives – unbeknownst to all but Dumbledore – is false. The memory we experience in the Pensieve informs the reader that there are six Horcruxes, but in fact – as will only be discovered at the very end of *Deathly Hallows* – there are seven. Even the final journey into the Pensieve – Harry's climactic entry into Snape's remembrances, his discovery of Snape's love for Lily and Harry's own fated death at Voldemort's hands – does not reveal the whole truth. When Harry returns from the Pensieve he thinks: 'finally, the truth' (*Deathly Hallows*, Chap 34, p.554). But we have been intentionally misled by the Pensieve into believing that Harry will meet his final end at Voldemort's hands.

THE PENSIEVE AND HOMERIC SYMPATHY

The name of the Pensieve puns not only on the way that the device 'sieves' through thoughts but also on the way that it renders the reader (as well as the user) 'pensive'. Although the word 'pensive' usually suggests serious or melancholy thought, it can mean simply thoughtful: 'full of thought; meditative, reflective' (*Oxford English Dictionary*). Rowling has given the Pensieve high prominence in interview, naming it as the magical object she would most like to own: 'I think the Pensieve would be tempting. Very tempting. To be able to go back and relive moments and look at them from different angles would be wonderful' (2007d). In the final, crucial, use of the Pensieve in *Deathly Hallows* Harry desires to escape from his own thoughts as he uses it, and this is a clue about how the Pensieve (and other flashbacks) functions within the narrative itself. It creates a hiatus, an escape from pre-formed modes of thinking and a pause for thought that provides a chance to make sense of what has gone before.

Embedded narratives are a storytelling technique that helps to create a three-dimensional world for the listener. But there is also an emotional and moral aspect to this three dimensionality. The vision in the Pensieve is not subjective – it records not what the 'rememberer' thinks has happened, but what did happen. Rowling has made this abundantly clear in interview: she has specifically rebutted the idea that the Pensieve reflects a personal perspective, saying that instead they show 'reality. It's important that I have got that across . . . what you remember is accurate in the Pensieve . . . and that's the magic of the Pensieve, that's what brings it alive . . . the Pensieve recreates a moment for you, so you could go into your own memory and relive things that you didn't notice at the time' (2005c). The importance of the Pensieve, surprisingly, turns out not to lie in the fact that it enables its users to see the past, but in the fact that it enables them to form a new perspective on it. In one of the most enigmatic moments in *Harry Potter* Dumbledore uses the Pensieve to probe the secrets of Voldemort's divided soul (*Phoenix*, Chap 22, p.416). In interview Rowling has described how 'Dumbledore is thinking aloud here, edging towards the truth with the help of the Pensieve' (2007f). The Pensieve allows even Dumbledore to think more clearly, and it also enables Harry to challenge his prejudices. In both *Phoenix* and *Deathly Hallows* Harry enters Snape's memories and learns new perspectives on his seemingly unshakeable beliefs about his teacher. In Harry's last entrance into the Pensieve he is finally brought to understand Snape: his fidelity to Lily's memory, his loyalty to Dumbledore and his bravery. This final challenge to his long-held prejudice means that he will eventually name his son after the man who had once been his arch-enemy.

Colin Burrow calls Homer's flashbacks 'the narrative form of Homeric sympathy' (1993, p.22). Burrow argues that Homer's epics are fundamentally concerned with the nature of sympathy and, in reference to the flashback about Odysseus' scar, states that 'it begins to look as though some version of compassion – sharing the experience of a sufferer – lies behind many of the most strikingly unseasonable of Homer's transitions' (1993, p.32). According to Burrow 'Homeric sympathy involves memory' and Homer's habit of breaking the main line of narrative to take the listener back into the past is connected with 'an effort on the part of the author to comprehend and embrace alien forms of feeling' (1993, pp.21, 4).

The most famous and powerful moment of Homeric sympathy is when Priam visits Achilles and begs for the return of his son's body. As the Trojan king, Priam is not only Achilles' enemy but one who risks his life in making this supplication. Achilles has killed Hector and then desecrated his body by dragging it round Troy's walls tied to his chariot wheels: 'foul deeds for noble Hector' (*Iliad*, Book 22, l.395). Achilles has reached this appalling pitch of wrathfulness because of the death of his friend, Patroclos, and it seems impossible that he will accede to Priam's request to return the body he has desecrated. But suddenly, astonishingly, he recognises a kinship of suffering with Priam. Priam asks Achilles to 'take pity on me remembering your father' and this request touches something within Achilles. The Greek warrior remembers that he too has a father, a father who will mourn his death as Priam mourns Hector, and in this moment of unexpected sympathy they sit and weep together:

> So he spoke, and in Achilles he roused desire to weep for his father . . ..
> So the two remembered – the one remembered man-slaying Hector and wept loudly, collapsed at Achilles' feet, but Achilles wept for his own father, and now again for Patroclus.
>
> (Book 24, ll.507–12)

Achilles has killed many others who have supplicated him earlier in the poem. Empathy has wrought an astounding change of heart in Homer's hero.

This is the climactic moment of the *Iliad* and it is one that *Harry Potter* remembers and responds to. Rowling has spoken of how, in *Goblet*, Harry 'can't save Cedric, but he wants to save Cedric's parents additional pain. He wants to bring back the body and treat it with respect' (2000j). The necessity of returning Cedric's body, and the fact that Harry risks his life to do it, responds to the importance that Homer places on the idea that Hector's body should be returned to Priam. (When an interviewer referenced this Homeric parallel, Rowling responded with enthusiasm: 'that's where it came from. That really, really, REALLY moved me when I read that when I was nineteen. The idea of the desecration of a body, a very ancient idea. . . I was thinking of that when Harry saved Cedric's body' [2000j].)

Homer, as discussed above, works repetition into the structure of his poems. This climactic moment of recognition between Achilles and Priam is prepared for by many moments of sympathetic recognition between enemies earlier in the *Iliad*. One such moment is when the Greek warrior Diomedes discovers that the Trojan Glaucus is tied to him through the guest-friendship of their forefathers. In one of Homer's many long interpolations, Diomedes discovers that he and this man whom he had thought his enemy are 'friends from our fathers' days' (*Iliad*, Book 6, l.231) because their forefathers had been friends. Harry, too, learns sympathy for his enemies through the Pensieve. Harry's journey into Snape's memories in *Phoenix* teaches him to appreciate his enemy's point of view. Harry is finally able to see the relationship between his father and Snape objectively, and realise that his father may not have been the paragon that he had always hoped and imagined. The Pensieve enables Harry to feel an unexpected emotion: '"I just never thought I'd feel sorry for Snape"' (Chap 29, p.592). *Harry Potter*'s use of Pensieves connects with Homer's flash-backs both in the way they enact the past as present and because they work to enable empathy. Diomedes and Glaucus discover that they are connected through a tie of guest-friendship by the digression into the past, a tie that prevents them from killing one another. As Burrow has argued: 'at the climactic moment of the [*Iliad*], in which Achilles is supplicated by Priam for the return of Hector's body, there is a similar movement of memory behind the sympathetic union of the two enemies: Priam asks Achilles not just to pity him but also to remember his own father' (1993, p.21). Achilles is suddenly enabled to see the humanity he shares with his enemies: Priam's resemblance to his father, his own resemblance to Hector and their common mortality.

Harry, too, is brought to some awareness of his connections with, and the shared humanity of, his arch-enemy Voldemort in the Pensieve. Harry's journeys into the Pensieve in both *Chamber* and *Half-Blood Prince* reveal a number of similarities between Harry and Tom Riddle. When Harry hangs back after class to speak to Slughorn, he reminds himself 'irresistibly of Voldemort' (*Half-Blood Prince*, Chap 18, p.355), whom he had seen doing exactly likewise in the Pensieve. This explicit parallel acts as a reminder of many other 'strange likenesses': they are similar looking, both half-bloods, both orphans raised unaware of their magical ancestry, and both Parselmouths (*Chamber*, Chap 17, p.233). Voldemort is Harry's gothic doppelgänger (see Chapter 6) and in their final battle, their ages will be mirror images of each other (17 and 71 [Harry Potter Wiki (2016e)]). When Harry first learns of these similarities, they terrify him, making him fear that he could be Slytherin's heir (*Chamber*, Chap 11, p.147). The gothic narrative frisson generated by unnerving reflections of the villain in the hero, however, deepens into something more generous and substantial by the end of the series.

As discussed earlier, *Chamber* is paired with *Half-Blood Prince* in the chiastic ordering of the series, and it is noticeable that this recognition of kinship, which is begun in *Chamber*, returns when Harry travels into the Pensieve in *Half-Blood Prince*. In the latter novel Harry learns that he shares with Voldemort the loss of his mother as a baby (and, as Rowling has said, 'everything would have changed if Merope had survived and raised him herself and loved him' [2007f]]). In a direct inversion of the mother who died to save Harry, Merope could not summon the will to live for her son:

'She wouldn't even stay alive for her son?'
Dumbledore raised his eyebrows.
'Could you possibly be feeling sorry for Lord Voldemort?'

(Chap 13, p.243)

The Pensieve evokes sympathy for Merope's suffering (Harry's first question on his return from Ogden's memory is, '"what happened to the girl in the cottage?"' [Chap 10, p.200]), but its vision of the past also rouses Harry's sympathy – instantly denied, but nonetheless clearly felt – for her son.

When Harry travels in the Pensieve to discover about Voldemort's origins he is unsure of what the benefit of all this time spent in Voldemort's past might be. When Dumbledore takes Harry back into Voldemort's past, he teaches him about the Horcruxes, but he also shows Harry Voldemort's terrible, abandoned start in life. In this way Dumbledore recalls and deepens the parallels between Harry and Riddle. For all that Voldemort and Harry have taken completely different paths, they share an essential kinship – the kinship of two boys who grew up alone without the people who should have loved them and who find the replacement for that love in a place rather than a person. They find it in Hogwarts; and it is part of Harry's kinship with Voldemort that he understands, in a way even Dumbledore does not, where the final Horcrux will be hidden.

Even after his first journey into the Pensieve Harry finds that the parallels between himself and Riddle have taught him sympathy. Burrow has noted the way in which 'Homeric sympathy is generally founded on memory of one's own suffering, and a sense that it is analogous to the suffering of the other' (1993, p.22). This is also how sympathy functions in *Harry Potter* as Harry recognises in Riddle another who shares both his own motherless condition and his love for Hogwarts. Harry identifies with Riddle as a boy who has been raised unloved in the Muggle world, who has had a miserable, parentless childhood and who has loved Hogwarts with the same deep sense that this is the first place he has belonged, his first and only real home (*Chamber*, Chap 13, p.185). It is a kinship that is remembered in the final novel when Harry argues that Voldemort will have hidden a Horcrux in Hogwarts – "'It was his first real home, the place that meant he was special, it meant everything to him'" – and Ron counters (with acerbic insight) that Harry could be talking about himself (Chap 15, p.238).

Harry's discovery about Voldemort's comparable beginnings – his parallel loss of maternal love – is a version of the discovery that Achilles makes about his enemy. Achilles, in the passage that Rowling found so very moving, suddenly understands that Priam is a father, just as his father is, and that Priam grieves for his son, just as he (Achilles) grieves for Patroclos: 'so he spoke, and in Achilles he roused desire to weep for his father . . .. So the two remembered – the one remembered man-slaying Hector and wept loudly, collapsed at Achilles' feet, but Achilles wept for his own father, and now again for Patroclus.' This is the kind of sympathy of which Voldemort is incapable but it is a sympathy that Dumbledore attempts to make Harry understand. It is, at its most basic, an awareness of man's common mortality.

It is, perhaps, the empathy for Voldemort that Harry has (however unwillingly) gained through the Pensieve that enables Harry not only to realise where the final Horcrux will be hidden, but to reach out to his enemy in his own heroic gesture of sympathy. As Harry and Voldemort circle each other in the final battle Harry tells his enemy to attempt to reconnect with his own humanity and feel remorse. Harry's attempt to bring Voldemort to repentance is deeply un-Homeric. Nonetheless, Harry's generosity towards his enemy has been enabled by the Homeric narrative aspects of the Pensieve and *Harry Potter*'s responsiveness to Homer's own deep concern with a recognition of kinship even (or especially) with one's enemy. Achilles returns Hector's body to Priam because he recognises the likeness between his father and his enemy's father, between Priam's suffering and his own. Homer's poetry strives towards an enabling of dialogue, of empathy; to bring listeners to the understanding that the pain of another's suffering is identical to their own. This is one of the things that literature can do and in this sense the Pensieve, like Homer's flashbacks, is a metaphor for literature as a whole: an attempt to see things from someone else's perspective.

This chapter's consideration of how *Harry Potter* is inspired by Rowling's own classical reading will be built on in the next chapter's exploration of Ovidian names. There are many classical names in *Harry Potter* and it is noticeable, for example, how many of the people whom Slughorn recalls in *Half-Blood Prince* have such names. Among Slughorn's recollections feature characters with names such as Hector Dagworth-Granger and Ciceron Harkiss; there is Cormac McLaggen's uncle Tiberius, Draco's grandfather Abraxas and Marcus Belby's uncle Damocles. Slughorn himself has the first name Horace, a Roman poet who was famous for nurturing a celebrated circle of influential friends and supporters (Spencer, 2015, p.157). These classical names from Hogwarts' past reflect Slughorn's own old-fashioned nature: his dated nightwear and notions (for example, on the acceptability of openly expressing favouritism) and his hankering for an outmoded 'old-boys' school network.

They also, however, work on a deeper level. Slughorn is the only teacher who seems obsessed with Hogwarts' past, or who retains regular links with the previous generations he has taught. Slughorn's primary plot-relevance is his memory of a question a student asked him fifty years earlier, and it could be argued that these classical names draw attention to the way the past is played out in the present. It is true both within the plot-dynamics of *Harry Potter* (and in the novels' own self-referential structure) that the past is 'parent' to the present narrative. Just as Harry embodies his parents' physical attributes, and his year group replay the dynamics of his parents' cohort, so these resurfacing classical names, like the epigraph from Aeschylus, suggest that old stories and familiar cycles will be replayed in this modern text.

Note

1 Dupree has an interesting discussion of the Aramaic and Hebrew sources of 'Abracadabra' (2011, pp.46–52).

2 Naming in *Harry Potter*

Plato, Shakespeare and Ovid

Rowling thinks very carefully about her names: 'names are really crucial to me . . .. And for some reason I just can't move on until I know I've called them the right thing' (1999e). The name of the Mirror of Erised, for example, is (as is well known) 'desire' spelt backwards. Inversion is a traditional naming technique and Rowling here joins an English satirical tradition of mirror-names that hide meaning in plain view. (One mid-sixteenth-century comic work, for example, contains the mendacious tales of the traveller Mendax, who tells of his faraway journeys in the humorous-sounding capital city of 'Nodnol' [Bullein, 1888, pp.105–106].) The Mirror of Erised is, however, a particularly satisfying example of the genre, as it uses a mirror-name to name an actual mirror. But it also does something even more subtle. The Mirror of Erised reflects the on-looker's desire but it also – as will be discussed in this chapter – fosters their desire for a mere reflection.

Harry Potter's names are an exuberantly joyful, as well as highly informative, part of its imagined world. Rowling drew inspiration from numerous sources – 'war memorials, telephone directories, shop fronts, saints, villains, baby-naming books – you name it, I've got names from it!' (2004–12a) – but her main source was books. These are often factual works: in one interview Rowling called *Culpeper's Complete Herbal* 'the answer to my every prayer' (2002b) and she has also noted that Hedwig's name came from a book of medieval saints (2004–12a). She describes Brewer's *Dictionary of Phrase and Fable* as 'a great source for names' and it is where she found Gilderoy Lockhart's Christian name: 'I knew his name had to have an impressive ring to it. I was looking through the *Dictionary of Phrase and Fable* . . . and came across Gilderoy, a handsome Scottish highwayman' (2002a). It is literature, however, that is probably the most important source for *Harry Potter*'s names.

To take one example – the surname of the Gryffindor ghost Sir Nicholas de Mimsy-Porpington. The word 'mimsy' first appears in 'Jabberwocky', a poem in Lewis Carroll's *Through the Looking Glass*. (This is a book Rowling knows well: when she described Luna as 'likely to believe ten impossible things before breakfast' [2003c] she was quoting the White Queen's airy description of herself as someone who has 'believed as many as six impossible things before breakfast' [Carroll, 1963 (1871), p.202].) 'Jabberwocky' is a nonsense poem and Carroll has great fun sending up literary critics in the scene when Humpty Dumpty explains the poem to Alice:

> *'Twas brillig, and the slithy toves*
> *Did gyre and gimble in the wabe;*
> *All mimsy were the borogoves,*
> *And the mome raths outgrabe.*

'That's enough to begin with,' Humpty Dumpty interrupted: 'there are plenty of hard words there. "*Brillig*" means four o'clock in the afternoon—the time when you begin *broiling* things for dinner.'

'That'll do very well,' said Alice: 'and "*slithy*"?'

'Well, "*slithy*" means "lithe and slimy." "Lithe" is the same as "active." You see it's like a portmanteau—there are two meanings packed up into one word . . . "*mimsy*" is "flimsy and miserable" (there's another portmanteau for you).'

(pp.218–9)

The portmanteau 'mimsy' – meaning 'flimsy and miserable' – is a perfect description of Nearly Headless Nick, who is both often upset and affronted and, being see-through, literally 'flimsy'. But in addition to being the source of Nick's surname, Humpty Dumpty's zestful discussion of portmanteau words recalls the way that Rowling compresses as much meaning as possible into the words she invents:

> 'When *I* use a word,' Humpty Dumpty said in rather a scornful tone, 'it means just what I choose it to mean—neither more nor less.'
>
> 'The question is,' said Alice, 'whether you *can* make words mean so many different things.'
>
> 'The question is,' said Humpty Dumpty, 'which is to be master—that's all . . ... I meant by "impenetrability" that we've had enough of that subject, and it would be just as well if you'd mention what you mean to do next, as I suppose you don't mean to stop here all the rest of your life.'
>
> 'That's a great deal to make one word mean,' Alice said in a thoughtful tone.
>
> 'When I make a word do a lot of work like that,' said Humpty Dumpty, 'I always pay it extra.'

(pp.216–7)

Rowling, like Humpty Dumpty, loves words that 'do a lot of work': 'Azkaban', for example, combines the island prison Alcatraz and the Hebrew word for the depths of hell, 'Abaddon' (Rowling, 2015a). And just possibly, Rowling was recalling Lewis's bravura description of word-creation when she gave Nick the surname de Mimsy-Porpington.

Nick's name perfectly suits his character and this chapter explores the literary concept of 'cratylic' naming – a name that fits the person's nature – before looking at the influence of Shakespeare and classical sources on a number of *Harry Potter*'s names. The chapter argues, in particular, for the influence of the Latin poet Ovid (whom Rowling studied at university (1998d, p. 260)). Ovid is the source of the first names of Remus Lupin, Merope Gaunt, Argus Filch and Narcissa Malfoy, and – as this chapter argues – the Ovidian myths of Narcissus and of Orpheus and Eurydice also influence *Harry Potter* in more fundamental ways.

Ovid's *Metamorphoses* tells stories about people and gods who 'metamorphose' into new and strange creations; and, as Spencer has shown, there are a number of close parallels between Ovidian transformations and those which characters undergo in *Harry Potter* (2015, pp.212–4). In Rowling's original plans for the subject of Transfiguration she named it 'Metamorphosis' (2015i) and the name of Ovid's epic is also echoed in the name of her Metamorphmagi. Ovid's poetic epic of transformed mortals and shape-shifting gods has been so perennially popular over the centuries that it has a good claim to be one of the most influential poems ever written. The planet Jupiter's moons, for example, are named after Jupiter's lovers in the *Metamorphoses* and Io, Callisto and Ganymede (three of these moons) turn up in Harry's O.W.L. homework. When Harry tries to remember the moons of Jupiter during his exams, therefore, he is sifting his memory for Ovidian names.

PLATO AND CRATYLIC NAMES

In having names that correspond to natures – a mirror with a mirror-name and a bank called Gringotts (with 'ingots' tucked away within it [Rowling, 2005e]) – *Harry Potter* is part of a tradition that derives, ultimately, from Plato's *Cratylus*. Plato's *Cratylus* is a dialogue between Socrates, Cratylus and Hermogenes in which Socrates explains the nature of language through an explanation of names. Cratylus believes in the divine origin of names and thinks therefore that the form of a name – its sound, for example – will 'fit' the thing named. Plato's dialogue suggests that if names have no inherent link to the things they signify then language is arbitrary, but if there is some intrinsic connection between the name and the thing named then language could be seen as a divinely inspired guide to reality.

The idea of an intrinsic connection between name and thing was often held to exist at the level of sound. This onomatopoeic theory of language has an obvious appeal for writers, and Gerard Manley Hopkins, a profound poet of sound, wrote in his journal: '*Grind, gride, gird, grit, groat, grate, greet* . . . . Original meaning to *strike, rub*, particularly *together*. To *greet*, to strike hands together (?) . . . . I believe these words to be onomatopoetic. *Gr* common to them all representing a particular sound. In fact I think the onomatopoetic theory has not had a fair chance' (1959, p.5). Names beginning with '*Gr*' – such as Griphook, Grindelwald, Gringotts and Grawp – are relatively common in *Harry Potter* and they highlight Rowling's own interest in onomatopoeic naming: '"*Gr*" words can sound quite aggressive . . . or even sinister . . . . I just thought it sounded that little bit intimidating' (2005e).

The onomatopoeic theory of language has not been generally accepted for – as Socrates notes in *Cratylus* – so few words 'sound' like the thing that they name. In Plato's dialogue, therefore, Socrates rejects the philosophical study of language as inferior to the study of things. Socrates' disappointment, however, is the writer's opportunity for in fiction writers have the chance to create names that fit their owners to perfection. Cratylic names are one of *Harry Potter*'s most ubiquitous and enjoyable forms of naming. Slughorn, for example, has a name that fits him perfectly: Socrates says in *Cratylus* that 'o' is best used when imitating roundness and 'g' when imitating something cloying or glutinous (as the sound stops the gliding of the tongue as it is spoken [427b, 427c]). The fitting – 'cratylic' – nature of *Harry Potter*'s naming, however, is not primarily about sound, but about the meaning of the words that combine to form these names. Slughorn's name suggests that he is well fed and possibly slightly repellent, like a slug, but it also gives a more important hint about his nature: his extreme caution. Slugs retract their horns at the first sign of danger. Slughorn's name is therefore a clue to the patience Harry will need to acquire the Horcrux-memory from him. Under the influence of Felix Felicis Harry learns to use enticements – the gold Slughorn can make from the Acromantula venom and the conviviality of alcohol-fuelled reminiscences – to tempt him out of his reluctance.

Rowling has described how much she likes the way English sounds – 'nobbily, and textured, and I love it' (2005g) – and how satisfying she finds it when characters' names work both in terms of their sound and their meaning: 'Gildcroy Lockhart, it just sounded perfect .... Impressive, and yet, in the middle, quite hollow, of course' (2005g). Rowling has picked out Mundungus Fletcher as a name with which she is particularly pleased: Mundungus means 'foul-stinking tobacco, which really suits him' (2005g). But there is also a possible pun in his very ordinary-sounding surname. A 'fletcher' is someone who adds the feathers ('flitches') to arrows and Mundungus is indeed a flighty individual: the first time the reader comes across him is when he has just deserted his post (he was meant to have been guarding Harry at the beginning of *Phoenix*) and he will also flee at the beginning of *Deathly Hallows* with more catastrophic results.

Dumbledore's name is another example of Rowling's excellence at cratylic naming. The sound of the name evokes a friendly dependability – the repeated '*d*' sounds solid and reliable, the soft '*um*' sounds warm – and it 'sounds endearing and strangely impressive at the same time' (Rowling, 2002a). As noted in the Introduction, the name derives from Hardy's dialect name for a bumblebee: 'I chose it because my image is of this benign wizard, always on the move, humming to himself' (2002a). Dumbledore's full name – Albus Percival Wulfric Brian Dumbledore – is a synthesis of ancient worth (the Latin for white, an Arthurian knight, and a medieval saint – Wulfric of Haselbury – who was famed for his gifts of healing and prophecy) and eccentricity. In the context of Dumbledore's other names 'Brian' is fabulously incongruous and, as Rowling adores Monty Python (see Chapter 5), may allude to Python's choice of 'Brian' as comically inappropriate for a Messiah. Dumbledore's name encapsulates his nature: it is authoritative, warm, witty, unconventional and suggestive of hidden depths.

Cratylic naming is ubiquitous in English comedy, and *Harry Potter* often uses cratylic names for comic effect; but cratylic names also encourage readers in a bit of sleuthing. Percy Weasley's middle name (Ignatius) suggests that, like Ignatius Loyola – who underwent a famous conversion –, he might switch sides. 'Scabbers' sounds at first as if it is nothing more than a comic name for a rather mangy rat, but as the reader discovers who Scabbers actually is, the term 'scab' (a slang word for traitor) becomes pertinent. 'Scabs' are strike-breakers, abused as those who have given up the unequal fight and thrown in their lot with the bigger, stronger, but morally wrong, side. There is a strong resonance in this for Scabbers, who, from his hero-worship of James and Sirius to his defection to Voldemort, is a coward who has always sought the protection of the biggest bully in the playground. The name of Ron's rat – as well as the meaning of 'rat' itself – is a hint as to the true identity of the traitor in their midst.

ROWLING'S SHAKESPEAREAN NAMES: HERMIONE, HERMES AND HERMENEUTICS

Shakespeare, one of Rowling's favourite writers, is the origin of one of *Harry Potter*'s most significant names. Rowling saw Shakespeare's *The Winter's Tale* as a teenager 'and that was where I found the name Hermione' (quoted in Fraser, 2001, p.31). Hermione is a feminisation of the name Hermes and in February 2007 Rowling left a message on the bust of Hermes in her room in the Balmoral Hotel: '*JK Rowling finished writing* Harry Potter and the Deathly Hallows *in this room (652) on 11th Jan 2007*' (Edinburgh-flats, 2016). Hermes – the messenger God – is given a message to carry by Rowling. But she may also have chosen this room, with its Hermes statue, in reference to her hero-ine; for – in a sly allusion to the fact that Shakespeare's Hermione famously ends *The Winter's Tale* as a statue – Hermione becomes a statue when she is Petrified in *Chamber*. Rowling strengthens the connection between her hero-ine and Hermes by giving her the initials HG – Hg is the chemical symbol for Mercury, the Latin name for Hermes (Granger, 2008, p.146; Granger, 2009, p.239). Hermes is the messenger-god and within *Harry Potter* this aspect of the deity is drawn attention to by having an owl (the message-carriers in the Wizarding world) with the name Hermes.[1] The Greek god Hermes' role as a messenger between heaven and earth means that he explains the actions and desires of the gods to humankind. For this reason he has given his name to the study of meaning: 'hermeneutics'. Hermione, as her name suggests, is the queen of hermeneutics in *Harry Potter*. She is constantly explaining to the others what is really going on.

Harry Potter pairs Hermione's love of reading with her intellect, her ability to read between the lines. Hermione is always darting off to the library and her love of books symbolises her ability to correctly grasp the meaning of things. Rowling has agreed emphatically with the observation by the *Harry Potter* screenwriter, Steve Kloves, that Hermione is a gift for a writer because 'she can carry exposition in a wonderful way because you just assume she'd read it in a book' (2014d). Hermione is an attentive reader (pleasingly, we know she even pays attention to footnotes [*Deathly Hallows*, Chap 6, p.89]). At the beginning of *Phoenix* Hermione reads the *Daily Prophet* carefully while Harry simply scans the front page. Her observant reading means that she understands what Harry has failed to notice: the way its editors are attempting to discredit him through a continual stream of subtly negative comments. In *Half-Blood Prince* Hermione works out that 'Prince' – the name written in Harry's Potion book – may be a surname not a title. She likewise decodes Professor Umbridge's speech at the beginning of the new school year in *Phoenix*. This speech is so full of cliché that Harry and Ron (like almost everyone else) immediately stop listening, but Hermione (alone of the students) hears the subtext of what Umbridge is saying.

Hermione detects the truth beneath Umbridge's fine-sounding words: that the Ministry will be instituting a repressively conservative curriculum. In *Phoenix* the Ministry of Magic (always a somewhat equivocal establishment) becomes a fully oppressive institution. Sarah Cocita Reschan (2015) has argued for *Phoenix* as a dystopian novel; and it is at this point in the series that echoes of the Ministry of Love and the Ministry of Truth (from George Orwell's dystopian novel *1984*) can be clearly heard in the name 'Ministry of Magic'. In *1984* the Ministry of Love spreads hatred and the Ministry of Truth spreads disinformation and, likewise, in *Phoenix* the Ministry of Magic tries to prevent students from learning magic. Umbridge is guilty of a similar falsifying of language as Orwell's government and it is Hermione, alone of the students at Hogwarts, who recognises the disjunction between the value Umbridge claims to place on education and what she actually plans to do.

Rowling has explained that Harry's glasses have 'a symbolic function . . . Harry is the eyes on to the books in the sense that it is always Harry's point of view, so there was also that, you know, facet of him wearing glasses' (2005d). It seems highly suggestive, therefore, that Hermione helps Harry when he cannot see through his glasses. She uses the *Impervius* spell to enable him to see through his rain-drenched glasses in *Azkaban* (Chap 9, p.133) (and Steve Kloves builds on this idea by having Hermione mend Harry's glasses when she first meets him in the film of *Philosopher's Stone*). If his glasses symbolise the way that 'Harry is the eyes on to the books' then Hermione's ability to help him see through his glasses symbolises the way that she helps both him and the reader to understand what is happening. As Rowling notes: 'you need to tell your readers something . . . there are only two characters you can put it convincingly into their dialogue – one is Hermione and the other is Dumbledore' (2014d). Like her namesake Hermes, Hermione has an explanatory – a hermeneutic – function.

Rowling's Shakespearean names: the Gaunts

'Gaunt', the surname of Voldemort's grandfather, is, like Hermione, another of *Harry Potter*'s Shakespearean names and it is one of the series' most subtle cratylic names. John of Gaunt is a historical figure, and in Shakespeare's *Richard II* he puns on his name: 'O how that name befits my composition!/ Old Gaunt indeed, and gaunt in being old' (2.1.73–4). In *Harry Potter*, likewise, the hollowed-out qualities of the name come to the fore. Fittingly, the main thing that has dried out loveless old Marvolo Gaunt is his obsession with this name. Marvolo Gaunt is fiercely proud of his descent: he shoves his ring into Bob Ogden's face: '"centuries it's been in our family, that's how far back we go, and pure-blood all the way! Know how much I've been offered for this, with the Peverell coat of arms engraved on the stone?"' (*Half-Blood Prince*, Chap 10, p.196). The reader finds out in the final book that this stone did indeed belong to Cadmus Peverell. However, the symbol scratched on its surface is not a coat of arms, but the sign of the Deathly Hallows. Marvolo's obsession with his aristocratic heritage means that he has misread this symbol; his bigoted obsession with the purity of his blood means that he fails to discover the true power of what he owns.

The chapter of *Half-Blood Prince* in which the reader is introduced to Marvolo and Morfin is called 'The House of Gaunt'. This title puns on the heraldic meaning of 'house' as a long-lived, noble family and puts it in ironic contrast with the hovel in which the Gaunts now live. The same pun is used in Chapter 6 of *Phoenix* ('The Noble and Most Ancient House of Black'). These chapter titles alert the reader to the way that the Gaunt and Black families have privileged past grandeur over present comfort, for both families now live in truly horrible homes. The Gaunts share with the Blacks their 'pure-blood mania', which, as Sirius puts it, is to be '"convinced that to be a Black made you practically royal"' (*Phoenix*, Chap 6, p.104). The name 'Gaunt' follows through this idea as it a genuinely royal name, for John of Gaunt was a member of the House of Plantagenet, a famous royal dynasty.

Shakespeare's John of Gaunt speaks proudly of his country in the famous 'sceptred isle' speech in *Richard II*:

> This royal throne of kings, this sceptered isle,
> This earth of majesty, this seat of Mars,
> This other Eden, demi-paradise,
> This fortress built by nature for herself
> Against infection and the hand of war,
> This happy breed of men, this little world,
> This precious stone set in the silver sea,
> Which serves it in the office of a wall,
> Or as a moat defensive to a house
> Against the envy of less happier lands,
> This blessèd plot, this earth, this realm, this England.

(2.1.40–50)

This speech is an astonishing single sentence and a lyrical evocation of national pride. But in giving Voldemort's family the name 'Gaunt' Rowling draws on the literally insular nationalism of John of Gaunt's most famous speech – with its image of England as an island, a separated nation, a 'precious stone set in the silver sea' – and transforms it into an unthinking 'little-Englander' outlook. In Marvolo and Morfin Gaunt the proud patriotism of John of Gaunt's most famous speech has withered into an embittered and abusive isolationism that gives rise to racially motivated violence. Their bigotry hardens into the fully fledged racial cleansing of Voldemort, who murders his "'filthy Muggle father'" (*Chamber*, Chap 17, p.231) before attempting to rid the Wizarding world of Mudbloods and blood traitors. Rowling's response to the question 'what vice do you most despise?' is 'bigotry' (2007l) and with the name 'Gaunt' *Harry Potter* draws subtle attention to the idea that what begins as nationalism can end as bigotry.

HARRY POTTER'S OVIDIAN NAMES: REMUS

One of the most cratylic of *Harry Potter*'s names is that of Remus Lupin for both parts of Lupin's name declare his wolfish ('lupine') nature. 'Remus' is connected with wolves because in Rome's foundation myth the twins Romulus and Remus were suckled by a wolf (before the elder of them grew up and founded Rome). But the name 'Remus' also expresses something less easy to define. Lupin is one of Rowling's most loveable creations, but he is also something of an outsider. His argument with Harry over his abandonment of Tonks and their future child, and his death in the battle of Hogwarts, reflect the bad luck and, possibly bad judgement, of the classical Remus.

The myth of Romulus and Remus is a strikingly ambivalent foundation myth. Surprisingly, it hints that Romulus may not have been, in fact, divinely chosen to found Rome and it ends in disturbing violence with the murder of his unsuccessful twin. In Ovid's version of the myth the brothers differ about where to build their new city and agree to decide the matter by divine augury: 'Romulus said: "There needs no contest. Great faith is put in birds, let's try the birds." The proposal was accepted. One of the two went to the rocks of the wooded Palatine; the other went at dawn to the top of the Aventine. Remus saw six birds, Romulus saw twice six, one after the other: they stood by their compact, and Romulus was accorded the government of the City' (*Fasti*, Book 4, ll.813–8).

In Ovid's version of the story Romulus is chosen by divine augury and Remus accepts his brother's victory. Other sources, however, suggest that Romulus' victory may have been the result of deception. In Plutarch's *Life of Romulus*, 'Agreeing to settle their quarrel by the flight of birds of omen, and taking their seats on the ground apart from one another, six vultures, they say, were seen by Remus, and twice that number by Romulus. Some, however, say that whereas Remus truly saw his six, Romulus lied about his twelve' (9.4–5). Plutarch suggests that Remus may in fact have had the superior claim and that, without Romulus's deceit, 'Rome' would have been 'Remuria'. Rowling studied Plutarch as an undergraduate (2008d) and she may be aware of this rather more equivocal account.

Remus' bad luck becomes even clearer later in the story when he is killed. In Ovid Romulus is innocent of Remus' death (he has – fittingly – been swiftly killed by someone called Celer because of his 'rash' behaviour) but this is not the case in Plutarch, who notes the rumour that Romulus had himself murdered his brother: 'when Remus knew of the deceit, he was enraged, and as Romulus was digging a trench where his city's wall was to run, he ridiculed some parts of the work, and obstructed others. At last, when he leaped across it, he was smitten (by Romulus himself, as some say; according to others, by Celer, one of his companions), and fell dead there' (10.1). Plutarch tells much the same story as Ovid – Remus leaps over the newly built city walls and is killed – but in a very different way. Plutarch's statement that Remus was enraged by Romulus' deceit strengthens the evidence that Romulus *did* trick him and it is strongly hinted – given this confirmation of the previous rumour – that the 'some' who say that Romulus has murdered his own twin are telling the truth. Ovid appears to whitewash the injustice against Remus that Plutarch reveals.

Wizarding society likewise closes ranks against Remus Lupin, who will – like the classical Remus – be murdered at the end of the series. *Harry Potter*'s Remus is a reminder of how the winners of history tend to rewrite the losers as morally bankrupt, while the truth may be quite the reverse. Ovid's Remus is merely unlucky but Plutarch's Remus is the victim of injustice. Remus Lupin grows up thinking that he is an Ovidian figure, unluckily bitten by an out-of-control werewolf, but he later discovers that he is, in fact, a Plutarchan-style victim of a politically motivated revenge (*Half-Blood Prince*, Chap 16, p.314).

There is a surprising link between city-building and fratricide in foundation myths. Not only does Romulus murder Remus in order to found Rome but the first man to build a city in the Bible is Cain, who also committed the first murder (Genesis 4.2–8, 16–7). Cain kills his brother Abel because he is jealous when Abel's offering gains divine favour and his does not – and if Rome's foundation myth is read in the light of this, older, story it might even be suspected that Remus won the augury of divine favour and was murdered by Romulus as a result. The story of Romulus and Remus, like that of Cain and Abel, speaks to the dark origins of civilisation.

Harry Potter has a strong, and slightly surprising, interest in the mechanics of society. Its heroes not only resist the evil of Voldemort but also the unjustly wielded bureaucratic power of the Ministry. After Voldemort has been defeated they will work to cleanse the Ministry of corruption. In an interview immediately after the ending of the series Rowling said that Harry became the head of the Auror Department and Hermione went 'pretty high up' (2007m) in the Department of Magical Law Enforcement. (In *Cursed Child* Hermione has become Minister for Magic, and Harry is Head of Magical Law Enforcement.) Rowling said that they will improve the Ministry beyond all recognition: 'they made a new world' (2007m). One of the aspects of Wizarding society that *Harry Potter* most strongly criticises is bigotry against the outsider: the oppression of house-elves, the prejudice against 'half-breeds', and the way that Hagrid and Lupin are made to suffer when people realise their 'otherness'. Remus' name marks him as an underdog, an 'outsider' in the stories society chooses to tell about itself. Rowling has written of how 'Lupin's condition of lycanthropy (being a werewolf) was a metaphor for those illnesses that carry a stigma, like HIV and AIDS' (2015q) and he battles Voldemort in the hope of founding a fairer, less prejudiced society.

When Lupin appears on Potterwatch he takes the alias Romulus. *Deathly Hallows* sees Lupin reach his lowest point, fleeing from the responsibility of his wife's pregnancy and rejected by Harry as a result. But Lupin's appearance on *Potterwatch*, suggests that he has turned a corner and his supportive message to Harry suggests that (as Ron will confirm) he has returned to Tonks. Lupin's generosity to Harry at this point is a mark of his redemption: '"I'd tell him to follow his instincts, which are good and nearly always right"' (Chap 22, p.357). 'Remus' is the name of the brother who was forgotten by history, the one who did not found Rome, the inauspicious 'other' who is murdered. The alias 'Romulus' that he takes on *Potterwatch* – the famous twin who founds Rome – intimates his new-found strength. Lupin will die, but not before he has witnessed the great joy of his son's birth. Teddy Lupin will not suffer as his father has done and when Voldemort is defeated, a new, fairer society will be born, which will banish the bigotry that afflicted his father.

OVIDIAN NAMES: MEROPE

There is a fashion among pure-blood families for naming their children after stars. Merope Gaunt and the brothers Sirius and Regulus Arcturus Black all have star-based names. Rowling's hand-drawn family tree of 'The Noble and Most Ancient House of Black' (made and auctioned for charity in 2006) shows that other members of the family have names derived from constellations, such as Orion and Cassiopeia. Draco Malfoy, likewise, shares his name with a constellation (the dragon [Rowling, 2015e]) and his son Scorpius Malfoy carries on this pure-blood tradition. This is, perhaps, an unsurprising pure-blood family tradition, for the most famous character to share his name with a star is Lucifer, whose name means 'light bearer'. (In a possible allusion to Lucifer's most famous attribute – his pride – Rowling has noted that the Black family tradition of naming their children after constellations is an apt expression of 'their lofty ambition and pride' [2015n]). The prince of darkness shares his name with the morning star: 'how art thou fallen from heaven, O Lucifer, son of the morning!' (Isaiah 14.12). The star imagery in the names of Merope, Sirius and Regulus Arcturus, however, has the capacity to break free from its implicitly satanic origins. While it might be natural for characters such as Marvolo Gaunt and Mrs Black to name their children after stars in honour of Lucifer, such stellar names nonetheless point to the possibility that these characters will, after all, learn to shine.

After the death of Dumbledore Harry discovers that a certain 'R. A. B.' has taken the locket Horcrux. This means that the trio are searching for someone with these initials, which brings all three of Regulus' names to the fore: '*Regulus Arcturus Black*' (*Deathly Hallows*, Chap 10, p.153). Regulus is a particularly bright star and Arcturus is even brighter: the fourth brightest star in the night sky (while Sirius is the brightest). Both of the Black sons have forenames that shine against the darkness of their unprepossessing surname. Regulus Arcturus and Sirius spring from 'black' parentage in metaphorical as well as literal senses – for they come from a family in thrall to the Dark Arts – and both are believed to be Death Eaters. But both, in their different ways, break free of their evil upbringing and the negative significance of their surname. Although Regulus joins the Death Eaters, he will sacrifice himself to defeat the Dark Lord. For Regulus, like Sirius, the bright potential of his stellar name ends up shining through the darkness of his Black parentage.

Merope Gaunt, likewise, shares her name with a star. Like Sirius (whose naming after the 'Dog Star' punningly alludes to the form he takes as an Animagus) the star after whom Merope is named has a strong relevance to her story. Merope was a beautiful nymph – one of the seven sisters who make up the constellation known as the Pleiades. She is sometimes known as the 'Lost Pleiad' because she shines less brightly in the night sky than the other Pleiades (it was some time before she was noticed and charted by astronomers). The myth that evolved to explain her relative faintness was that while her sisters married gods she married a mere mortal. Her pale beams were the result, therefore, either of the loss of power that this lowly marriage entailed, or because she repented of her choice and hid her head in shame:

> The Pleiades will commence to lighten the burden that rests on their father's shoulders; seven are they usually called, but six they usually are; whether it be that six of the sisters were embraced by gods . . .. [T]he seventh, Merope, was married to a mortal man, to Sisyphus, and she repents of it, and from shame at the deed she alone of the sisters hides herself; or whether it be that Electra could not brook to behold the fall of Troy, and so covered her eyes with her hand.
>
> (*Fasti*, Book 4, ll.169–78)

Ovid's Merope's marriage to a mortal parallels Merope Gaunt's union with a Muggle. Ovid's culture looked no more kindly than the Gaunts on 'mixed' marriages and Ovid states that Merope repents of marrying beneath her and hides her head in shame. It is noticeable, however, that this is not the only explanation given in the *Fasti* as to why the Pleiades (a group of seven sisters) often appear as only six stars in the night sky. Ovid's other explanation is that it is in fact Electra who is the 'Lost Pleiad' because she hides her face in grief. This means that the reader is, after all, free to believe that Merope is neither weakened by, nor ashamed of, her choice of a mortal husband.

Harry Potter's Merope shares with Ovid's in the way that her story is liable to different interpretations. Merope Gaunt, too, may or may not hide her head from shame. Unusually for *Harry Potter*, there is no definitive answer given to the puzzle as to why Merope fails to use magic to prevent her death: is she ashamed like Ovid's Merope or grieving like Ovid's Electra? Harry and the reader are left to rely on Dumbledore's guesses to piece together Merope's story. Did her magical powers increase when not suffocated under the abuse of her male relatives? Did she cease to enslave her husband because she loved him? Did the consequent depression caused by his leaving her rob her of her newly acquired magical abilities? Or did she just decide that she wanted to die?

Such alternative explanations are known in Ovidian criticism as 'multiple aetiologies' and they are a significant feature of Ovid's *Fasti*. Modern explanations of phenomena – in scientific papers, for example – rarely proffer competing theories without choosing among them, but in this poem Ovid often gives more than one reason for why things might be as they are. Ovid's fluidity of explanation may be something on which *Harry Potter* draws as it allows readers to make their own decisions about Merope's story.

Merope is one of the series' most ambiguous characters. She enslaves Tom Riddle Snr and her abandonment of her baby is one reason for his subsequent psychopathy. Nonetheless, there is a natural tendency for a reader to support the underdog and Merope gropes for personal fulfilment out of the violent misery in which she is raised. She is an oppressed young woman who does not share in the anti-Muggle prejudice of her bigoted family. In an inversion of Ovidian morality (in which the author assumes that his Merope will be ashamed of marrying a mortal) *Harry Potter* presents Merope's lack of race-prejudice against Muggles as a moral strength. *Harry Potter* also uses literary archetypes to strengthen the reader's sympathy for Merope. She shares the Ovidian name of a beautiful and poignant nymph-star and (as will be discussed in Chapter 7) her story echoes the hopeless pathos of Hardy's deserted, poverty-stricken heroine Fanny Robin. These sympathetic analogues work to give a complex and morally nuanced hinterland to a woman whom the reader meets only through the medium of others' memories, but whose tragic tale is the dark reflection of Harry's own mother's death.

OVIDIAN NAMES: NARCISSA

Narcissa, like Merope, is a refraction of the perfect maternal love embodied by Lily Potter. Like Merope she is also named after an Ovidian story about the unprosperous love of a beautiful nymph. The youth Narcissus is loved by the nymph Echo but, wrapped up in self-love, he ignores the possibility she offers of a reciprocal relationship. Just as Narcissus' beauty is destroyed as he wastes away through his obsessive self-regard, Narcissa Malfoy's beauty is marred by her disdain of others (*Goblet*, Chap 8, p.92).

The story of Narcissus and Echo is first alluded to in *Philosopher's Stone*. In this book, a mirror is presented, which, like Narcissus' pool, leads the gazer to waste away with longing for what they see there (Spencer, 2015, pp.56–60). Harry falls under the thrall of the mirror but he is warned by Dumbledore that "'this mirror will give us neither knowledge or truth. Men have wasted away before it, entranced by what they have seen . . . . It does not do to dwell on dreams and forget to live, remember that'" (Chap 12, p.157). The link between Narcissus' pool and the Mirror of Erised is made explicit in Dumbledore's description of the way in which '"men have wasted away'" from desire for Erised's reflections, like Narcissus who 'wasted [away] with love' out of desire for his own reflection. *Harry Potter* suggests that an excessive preoccupation with the past – the parents who have gone and the happy childhood Harry has lost – is, like Narcissus' far more self-obsessed desire, essentially sterile. Harry's first vision in the mirror is solipsistic – he sees the fulfilment of his own desires – but by the end of *Philosopher's Stone* he manages the heroic feat of seeing something fundamentally un-narcissistic in the mirror.

Ovid's *Metamorphoses* tells the famous story of Narcissus falling in love with his own reflection. Narcissus, having scorned Echo's love, stops to drink at 'a clear pool with silvery bright water':

> While he seeks to slake his thirst, another thirst springs up, and while he drinks he is smitten by the sight of the beautiful form he sees. He loves an unsubstantial hope and thinks that substance which is only shadow. He looks in speechless wonder at himself and hangs there motionless in the same expression, like a statue carved from Parian marble . . . . Unwittingly he desires himself . . . . How often did he offer vain kisses on the elusive pool? How often did he plunge his arms into the water seeking to clasp the neck he sees there, but did not clasp himself in them! What he sees he knows not; but that which he sees he burns for, and the same delusion mocks and allures his eyes. O fondly foolish boy, why vainly seek to clasp a fleeting image? What you seek is nowhere; but turn yourself away, and the object of your love will be no more. That which you behold is but the shadow of a reflected form and has no substance of its own. With you it comes, with you it stays, and it will go with you – if you can go.
>
> No thought of food or rest can draw him from the spot; but stretched on the shaded grass, he gazes on that false image with eyes that cannot look their fill and through his own eyes perishes . . . and loses himself in his own vision . . . . [H]alf distraught, [he] turned again to the same image . . . he can bear no more; but, as the yellow wax melts before a gentle heat, as hoar frost melts before the warm morning sun, so does he, wasted with love, pine away, and is slowly consumed by its hidden fire . . . . [Echo] felt pity; and as often as the poor boy says 'Alas!' again with answering utterance she cries 'Alas!' and as his hands beat his shoulders she gives back the same sounds of woe. His last words as he gazed into the familiar spring were these: 'Alas, dear boy, vainly beloved!' and the place gave back his words.

When his sisters come to bury him they find there is no body, only a flower. Narcissus has become a narcissus: 'in place of his body they find a flower, its yellow centre girt with white petals' (Book 3, ll.415–510).

There are a number of parallels between this passage and the Mirror of Erised: Harry, like Narcissus, is initially confused by the reflection into thinking that someone else is present; Harry, like Narcissus, 'thinks that substance which is only shadow.' Both young men get as close as possible to the people they see reflected – Narcissus kisses his own lips on the surface of the water, and Harry 'was so close to the mirror now that his nose was nearly touching that of his reflection' (p.153). Narcissus reaches out and touches only water, while Harry 'reached out a hand' (p.153) but touches only air. Harry's obsession with this insubstantial reflection, like Narcissus', causes him to lose both his sleep and his appetite. Narcissus is no longer responsive to normal appetites – 'no thought of food or rest can draw him from the spot' – and Harry too, after seeing the mirror, 'couldn't eat' (p.154) and when he visits the mirror for the third time he determines to forgo his sleep and sit in front of it all night. Ron advises Harry not to return to the mirror, but Harry, like Narcissus, cannot draw himself away. *Harry Potter* also draws on Ovid's moral here. Narcissus' fruitless choice to love a bodiless dream is recalled in Dumbledore's advice to Harry: 'it does not do to dwell on dreams and forget to live, remember that.' The authorial voice addresses Narcissus with much the same authority, and exactly the same advice: 'O fondly foolish boy, why vainly seek to clasp a fleeting image? . . . That which you behold is but the shadow of a reflected form and has no substance of its own.'

Even in this first encounter with the mirror, however, Harry's desire for his family is not 'narcissistic' in the modern sense of the term. While Narcissus focuses first on the beauty of his own eyes and hair ('he gazes at his eyes, twin stars, and on his locks, worthy of Bacchus, worthy of Apollo' [Book 3, ll.420–21]), the first aspects of the reflection that Harry notices are the eyes and hair of others. Gazing at his mother and father he feels a different type of love as he glimpses himself in others: 'her eyes – her eyes are just like mine, Harry thought, edging a little closer to the glass . . .. [H]is hair was very untidy. It stuck up at the back, just like Harry's did' (p.153).

Nonetheless the echoes of the myth of Narcissus are a warning. Harry's vision is not literally narcissistic (he is not falling in love with himself) but this reflection does represent a similarly fruitless desire for an impossibility. It is a desire that Harry, unlike Narcissus, manages to draw away from. Harry's successful internalisation of Dumbledore's message is shown by the fact that he does not search for the mirror again after it has been moved and in his ability to use the Mirror of Erised for the good of others at the climax of *Philosopher's Stone*. This moment is remembered and celebrated by Dumbledore five books later as proof of Harry's purity of heart: '"Harry, have you any idea how few wizards could have seen what you saw in that mirror?"' (*Half-Blood Prince*, Chap 23, p.478). Harry learns the lesson of Narcissus: the lesson that love must be given to others. Rather more surprisingly, however, this is also a lesson that is learnt by the character who bears Narcissus' name.

Narcissa is named after Ovid's youth, but also after the flower into which Narcissus transforms at the end of the story. This flower-name connects her with Lily Potter, the series' flawless emblem of maternal love. Like Merope, Narcissa seems at first a dark reflection of Lily: her love for her son is obsessively protective and it seems a narcissistic form of love (confined to her family, for those who are like her).

It is regularly stressed how much Narcissa loves her son. In *Goblet* Malfoy boasts that he would have attended Durmstrang, if only his mother could have borne to part with him. Ron muses on the rich opportunities for disposing of Malfoy that Durmstrang would have presented: "'Ah, think of the possibilities," said Ron dreamily. ". . . [S]hame his mother likes him'" (Chap 11, p.148). This is a comic moment, but it also connects with one of *Harry Potter*'s central concerns – the saving nature of parental (and particularly maternal) love. Rowling has commented on how the talismanic power of maternal love in the series – 'the power that you give someone by loving them' (2007h) – is related to her own experience of grieving for her mother (see Chapter 8). Molly Weasley, who is the living exemplar of maternal love in the series, saves Ginny at the climax of *Deathly Hallows* and Lily's love for her son likewise saves him, both when Voldemort first tries to kill him as a baby and at the end of *Philosopher's Stone*. (Even Hagrid's mother has passed on to her son toughened skin that will save his life in his duel with a Death Eater at the end of *Half-Blood Prince*.) Lily's decision to die for Harry protects him in a magical way: "'to have been loved so deeply, even though the person who loved us is gone, will give us some protection for ever. It is in your very skin'" (*Philosopher's Stone*, Chap 17, p.216).

Although Narcissa is ideologically committed to the dark side, this allegiance turns out to be meaningless to her compared with her love for her son. Rowling has called Narcissa's saving of Harry 'quite a conscious echo of what Lily did' (2012h). The fact that Narcissa's maternal love will enable her to resist Voldemort is signalled at the beginning of *Half-Blood Prince* when Narcissa disobeys Voldemort in order to protect her child. The knowledge of how far Narcissa will go to shield Draco points forward to the dénouement in which her desire to save her son – who is trapped within Hogwarts – enables Harry's survival. Lily and Narcissa's maternal love lead both to resist Voldemort, and in both cases this resistance saves Harry's life. Narcissa may be named after Narcissus but it is Echo whom she finally reflects. Her love for Draco enables her to resist evil and at the end of *Harry Potter* she and her husband run through the castle heedless of the battle raging around them: 'Lucius and Narcissa Malfoy running through the crowd, not even attempting to fight, screaming for their son' (Chap 36, p.589). When Narcissa runs through Hogwarts calling out the name of her son, she is not Narcissus, but Echo calling out the name of her beloved. Narcissa's change of heart saves Harry's life and enables the Malfoys to be included in the final unification of Hogwarts. As families grieve and embrace, the divisions signalled by the house tables are removed and wizards, centaurs, Slytherins, Gryffindors and house-elves finally mingle as one. The Malfoys are part of this new, Utopian togetherness as they join, unremarked on, in the general reunion of families (Chap 36, p.597).

Harry Potter takes Ovid's famous story about metamorphosis effected by love, and changes its meaning. The irony of Narcissa's name will only become evident at the very end of the series when her love effects her metamorphosis. In *Harry Potter*'s redemptive re-reading of Ovid, Narcissa – like Narcissus, but in a very different way – flowers under the influence of love.

CORRIDORS, UNDERGROUND CHAMBERS AND THREE-HEADED DOGS

As has been noted above, Rowling studied Greek and Roman Studies as an undergraduate and she has continued to draw inspiration from classical literature. In her post-*Potter* detective novels her hero is a Private Eye who quotes the Latin poet Catullus and in her 2008 Harvard Commencement Address she quotes from both Seneca ('as is a tale, so is life: not how long it is, but how good it is, is what matters') and Plutarch ('what we achieve inwardly will change outer reality'). In this address Rowling described her choice of Greek and Roman Studies as a fleeing 'down the Classics corridor, in retreat from career ladders, in search of ancient wisdom.' It is no coincidence that she makes her quest for intellectual fulfilment sound like a Hogwarts-style adventure as she set out 'in search of something I could not then define' (2008d). Rowling holds up intellectual enquiry as an adventure that is open to all.

The Classics corridor in Exeter University is a literal place, but Rowling also encourages her listeners to hear it as a metaphor by contrasting it with the metaphorical 'career ladders' from which she was fleeing. It is a corridor that is the start of her adventure, as are the corridors of Hogwarts for her hero. Harry and Rowling share a birthday; they also share a certain taste for adventure. When he breaks the rules and enters the forbidden third-floor corridor in *Philosopher's Stone*, Harry's real adventures at Hogwarts begin; and fleeing down the Classics corridor was likewise an act of rebellion for Rowling. It was a privileging of her desire for knowledge over the parental pressure to get a degree that would more obviously lead to financial security: '[my parents] hoped that I would take a vocational degree; I wanted to study English Literature. A compromise was reached that in retrospect satisfied nobody, and I went up to study Modern Languages. Hardly had my parents' car rounded the corner at the end of the road than I ditched German and scuttled off down the Classics corridor' (2008d). What Rowling finds at the end of her prohibited Classics corridor is 'ancient wisdom', most profoundly for her in the form of ancient myth.

One of the mythic creatures Rowling learnt about at the end of her Classics corridor was Cerberus, the three-headed dog who guards the underworld. What Harry finds at the end of his forbidden corridor in *Philosopher's Stone* is, likewise, a three-headed dog. Cerberus, like Fluffy, is a threshold guardian (Boll, 2013, p.91) and he symbolises the absolute nature of death and the unknowability of what lies beyond the grave. Cerberus allows people to enter the underworld, but the vigilance of his six eyes and the violence of his three slavering mouths means that none can get past him and back into the light.

But Rowling is interested in myth not so much as metaphor, but as story. She comments on her undergraduate degree that 'a thrilling tale of kidnap starring one Persephone had turned out to be about crop storage' (1998d, p.26). Persephone is a beautiful goddess who is abducted by Pluto and taken down to Hades. Her mother Demeter (the goddess of Harvest) searches in vain for her and, in her mourning, forbids any plants from growing. Persephone comes back to the upper world but Pluto has tricked her into eating six pomegranate seeds and having tasted the food of the underworld she is forced to return for six months every year. In ancient Greece corn was kept cool and dark by being stored underground, and at the time of sowing Persephone's return to the world was celebrated as a symbol of the corn ascending from its underground storage.

Rowling, however, rebelled against this literalist reading of the 'thrilling tale' of Persephone's abduction as merely an explanation for the underground storage of corn; and *Harry Potter*, likewise, rejects this rationalist reduction of myth. When Hermione argues with Professor Binns that there must be a kernel of truth in the legend of the Chamber of Secrets, she appears to be following the reasoning of Rowling's Classics tutors. Professor Binns (who was based on one of Rowling's most boring lecturers [Rowling, 1998d, pp.25–7]) must accept Hermione's point about the literal underpinning of myth because it is his own. But Rowling is here brilliantly turning the tables on dry tutors who evacuated myth of narrative excitement. In *Harry Potter*'s magical world such academic interpretation retains, rather than undoes, the fundamental joy of the story, for the literal underpinning of the myth of the Chamber of Secrets is not an explanation of crop storage but the existence of a *real* Chamber of Secrets. Rowling puts the magic back into myth and doing so is her own, witty act of rebellion against the hyper-literalist interpretative school she felt had stripped Ovidian myth of its wonder. In the world of *Harry Potter* apparently mythic places (such as the Chamber of Secrets) and apparently mythic objects (such as the Hallows) turn out, in fact, to be real.

Fluffy's connection with Cerberus is a clue to how to solve the problem of how to get past him: for Fluffy, like Cerberus, can be charmed by music. As the trio sit in Hogwarts' library, 'Ron, looking up at the thousands of books surrounding them', says, '"I bet there's a book somewhere in here, telling you how to get past a giant three-headed dog"' (*Philosopher's Stone*, Chap 15, p.180). That book is Ovid's *Metamorphoses*.

In a hauntingly beautiful passage the incomparable poet Orpheus goes down to the underworld and such is the wonder of his song that Cerberus allows a living person to pass into the land of the dead. This story of Orpheus and his lyre (to which Fluffy and the harp that charms him allude) is a story about the intertwined power of love and the creative artist. Orpheus' new bride Eurydice has been bitten by a snake as she walked through the grass and has died. Orpheus decides to follow her to the underworld to see if he might not move the dead and win her back:

> He came to Persephone, and to him who rules those unlovely realms, lord of the shades. Then, singing the music of his lyre, he said: 'O ye divinities

who rule the world which lies below the earth, to which we all fall back who are born mortal, if it is lawful and you permit me to lay aside all false and doubtful speech and tell the simple truth: I have not come down hither to see dark Tartara, nor yet to bind the three necks of Medusa's monstrous offspring, rough with serpents. The cause of my journey is my wife, into whose body a trodden serpent shot his poison and so snatched away her budding years. I have desired strength to endure and I will not deny that I have tried to bear it. But Love has overcome me . . .'. As he spoke thus, accompanying his words with the music of his lyre, the bloodless spirits wept . . . nor could the queen nor he who rules the lower world refuse the suppliant. They called Eurydice. She was among the new shades, and came with steps halting from her wound. Thus then the Thracian hero received his wife and with her this condition, that he should not turn his eyes backward until he had gone forth from the valley of Avernus, or else the gift would be in vain. They took the up-sloping path through places of utter silence . . . now they were nearing the margin of the upper earth, when he, afraid that she might fail him, eager for sight of her, turned back his longing eyes; and instantly she slipped into the depths. He stretched out his arms, eager to catch her or to feel her clasp; but, unhappy one, he clasped nothing but the yielding air.

(Book 10, ll.1–59)

The intangible desirability of Eurydice – 'he stretched out his arms, eager to catch her or to feel her clasp; but, unhappy one, he clasped nothing but the yielding air' – is similar to that of the reflection in Narcissus' pool. The image of the desired dead in the Mirror of Erised echoes both these myths as Harry 'reached out a hand . . . but he felt only air' (*Philosopher's Stone*, Chap 12, p.153).

The classical underworld resonates throughout *Harry Potter* in the repeated formula of Harry's yearly struggle with the forces of darkness in an underground space (Granger, 2009, pp.91–8). In the first novel of the series the connection of these spaces with the classical underworld is made explicit through the guardianship of this space by a three-headed dog who is charmed by music, but there is also a more subtle parallel. In *Philosopher's Stone* the trio enter this underground chamber in a chapter that begins with Snape's asking them to make a Forgetfulness Potion (Chap 16, p.191). Like figures from classical myth they cannot enter the underworld until they have drunk from the waters of Lethe: the river of Forgetfulness. The explicit connection with the Orpheus myth in *Philosopher's Stone*, in the three-headed dog who is charmed with music, links the underground spaces of Hogwarts with the classical underworld. It opens up the possibility of reading the similar underground chamber of the following novel as containing a more subtle Orpheus allusion. In *Chamber*, in an optimistic rewriting of Ovid's story, Harry goes down to the underworld and succeeds in rescuing the woman who will become his beloved from death.

The sheer inventiveness of Ovidian poetry fires Rowling's imagination and the secret places within Hogwarts are responses to her reading of classical myths as thrilling tales, not (as Binns would have it) mere stand-ins for something else. Hogwarts' hidden chambers resonate with the stories of the classical underworld – of the loss of Eurydice and the abduction of Persephone (Spencer, 2015, p.73) – and transmit some of the exhilaration Rowling felt when reading these myths. In a comic touch, when Hermione, Ron and Gabrielle are 'taken hostage' in the uncanny, underwater world of the lake in *Goblet*, Rowling reuses a phrase she had earlier employed about the myth of Persephone being taken down to the underworld. As noted above, Rowling wrote in 1998 of this abduction of Persephone as 'a thrilling tale of kidnap': when Ron tells tall tales about his underwater trials in the Triwizard tournament, 'at first, he gave what seemed to be the truth . . .. One week later, however, Ron was telling *a thrilling tale of kidnap* in which he struggled single-handedly against fifty heavily armed merpeople' (Chap 27, p.442).

This recurring phrase is suggestive of the way that the dark places and underground spaces of Hogwarts recall the classical underworld. But these areas are likewise influenced by a much wider network of traditional stories about forbidden or secret spaces. The Forbidden Forest, for example, builds on the forests that have always lain on the periphery of folk tales. It has been argued that in the Grimms' Tales this forest 'represents ancient law and custom based on communal folk heritage; it is the landscape which the Grimms saw as the origin and unifying factor of German culture . . . [and] the Tales, like the forest, provide a space in which social and political change can be stimulated' (MacKenzie, 2015, pp.76–7). Harry enters the Forbidden Forest at a crucial point in the narrative in all bar one of the *Harry Potter* novels and, as Garry MacKenzie argues, 'what is at stake in the Grimms' forest is also at stake in Rowling's Forest – access to the transformative influence of forces that exist outside the mainstream of urban, rationally governed society' (2015, p.78).

The next two chapters will look at the way that medieval poems, stories and folk tales influence *Harry Potter*. The forest as a location for testing the hero, which is familiar from texts from Spenser's *Faerie Queene* to Grimms' Tales, also has a particular resonance with a famous, fourteenth-century, Arthurian romance. There are a number of Arthurian names in *Harry Potter*: Arthur Weasley, Percival Dumbledore, Aunt Muriel's cousin Lancelot and Gawain Robards (the new head of the Auror Office in *Half-Blood Prince*). The next chapter argues that Harry's final confrontation with Voldemort in a clearing in the Forbidden Forest recalls the climax of the poem *Gawain and the Green Knight* in which the Arthurian knight encounters his adversary in a clearing in a woodland. Both heroes meet their nemesis in a wild place outside society and its rules, and are tested in a single combat in which they allow their enemy to strike them without lifting a hand to defend themselves.

Note

1 Steve Kloves may allude to this link when he has Hermione say 'I'm not an owl!' in the screenplay of *Goblet*.

3   *Harry Potter*'s Medieval Hallows

Chaucer and the *Gawain*-poet

Medieval folklore is full of mysteriously powerful and dangerous objects. Such magical objects also hold a sway over Rowling's imagination: from the seven cursed diamonds of her first long story (written when she was eleven) to the seven Horcruxes, four Hogwarts' founder's objects and three Deathly Hallows of *Harry Potter*. Rowling has cited a number of mythic and literary sources for *Harry Potter*'s Hallows and Horcruxes: medieval Arthurian legends, the late medieval Welsh tradition of the Thirteen Treasures of Britain and the medieval Irish myth of the Four Jewels (2015r). Rowling has noted how, in common with the Thirteen Treasures and Four Jewels (both of which include a magic cauldron), she had considered 'making Helga Hufflepuff's hallow [sic] a cauldron' (2015c). Rowling's mistaken use of the word 'hallow' here (which is incorrect in terms of *Harry Potter*'s own mythology – Hufflepuff's cup is a founder's object and it becomes a Horcrux not a Hallow) suggests that she knows, and is unconsciously using, the more general meaning of 'hallow'. The *Oxford English Dictionary* defines 'hallow' as 'to consecrate, set apart (a person or thing) as sacred to God; to dedicate to some sacred or religious use or office' and a 'hallow' is a traditional name for objects that have been set aside for a sacred purpose. Rowling's 'slip' increases the evidence for the influence of these traditional myths on her own creation of the Deathly Hallows. Irish mythological cycles, for example, tell of how the Tuatha Dé Danann were instructed in magical arts in the northern isles, returning to Ireland with their four 'hallows': a Stone, an unbeatable Spear, an irresistible Sword and a Cauldron that would never leave any unsatisfied. These Four Irish 'hallows' have a clear relation to Rowling's own Deathly Hallows: the unbeatable weapons of Irish myth are reworked into the Elder Wand, and the Stone into the Resurrection Stone. The third Deathly Hallow finds its forebear in the Thirteen Treasures of Britain, which include the Cornish Mantle of Arthur (which renders the wearer invisible).

The mythology of the Four Jewels and the Thirteen Treasures is primarily about powerful, rather than explicitly dangerous, magical treasures. It is, however, the simultaneous allure and menace of magical objects that is crucial in *Harry Potter*. Rowling's first long story revolved around cursed diamonds and, as she has noted, 'there are echoes of that story – I suppose – in *Harry Potter*' (2008e).

From the glittering opal necklace that almost kills Katie Bell to the dark magic of the Horcruxes and the deeply equivocal nature of the Deathly Hallows, *Harry Potter* is drawn to objects with a dark side. The Hallows are desirable, but they are also dangerous, and the owners of both the Resurrection Stone and the Elder Wand are often cut off in their prime. Rowling has written, 'the *Harry Potter* books are full of dangerous sparkling objects, and in this, they are like the fairy tales of every culture in the world' (2013c). This chapter argues for a specific connection between *Harry Potter*'s most 'tempting objects' (*Deathly Hallows*, Chap 35, p.577) – the Hallows – and three dangerous glittering treasures of medieval literature: the magical green and gold girdle of *Gawain and the Green Knight*, the thirty pieces of silver that persuade Judas to betray Jesus and the deadly pile of gold in Chaucer's 'Pardoner's Tale'. The convincing past that *Harry Potter* creates for its Hallows is strengthened by a literary heritage rooted in medieval myth and poetry.

GAWAIN AND THE GREEN KNIGHT

Rowling has explained that the powerful potential of magic can be problematic for narrative: 'an essential problem from the beginning was to establish the limits. Not what magic could do but what it couldn't do . . . . You had to put the walls in place and contain the action. Otherwise you have no conflict and without conflict you haven't got a story' (2007c). It is a difficulty shared by other magical genres, such as medieval romance, which is likewise populated by wizards, powerful potions and magical objects (Arden and Lorenz, 2003). *Gawain and the Green Knight*, one of the greatest of these romances, places one such magical object at the heart of its narrative.

J. R. R. Tolkien called *Gawain* 'one of the masterpieces of fourteenth-century art in England, and of English Literature as a whole', and he was interested by its relation with more naïve folktales: 'it is made of tales often told before and elsewhere, and of elements that derive from remote times' (1997, p.72). In *Gawain* a Green Knight arrives at a Christmas feast in Camelot and challenges Gawain (a Knight of the Round Table) to a beheading 'game'. In this contest Gawain will behead the Green Knight on the condition that he will submit himself to a single stroke of the Green Knight's axe in a year's time. The assumption among Arthur's knights is that no reciprocal beheading will be possible as the Green Knight will already have died, but he magically survives his beheading and leaves the court reminding Gawain of his promise to seek him in a year's time. A year later Gawain leaves the court and searches for the Green Chapel where he meets the Green Knight and, in a climactic trial of his bravery, submits to his own beheading. On the way, he meets a woman who offers him a 'magic' girdle that will save him from death and he decides to wear it when he faces the Green Knight (although he will in fact survive this encounter for quite a different reason).

The poem – initial test, quest, climactic test – follows a traditional formula, yet it 'rethinks every technique or convention of the genre' (Cooper, 2004, p.159).

When Gawain gives into temptation and accepts the magical girdle (in order to save himself from the threatened beheading) it turns out that – uniquely among the 'magical' objects in medieval romance – the girdle does not in fact have any supernatural power. As Helen Cooper drily notes: 'the *Gawain*-poet's solution to the problem of how to make a talisman that bestows invulnerability interesting is peculiarly drastic' (2004, p.159). *Harry Potter* faces much of the same problem with the Deathly Hallows. In both *Harry Potter* and *Gawain* the presiding and somewhat inscrutable figure who controls the heroes' destiny (Dumbledore in *Harry Potter*, the Green Knight in *Gawain*) allows the hero to believe that he will face death in the forest, in order that he may be fully tempted by the talisman of invulnerability. In both *Gawain* and *Deathly Hallows* the heroes are presented with this magical object moments before they face (what seems to be) certain death at the hands of their adversary and in both texts their final trial is the bravery to face death without resorting to the protection of this talisman.

For both heroes the easy, magical way out of the final, fatal encounter is a temptation to be avoided. The trial turns out to be a very human test of the heroes' own courage and integrity. Rowling states that 'Sir [James] Frazer (in *The Golden Bough*) says that in religion the man depends on God, but in magic the man depends on himself, which allows us to measure the capacity of man' (2008b). Such self-reliance is even more striking when the hero has magical power that he chooses to relinquish. Harry has a magical way to evade death but he does not choose to take it. Gawain, on his side, fails his final test. He tries to elude his imminent beheading with a magical object, and in doing so finds that magic is not to be relied on. But Harry does not rely on magical objects for his reckoning with Voldemort. He chooses not to seek the Elder Wand, he drops the Stone, stows away his wand and steps out from under the cloak – and in doing so proves his heroism.

The parallels with *Gawain*, however, go deeper than this temptation to use a magical, talismanic object to avoid death (Prinzi, 2009, p.92). *Gawain*, like *Harry Potter*, charts the development of its hero from childish ignorance to maturity and self-knowledge. Both heroes pass through trials that teach them surprising truths about friends, enemies and themselves as they grow from naivety to self-awareness. *Gawain* is a sophisticated version of the traditional romance form in that both its quest and trial centre on the psychological growth of the hero. At the beginning Arthur's knights are mocked as 'beardless boys' ('berdlez chylder') and described as 'somewhat boyish' ('sumquat childgered') (Tolkien et al., 1966 [c.1390], ll.280, 86) in their desire for tales of adventure. But Gawain returns home as a chastened, older and wiser hero at the end of the poem. In *Harry Potter*, likewise, the hero grows up over the course of the series and the way each novel is structured – a departure, a subsequent quest or trial, and a return – echoes the overarching structure of the series itself in its journey from Harry's first accidental, childish encounter with Voldemort in the Forbidden Forest to his final, mature decision to face Voldemort there again. Gawain's journey, like Harry's, takes him to a final reckoning in a forest clearing and the specific nature of this encounter – a beheading that does not happen – is replicated by *Harry Potter* in which (as we shall see) a threatened beheading likewise hangs over the hero.

Gawain and the Green Knight: plot synopsis

The beheading-plot of *Gawain* is the result of a deadly, magical challenge that is presented as a Christmas game. The poem opens at Camelot at Christmas time. The feasting cannot begin until Arthur has seen or heard something wonderful: 'some adventurous matter, or uncouth tale of some great marvel he might be able to believe in, of kings, of knightly combat, or other adventures' ('Of sum auenturus thyng an vncouthe tale,/ Of sum mayn meruayle, that he myght trawe/ Of aldere, of armes, of other auenturus' [ll.93–5]). Arthur asks in fact for a 'tale' and the tale he is told is that which the reader is reading. As Arthur asks for a tale, a huge Green Knight rides in bearing an axe in one hand and a branch of holly in the other. The Green Knight challenges Arthur's knights to a 'Christmas game' ('Crystemas gomen' [l.283]): he will give one of the knights a free blow with his axe on the condition that the Green Knight will return the blow in a year and a day. At first no-one rises to the challenge but then Gawain – one of the youngest and least experienced of the knights – steps forward. He beheads the Green Knight with a single stroke; but to everyone's shock the knight simply picks up his head and holds it in his hands. The Green Knight's head challenges Gawain to receive his return stroke at the Green Chapel in a year and a day's time, and the knight leaves; with no-one knowing where he had returned to any more than they understood where he had come from ('to quat kyth he becom knwe non there,/ Neuer more then thay wyste from quethen he watz wonnen' [ll.460–461]).

The year passes swiftly, and after Gawain has enjoyed Camelot's Halloween ('Al-hal-day' [l.536]) feast, he leaves the court to seek the Green Chapel. He travels through the woods and hills of North Wales fighting wild animals and sleeping out in the cold, but when Christmas Eve arrives he fervently prays that he may find somewhere where he can hear Mass. Suddenly he sees, shimmering through the trees, the most glorious castle he has ever set eyes on. He receives a warm welcome at the castle from Bertilak de Hautdesert and his beautiful wife (although there is a mysterious, ugly old lady lurking in the background) and joins them in their Christmas observances. Gawain explains that he is seeking the Green Chapel, and is told that it is close by, so he can rest and enjoy Christmas at the castle because his quest is almost over. Gawain's host Bertilak then proposes a pact (a 'couenauntez' [l.1123]): each day he will hunt and bring back to Gawain what he kills, while on his side Gawain must give to his host whatever he 'wins' during his day. Gawain agrees (seemingly having forgotten how badly his last 'Christmas game' ended).

The section that follows is the most celebrated passage of the poem: the poet interlaces Bertilak's hunts in the forest, and the twists and turns of the animals he pursues, with his wife's attempted seduction of Gawain, while Gawain – like the hunted animals – attempts to escape her advances (without compromising either his courtesy or her honour). Lady Bertilak sits on Gawain's four-poster bed and tells him, 'I've come to you all alone, to sit and learn from you; teach me about the game of love while my husband is away from home' ('I com hider sengel, and sitte/ To lerne at yow sum game;/ Dos, techez me of your wytte,/ Whil my lorde is fro hame' [ll.1531–4]). She taunts him about his boldness and appears to advocate making the 'game' between her and Gawain as physical as the 'sport' between her husband and his quarry.

On the first two days Gawain skilfully and virtuously parries the lady's seductive game, accepting just one kiss, which he then bestows – as promised – on her husband. But on the third day he finds it more difficult to resist her: waking from sleep he finds her bending over him and is sorely tempted to pursue matters. He succeeds in rebuffing her advances, but (after turning down a gold ring set with a precious stone) accepts her green and gold girdle, which, she claims, will protect whoever wears it from death. The lady describes the magical girdle as a 'jewel against danger' ('a juel for the jopardé' [l.1856]). Tempted by the possibility that it will save him from the beheading that awaits him in the Green Chapel, Gawain accepts and in the evening he gives to Bertilak the kisses that he has taken from his wife but not the 'grene lace' (l.1851), which he keeps hidden about his person.

The next day Gawain sets out to meet the Green Knight and discovers that the Green Chapel for which he has been searching is not a building, but simply a clearing in the woods. There he encounters the Knight and bares his neck but when the Green Knight brings down his axe Gawain flinches. Ashamed, Gawain asks the Green Knight to strike again; but again the Green Knight stops short of an actual blow. The third time the Knight makes a little nick in Gawain's neck and when Gawain sees his blood on the snow he knows that he has survived the 'beheading game': he leaps up to defend himself from further attack only to find that the Green Knight is laughing. He reveals himself as Bertilak – Gawain's host at the castle – whom the witch Morgan le Fay (whom Gawain had noticed in her disguise as an old lady at Bertilak's castle) has magically transformed into the invincible Green Knight.

It was Morgan le Fay's magic that protected the Green Knight at his beheading and it is at her behest that Bertilak and his wife have put Gawain to the test. This revelation makes Gawain ashamed that he kept the girdle but Bertilak is gracious in victory. Gawain returns to Arthur's court and ruefully tells his story. He declares that he will wear the girdle always as a token of his shame, and the Knights of the Round Table decide that they too will all wear a sash in solidarity with Gawain.

The poem ends with the phrase 'Hony soyt qui mal pence' ('shame be on him who thinks it'), which is the motto of the Order of the Garter. In the legend of the founding of this order, Edward III was dancing with the Countess of Salisbury when her garter fell to the floor; and when courtiers laughed suggestively as he stooped to pick it up, he gave this retort (Friedman and Osberg, 1977, p.314). The text appears to compare Gawain's girdle with the knightly Garter and *Gawain* may be intended as a foundation myth for this most honourable (but equivocal sounding) Order. In Rowling's fictional honour's system, the Order of Merlin, first class, also has a green ribbon (2015o) presumably to recall the Scottish version of the Order of the Garter, which is sometimes known as the 'Green Garter' or the 'Green ribbon' (Matikkala, 2008, pp.86–7). The Order of Merlin, therefore, also recalls the Order of the Garter in its first fictional incarnation, as the 'grene lace' worn by the knights in *Gawain*.

Gawain and *Harry Potter*

The conclusion of *Gawain* resonates with Harry's encounter with Voldemort in the forest at the climax of *Deathly Hallows*, but the poem also echoes through *Chamber*. Hogwarts' collection of (often knighted) headless ghosts recalls the uncanny headless Green Knight. Hogwarts' headless ghosts, like the Green Knight at Camelot's Christmas feast, make a dramatic, horse-back entrance into the Hogwarts festivities (*Chamber*, Chap 8, p.104). While the Green Knight is not a ghost, the poet notes the ghostly effect of his disembodied head speaking: 'that same man spoke like a ghost, with his head held in his hand' ('that ilke gome that gostlych speked/ With his hede in his honde' [ll.2461–2]). *Harry Potter* likewise deploys this eerie effect as many of the headless ghosts speak while their heads are detached from their shoulders (see below).

The Headless Hunt's charismatic but somewhat overbearing leader shares a number of characteristics with the Green Knight. Like the Green Knight, Sir Patrick Delaney-Podmore exerts a charismatic control over his audience. Both are rather bluff and domineering and yet clear sighted: the Green Knight knows far more about what is happening to Gawain than Gawain does and Patrick sees immediately through Nick and Harry's attempts to deceive him. Both exude a rather insensitive *bonhomie*: the Green Knight having put Gawain in fear of his life, subjected him to various trials and made him deeply ashamed of his own short-comings, embraces him and invites him to 'make merry in my house' ('make myry in my hous' [ll.2472, 68]). Gawain is still smarting from the trick that has been played on him, as is made clear from his less than gracious response: 'he told him no, not by any means' ('he nikked him naye, he nolde bi no wayes' [l.2471]) and the emphatic negative of all those 'n's (*nicked, naye, nolde, no*) give this phrase a sulky air. The Green Knight's jollity rather grates on Gawain after he has given him his 'nick' on the neck and the hearty, guffawing Sir Patrick, likewise, piques Nick in his continued puns about the partially severed ('nicked') neck about which Nick is so sensitive.

Gawain and *Chamber* share the uncanny presence of headless knights and they are also connected through the fact that a woman called Guinevere/ Ginevra (Ginny's full name) turns out, rather surprisingly, to be crucial to the plot. After the beheading-game at the beginning of *Gawain* the men refuse to take the event very seriously. Guinevere is upset by it, but Arthur dismisses her fears: 'dear dame, do not be perturbed, such tricks belong to the Christmas season' ('Dere dame, to-day demay yow neuer;/ Wel bycommes such craft vpon Cristmasse' [ll.470–471]). Arthur and Gawain treat it as a joke (they 'laughed and grinned', 'laghe and grenne' [l.464]) despite the fact that Gawain is now living under sentence of death. In *Chamber*, likewise, the boys seem not to have grasped the seriousness of what has happened. While Ginny is terribly upset, her male relations downplay the danger and try to jolly her along with practical jokes. In both texts, however, female alarm is a more accurate response than male bravado. The boys of Hogwarts, like the 'beardless boys' of Arthur's court, undervalue what is in reality a mortal threat. In both texts it turns out that Guinevere/Ginevra (who had seemed entirely incidental to the plot) is in fact the person who is directly threatened. While it is Ginny who has been possessed by Voldemort and is nearly murdered by him, the entire plot of the Green Knight's beheading-game turns out, in a startling *volte face*, to have been planned by Morgan le Fay in order to frighten Guinevere to death ('For to haf greued Gaynour and gart hir to dyghe' [l.2460]). In the predominantly male world of both texts[1] it is a female who turns out to have been both the instigator and the target of all the mischief.

Christmas at Camelot

The ability of magic to conceal identity is as central to *Gawain* as it is to *Harry Potter*. In *Gawain* Morgan le Fay's magic means that the uncanny Green Knight and the avuncular Bertilak turn out to be the same person. In *Chamber* Polyjuice Potion is first introduced. Harry, Ron and Hermione first take this shape-changing brew on Christmas Day and the transformation of the Green Knight, likewise, takes place at Christmas.

Christmas is an important social and festive season in both *Chamber* and *Gawain*. The halls of Hogwarts and Camelot ring with carols and feasting and in *Gawain* the Green Knight carries a holly branch, while the Great Hall of Hogwarts is likewise hung with boughs of holly. In *Chamber* it is noted that Hogwarts' Christmas feast is so wonderful that the task hanging over Harry can be forgotten for a time and despite the terrible shock that Gawain has received and the sentence of death that now hangs over him, he is likewise caught up in the Christmas festivities, grinning and laughing with the others. The holly, the carols and the joy are all part of a traditional Christmas season, but all – like the Christmas transformations of both texts – also have a theological undertow. Polyjuice Potion is created from ingredients that express 'the idea of duality': the 'intertwining or binding together of two identities' (Rowling, 2015p). Such a transformation is at the heart of the Christmas message. At Christmas, through 'intertwining or binding together of two identities' in the Incarnation, God becomes human. This makes both the transformation of Bertilak into the Green Knight and the first trial of Polyjuice Potion peculiarly fitting events for Christmas. As Arthur declares – unaware of the full accuracy of his words – such tricks belong to the Christmas season.

Christmas is important throughout *Harry Potter*. The word alone occurs 234 times in the series (Villaluz, 2008, pp.212–3) and it is the day on which Harry is given the Firebolt, the day of the Yule Ball, the day on which he receives the invisibility cloak and the day on which he first sees the Mirror of Erised (Prinzi, 2009, pp.106–107). But it is only in *Deathly Hallows* that the events of Christmas Day take on an explicitly Christian symbolism. This deepening of the religious import of Christmas over time also takes place in *Gawain*, where the feasting and games of the opening Christmas festivities take on a more explicitly Christian meaning in the final Christmas of the poem.

In both *Gawain* and *Deathly Hallows* as the more serious, holy, nature of the season is stressed, the desire for a traditionally festive Christmas is presented as having the potential to lead people astray. The inhabitants of Bertilak's castle, which Gawain reaches on Christmas Eve, wonder that Gawain should be so far from his comfortable home at Christmas time and suggest a new Christmas game that turns out to be full of temptation (ll.1046–9). In *Deathly Hallows*, likewise, Ron's desire for the traditional creature comforts of the season lead him into a dangerous path as he abandons the Horcrux-quest.

Gawain (like Harry in the *Deathly Hallows*) spends the autumn wandering through the wilds of the western part of the kingdom – North Wales, Anglesey, Holy Head and 'the wilderness of the Wirral' ('the wyldrenesse of Wyrale' [ll.697–701]). Gawain camps out in ancient Welsh woodland thick with oak trees and hung with 'iisse-ikkles' ('icicles' [l.732]) as he seeks the unknown destination where he will meet his nemesis. In *Deathly Hallows*, likewise, Harry spends the autumn wandering and searching – most memorably in the Forest of Dean, which (like Gawain's 'forest ful dep' [l.741]) is in the West of Britain. In both cases this rather aimless journey through Welsh and West-country forests (for neither hero knows where they are going) takes a decisive turn on Christmas Eve when Gawain comes upon Bertilak's castle and Harry finally decides to visit Godric's Hollow.

In both *Gawain* and *Harry Potter* this crucial Christmas Eve is the most explicitly Christian moment of the text. Gawain, lost questing in the woods, penitently prays that he may reach a dwelling where he will be able to hear Mass: 'he prayed as he rode, and wept for his sins; he crossed himself repeated and said "Christ's cross bless me"' ('He rode in his prayere,/ And cryed for his mysdede,/ He sayned hym in sythes sere,/ And sayde "Cros Kryst me spede!"' [ll.759–62]). Harry and Hermione arrive in Godric's Hollow to the sound of carols, read significant biblical quotations on gravestones and narrowly escape Voldemort's clutches while the church bells are 'ringing in Christmas Day' (*Deathly Hallows*, Chap 17, p.279). In addition to the explicitly Christian aspects of this Christmas Eve, Harry's story also resonates with Christian significance at this point for he is returning to the village of his birth. As in *Chamber*, Polyjuice Potion is once again taken at Christmas, and Harry and Hermione transform into a man and his wife returning – like Joseph and his wife in the original Christmas story – to the place of the man's birth on the night before Christmas (Granger, 2008a, p.104).

In both *Gawain* and *Harry Potter*, however, these explicit Christian references do not provide interpretative simplicity. Gawain is relieved to find Bertilak's castle, and believes that it will provide shelter, comfort and the resolution of his quest as its residents point the way to the Green Chapel. Gawain reads the appearance of Bertilak's castle as the answer to his prayer – but he has been led to a place not of safety, but of danger. In *Deathly Hallows*, likewise, Harry and Hermione believe that they can perceive Dumbledore's guiding hand behind their decision to visit Godric's Hollow. Harry thinks that this is the place where he will find both the answers for which he has been seeking and the sword that will enable him to complete his quest. Like Gawain at Bertilak's Castle, Harry believes that in journeying to Godric's Hollow he is going to the place where his protector has sent him, but in both cases the hero is walking into a trap.

Bertilak's castle and Godric's Hollow are not places of safety, marking the resolution of the hero's quest (as they hope) but the site of yet another trial. It is a trial, moreover, that takes a strikingly similar form. In both texts the hero talks to a woman, in a bedroom alone, unaware of the potentially deadly game she is playing. Gawain, visited by Bertilak's wife in his bedroom, awakes to find that she is startlingly close 'bending low over his fair face' ('felle ouer his fayre face' [l.1758]). Bathilda likewise talks to Harry in a bedroom and she suddenly appears, out of nowhere, alarmingly close to him. Both heroes are perhaps in greater danger at this point than at any other time in their adventures: Gawain is in 'great peril' ('gret perile' [l.1768]) and the danger to Harry is soon horribly clear as a great snake pours out of what had been the woman's neck (*Deathly Hallows*, Chap 17, pp.277–8).[2]

The final connection between Harry and Gawain's quests is found in their climactic confrontation with their adversary in the forest. Gawain leaves Bertilak's castle to face certain death in the Green Chapel; like Harry's meeting-place with Voldemort, this is a clearing in the woods. Each of Harry's adventures and encounters with Voldemort leads up to this final test, this final encounter. Each of his trials foreshadows his ultimate self-sacrificial act: 'everything, everything I've written, it was intended for the precise moment when Harry goes into the forest' (Rowling, 2008a). The whole of *Gawain*, likewise, is governed by the knowledge that Gawain must face this deadly encounter in the woods, an encounter in which – like Harry – he will not raise a weapon to defend himself from (apparently) certain death.

Gawain, however, is secretly wearing his girdle whereas Harry has learnt not to put too much faith in magical objects. Harry's crucial choice – 'Horcruxes or Hallows?' (*Deathly Hallows*, Chap 24, p.392) – is a decision about whether to put faith in dangerous sparkling objects or to seek to destroy them. Harry makes a momentous decision not to seek the Elder Wand and the importance of this choice is marked with unusually mystical language: 'he looked out over the ocean and felt closer, this dawn, than ever before, closer to the heart of it all' (Chap 24, p.391). The Resurrection Stone's double-nature, likewise, embodies this choice between Hallows and Horcruxes: the division between

Voldemort's acquisitive desire for trophies and Harry's heroic ability to resist their power and finally relinquish both the Elder Wand and the Stone. It is a decision that Gawain is unable to take and he places mistaken faith in the magical ability of the girdle to defend him from death and trusts in it to be 'a jewel to protect against danger'. In a startling turn, it is in fact Voldemort – with his materialistic desire, expressed in the trashy trophies he stole as a child and his double 'possession' of the ancient treasures he kills for as an adult – who (like Gawain) will mistakenly rely on magical objects to protect him from death.

The beheading motif

There are many people, animals and things that lose their heads in *Harry Potter*. The first password that Harry uses to enter the Gryffindor Common Room is '*Caput Draconis*' (dragon's head) (*Philosopher's Stone*, Chap 7, p.96) and each novel has at least one actual, or metaphorical, beheading. In the first novel Harry meets Nearly Headless Nick and hears about his botched beheading. The Headless Hunt is introduced in *Chamber*. In *Azkaban* not only does Buckbeak stand under a sentence of decapitation, but – in a comic riff on this plot – Harry's seemingly decapitated head terrifies Crabbe, Goyle and Malfoy in Hogsmeade. In *Goblet* Harry predicts his own death by decapitation in a homework assignment for Professor Trelawney and his fake wand turns into a rubber haddock whose neck is severed by Ron. In *Phoenix* Harry first visits the Hog's Head pub, Fred and George invent Headless Hats, the wizard's statue from the Fountain of Magical Brethren is decapitated, Ginny pretends there is Garrotting Gas loose in the corridors of Hogwarts and Harry visits Grimmauld Place with its macabre rows of shrunken, decapitated elf heads. In *Half-Blood Prince* Snape describes the power and infinite variety of the Dark Arts as 'a many-headed monster, which, each time a neck is severed, sprouts a head even fiercer and cleverer than before' (Chap 9, p.169). Snape is comparing the Dark Arts with the Hydra, the mythical, many-headed beast whose snaky heads multiplied each time they were removed.

This decapitation motif creates a nebulous, but insistent, threat that hangs over the hero and many fans were convinced that a beheading awaited Harry in the final novel of the series (Granger, 2008a, pp.250–253). In *Deathly Hallows* the motif returns when a gargoyle is decapitated during the Battle of Hogwarts and Ron muses fondly over how he used to daydream about cutting off Kreacher's head and placing it alongside the other elf heads in Grimmauld Place. But – in a characteristic wrong-footing of the reader – it turns out that all these beheadings pointed not to Harry, but to Neville and to Snape. Neville is given a heroic moment in the limelight when, like Hercules defeating the Hydra or the Redcrosse Knight beheading Error (Hardy, 2011), he slices off Nagini's head. Snape, meanwhile, endures a terrible, surreal form of decapitation as Nagini bites him in the neck as his head is encased within her cage (a death that, perhaps, could have been predicted: 'Severus Snape = sever his nape = cut off his head' [Skyinsane, 2013]).

There are other literary sources for Snape's death (see Richards, 2015 and Chapter 7) but most of the beheadings in *Harry Potter* – from the accidental beheading of dead caterpillars in Potions lessons to the idea that it is Kreacher's life's ambition to have his decapitated head mounted on the wall – are at once grotesque and comic. The macabre comedy of the botched decapitation of Nearly Headless Nick, for example, is very close to the bone (see, in particular, the Ballad of Nearly Headless Nick, from an early draft of *Chamber* [Harry Potter Wiki, 2016c]).[3]

This threatening yet comic grotesque recalls the festive and uncanny world of *Gawain* where the beheading is likewise both comic and macabre. In *Azkaban* McNair lovingly fingers his axe as he arrives in a manner that suggests Buckbeak's appeal is not going to go well. The narrative of *Gawain*, likewise, dwells in horrified fascination on the cutting-edge of the Green Knight's giant axe. It is described as having been chiselled to razor-sharpness – 'schapen to schere as scharp rasores' (1.213) – with alliterative '*sch*' sounds suggestive of the sharp swishing of the axe. These sounds return at the moment that the axe severs the Green Knight's head: 'that the scharp of the schalk schyndered the bones,/ And schrank thurgh the schyire grece, and scade hit intwynne' ('the man's sharp blade splintered the bones, and sank through the fair flesh, and split it in two' [ll.424–5]). The moment of the Green Knight's beheading is horrific and visceral, but it is also comic. The decapitated head rolls across the floor and is kicked away by the knights and ladies like a football: 'the fair head fell off its neck to the earth, and many people kicked it with their feet as it rolled about' ('the fayre hede fro the halce hit to the erthe,/ That fele hit foyned wyth her fete, ther hit forth roled' [ll.427–8]). In *Azkaban*, likewise, there is a grotesque comedy in Trelawncy's prurient and lurid imagining of Buckbeak's beheading: '"does the Hippogriff appear to . . . have its head? . . . You don't see it writhing on the ground, perhaps, and a shadowy figure raising an axe behind it? . . . No blood? No weeping Hagrid?"' (Chap 16, p.237). In both texts comedy exists alongside violence because, through the operation of magic, the violence – bloody as it is – results in neither pain nor death. Until *Deathly Hallows* almost none of *Harry Potter*'s 'beheadings' actually kills anyone: Fred and George are alive and well under their Headless Hats, as is Harry under the invisibility cloak in Hogsmeade, while the headless ghosts and the headless statues are – like the Green Knight – animated in a more uncanny form.

The eerie moment when the Green Knight picks up his own head by the hair after his beheading and addresses the company, is recalled in the loquacious decapitated heads of *Harry Potter*. The Headless Hunt rush into battle with 'their heads screaming with bloodlust under their arms' (*Deathly Hallows*, Chap 31, p.510) and Sir Patrick's head carries on a conversation from the floor during the Deathday party in *Chamber*. These separated heads, like the irritable and easily offended Nearly Headless Nick, are often rather grumpy, which encourages the reader not to take their predicament too seriously. The disembodied head of a gargoyle that has been blasted off during the Battle of Hogwarts comments crabbily from the floor: '"Oh, don't mind me . . . I'll just lie here and crumble"' (*Deathly Hallows*, Chap 31, p.498).

The comic, uncanny aspect of decapitation in *Harry Potter* resonates with the way that the beheading-challenge in *Gawain* is presented as a game. At Camelot's Christmas feast the Green Knight calls his beheading a 'Christmas game' and at Hogwarts' feasts likewise decapitation is treated as a form of entertainment, with displays of Horseback Head-Juggling and games of Head Hockey and Head Polo. Hogwarts' headless ghosts provide the entertainment at Halloween feasts including – an episode that strikingly recalls *Gawain*'s grisly Christmas game – Nearly Headless Nick's highly successful 're-enactment of his own botched beheading' (*Azkaban*, Chap 8, p.120).

This comedic, yet uncanny, aspect of the beheading-motif in both *Harry Potter* and *Gawain* interacts with the latent Christian aspect of both stories. The Green Knight appears at Christmas, carrying a branch of holly, 'resurrects' from a fatal blow and then tells Gawain to seek him at the Green Chapel. Gawain expects this to be a conventional Christian place of worship; however, it turns out not to be a building but a natural clearing in the wood. The Green Knight's magical survival of his decapitation, likewise, links with the natural virility of his greenness. This greenness connects him both with the natural world and with 'Green Men', grotesque carvings of faces spewing foliage out of their mouths, often found in the decoration of medieval churches.[4] While their symbolism is not entirely understood, their presence in churches appears to link the seasonal cycle of birth, death and regeneration with the Christian concept of resurrection.

The Green Chapel forms one part of the poem's synthesis between natural and Christian imagery. The Green Knight's branch of holly ('holyn bobbe'), likewise, carries associations with both Christianity and the natural world. As the poem notes, this is a tree 'that is greenest when the thickets are bare' ('that is grattest in grene, when greuez ar bare' [l.207]). Tere Stouffer has noted holly's popular etymology from 'holy' (2007, p.48) and its winter flourishing is traditionally linked with the mid-winter birth of Christ. This branch of holly, therefore, brings Christian associations to the Green Knight's survival of his 'death'; and in this regard it seems particularly pointed that Harry's wand is made from holly. (Rowling, in a nod to the traditional Christological connections of the tree, has noted that 'holly wands often choose owners who are engaged in some dangerous and often *spiritual* quest' [2015u, italics mine].)

The Green Knight is an ambiguous and suggestive figure and critics argue over whether he is an alarming, witchy character or something closer to a saviour figure who brings Gawain to repentance and a knowledge of himself while protecting him from harm. The end of the poem reveals that Morgan Le Faye's malice is the source of his transformation and yet he retains something of his mystique as he leaves by dissolving into the scenery in an echo of his enigmatic departure from Camelot at the beginning of the poem: 'and the knight into the bright green, whichsoever way he would' ('and the knyght in the enker-grene,/ Whiderwarde-so-euer he wolde' [ll.2477–8]). The Green Knight – darkly funny, cryptic, magical and spiritually suggestive – resonates both with the numerous comic and uncanny beheadings in *Harry Potter* and with the latent Christian potential of Harry's own mysterious death and resurrection at the end of *Deathly Hallows*.

JUDAS AND THE ELDER WAND

The Elder Wand is crucial to *Harry Potter*'s dénouement, its unexpected switch of allegiance being the providential 'flaw in the plan' that enables Harry to win the final battle against Voldemort (and its importance meaning that *Harry Potter and the Elder Wand* was a working title for the final novel [Rowling, 2007f]). Its name is a pun: it is the wand belonging to the eldest brother in the 'Tale of the Three Brothers' but it is also made from the wood of the elder tree (*Deathly Hallows*, Chap 21, p.331). But there is also another reason hidden in medieval folk-lore why Death fashions the Deathstick from the wood of the elder tree. After the trio hear the 'Tale of the Three Brothers' Ron reflects that this story has probably influenced the Wizarding proverb '"Wand of elder, never prosper"' (*Deathly Hallows*, Chap 21, p.336). Hermione and Harry have never heard this proverb (as Hermione reminds Ron, having been raised by Muggles they were taught different superstitions) but, in fact, the elder tree is also proverbially unlucky in the Muggle world.

The Bible states that Judas hanged himself (Matthew 27.5) but, as it does not specify a tree, medieval folk-lore filled in the gap. It chose the elder as it was a tree of notoriously poor-quality wood. It is a myth that turns up regularly in medieval literature, which tells of how 'upon an elder tree [Judas] hung himself in secret' (Herbert, 1905, ll.4851–2). (The myth remains to the modern day in the name of the Jew's Ear fungus, a brown gelatinous fungus that grows almost exclusively on elder trees, and whose name is probably a corruption of 'Judas' Ear fungus'.) Rowling could have discovered this tree-lore from many places (it turns up, for example, in Christopher Marlowe's *Jew of Malta*) but one of the most entertaining possibilities is a mid-fourteenth-century narrative called *The Travels of Sir John Mandeville*. This is a traveller's tale in which the author claims to have traversed most of the known world. Like Gilderoy Lockhart, however, Mandeville seems to be gilding his own narratives by appropriating the adventures of other people. Modern critical opinion agrees that its author may never, in fact, have left his study. The exoticism of Mandeville's travels – and his amazing flights of fancy – meant that his book remained immensely popular for hundreds of years and his work is one source for the myth that it was a 'tree of elder that Judas hanged himself upon, for despair that he had, when he sold and betrayed our Lord' (Seymour, 2002, p.68).

The myth linking Judas to the elder tree is also found in one of the greatest of medieval poems, Langland's *Piers Plowman*. Langland describes how the devil 'tempted Judas with Jewish silver, and he hanged himself on an elder tree afterwards. The devil thwarts love and is full of lies: whoever trusts in his treasure is the soonest betrayed' ('Judas he japed with Jewen silver,/ And sithen on an eller hanged hym after./ He is lettere of love and lieth hem alle:/ That trusten on his tresour bitrayed arn sonnest' [Langland, 1995 (c.1370–90), Passus 1, ll.67–70]). The devil tempts Judas with a pile of silver 'tresour' but

Langland stresses that it is a mistake to trust such treasure, just as it is unwise to place your faith in the 'fabulous treasures' and 'dangerous sparkling objects' (Rowling, 2013c) of folk tales.

The story of Judas is in one sense a story about the fatal nature of greed. Judas asks the High Priests: '"What are you willing to give me if I deliver him over to you?"' (Matthew 26.15). Judas had always had an unhealthy interest in money (John 12.6) but only after he has betrayed Jesus does he realise that his love of money has led him astray: 'he felt remorse and returned the thirty pieces of silver to the chief priests . . . . And he threw the pieces of silver into the temple sanctuary and departed; and he went away and hanged himself' (Matthew 27.3–5).

As Shira Wolosky notes, the word 'treasure' – from its first appearance in the series inscribed over Gringotts as a warning against greed to its crucial appearance in the biblical quotation on the Dumbledore family tombstone – is 'one of the books' important wordplays' (2010, p.45). Wolosky argues, 'the Gemini and Flagrante spells put on gold things in Gringotts so that they multiply, crush, and burn whoever touch them show the ultimate effects of gold on those who yearn for and seek it' (2010, p.45). Among these golden objects is Helga Hufflepuff's drinking cup, the Horcrux that the trio seek. As mentioned above, Rowling's first thought was to make this founder's object a cauldron (like the mythical cauldron of the Tuatha Dé Danann, which left no-one unsatisfied) and the object that she did choose has similar ancient links with feasting and conviviality. It is a drinking cup, likewise, that seals the guest-friendship between the forefathers of the Greek warrior Diomedes and the Trojan Glaucus in the *Iliad*: 'a two-handled cup of gold' (Book 6, 1.220). Hufflepuff's founder's object – likewise a gold, two-handled drinking cup (*Half-Blood Prince*, Chap 20, p.408) – also expresses the importance placed on friendship in *Harry Potter*. Double-handled drinking vessels are known as 'loving cups' because they can be drunk from simultaneously by two people and the double handles are an emblem of sharing and togetherness. The cup's embodiment of friendship has been brutally misappropriated in its transformation into a Horcrux and its presence among all the burning, crushing gold in Bellatrix's vault marks the ironic contrast between real and material worth.

The mythic background of the Hallows (and Horcruxes) is rooted in stories about over-reliance on material things: Gawain's misapplied faith in the golden girdle as a 'jewel against danger' and Judas' fatal love of money and his infamous 'thirty pieces of silver'. One further example is the traditional folk tale about a mysteriously appearing pile of gold that leads all who desire it to their deaths. This is the story that underlies Chaucer's 'Pardoner's Tale' as well as *Harry Potter*'s 'Tale of the Three Brothers'.

THE DEATHLY HALLOWS AND CHAUCER'S *CANTERBURY TALES*

A number of *Harry Potter*'s chapter titles recall Chaucer's *Canterbury Tales* – 'Hagrid's Tale', 'Kreacher's Tale', 'The Prince's Tale' – and 'The Tale of the Three Brothers' itself is, as Rowling has acknowledged, directly inspired by Chaucer's 'Pardoner's Tale' (2007f; see also: Fidelia, 2008). Both stories involve three 'brothers' who meet Death. In both tales this encounter is imagined as a fatal failure to resist powerful, desirable objects (a pile of gold in Chaucer; the Elder Wand and Resurrection Stone in Rowling). But *Harry Potter* recasts the moral of the 'Pardoner's Tale', for while Chaucer's story is a tale about the evils of greed, Rowling's version is a meditation on the right response to death. *Harry Potter* argues that an ability to face one's own mortality is the ultimate power.

The 'Pardoner's Tale' tells the story of three drunken young men who, hearing that someone has been killed by Death, band together as three sworn 'brothers' to set out and kill Death in revenge. They meet an old man on their journey who tells them that Death can be found at the foot of an oak tree, but on reaching the tree they discover only a vast hoard of gold. Delighted, they agree to take away the gold in the morning and draw lots as to which of them should go and fetch wine and food while the other two stay and guard the gold. The youngest draws the short straw and while he is away the other two plot to kill him when he returns so that they only have to split the gold two ways. After the youngest returns he is murdered by the elder two, who then carouse with the wine he has brought back, only to die in their turn, for the youngest had poisoned the wine intending, as they had, to keep all the gold for himself.[5]

Chaucer's bleak, elegant tale is a sophisticated engagement with a well-known folk story. An account of a mysterious and fatal pile of gold belongs to ancient Buddhist, Persian, Arabian, Tibetan, European and African folk traditions, and one critic has gone so far as to say that 'few stories were more widely diffused over Europe during mediaeval times' (Furnivall et al., 1872, p.417). Although most of the versions involve the death of all who set eyes on the gold, in the Buddhist original (from which Chaucer's version probably derives [Furnivall et al., 1872, pp.417–36]) the Bodhisattva – the pre-incarnation of the Buddha – is able to take home the treasure that has killed everyone else: 'he deftly removed the wealth to his own house, and continued the rest of his life giving alms, and doing other righteous acts, and when he died, he attained heaven' (Furnivall et al., 1872, p.422). While Chaucer's version – which is the direct source of the 'Tale of the Three Brothers' – involves the death of all three brothers, in *Harry Potter* the youngest brother lives safely with his deathly gift. This echoes the structure of the oldest version of the tale (and also adds to it the classic folk-tale motif of the 'modest choice' [Ostry, 2003, p.91] when Ignotus asks for a gift that appears so much less powerful than those of his brothers). The ability to live unscathed by the dangerous sparkling objects of folk-lore belongs only to the pure in heart. The Bodhisattva can safely own the gold because he is using it for the good of others, just as Dumbledore tells Harry that the cloak is the greatest Hallow because it can be used to protect others. In the 'Tale of the Three Brothers', as in the Buddhist version of the folk tale, the ability to live unharmed by the fatal treasure resides in the virtue of the possessor and it is Harry's purity that has enabled him to both own the cloak safely and to finally unite the Hallows (*Deathly Hallows*, Chap 35, p.577).

Harry Potter and fairy tales: 'The Tale of the Two Brothers'

Harry Potter elevates fairy tales to a high moral level when Dumbledore places them – alongside love – as that which is beyond Voldemort's comprehension (*Deathly Hallows*, Chap 35, p.568). Folk and fairy tales are important to Rowling, and after completing *Harry Potter* she decided to write *The Tales of Beedle the Bard* – the Wizarding book of fairy tales from which 'The Tale of the Three Brothers' came, and which she describes as 'a distillation of the themes found in the Harry Potter books' (2007j). Rowling has spoken of another fairy-tale author (Hans Christian Andersen) as 'a writer I revere, because his work was of that rare order that seems to transcend authorship. He created indestructible, eternal characters. The Ugly Duckling, The Little Mermaid, The Snow Queen, and The Naked Emperor have become so deeply embedded in our collective consciousness that we are in danger of forgetting that we were not born knowing about them, that Andersen gave them to us' (2010c). She has argued, 'there are good reasons why fairy tales endure. They appeal to us on such a subconscious and emotional level. I think you could say many of the same things about Harry. You have the changeling, you have the wicked stepparents . . . . You even have an ugly brother, in a way' (1999c; see also: 2010a). Alison Lurie calls Harry a 'classic Cinderlad' (1999, p.6) and Elaine Ostry writes that 'the Harry Potter series is positively soaked in an understanding of the fairy-tale form' (2003, p.90). This view of *Harry Potter* is supported by J. Hunter's structural analysis of the series, which argues that it 'casts its spell over readers by closely adhering to the formal organization of folktale structure', successfully tracing the 'ancient and enduring "cultural script" found in folk narratives we learn from childhood' (2015, p. 111; see also: Grimes, 2002).

Some aspects of *Harry Potter* draw directly on fairy tales – such as the house-elves, who, like the elves in 'The Elves and the Shoemaker', are freed when they are given clothing (Rowling, 2001a). The talking mirror that tells Harry the truth about his appearance ('"you're fighting a losing battle there, dear"' [*Azkaban*, Chap 4, p.46]) references the speaking mirror in 'Snow White' and the slugs that Ron burps up in *Chamber* recall the toads and snakes that the bad daughter is cursed to cough up every time she speaks in 'Diamonds and Toads'. Each of these examples, however, is a comic riff on the familiar story, which softens the punitive morality of the original. For *Harry Potter* both engages with, and critiques, traditional fairy tales. The series, for example, interrogates the assumptions of the fairy-tale genre by presenting lovable examples of its fearful creatures, such as giants and werewolves, and creating Marxist Goblins whose morality is at least more straightforward than that of the wizards who attempt to trick them. Fairy tales tend to accept that those who are different ought to be outcasts but, as Travis Prinzi has argued, 'traditionally evil and scary characters . . . serve in *Harry Potter* as examples of the plight of the oppressed rather than creatures who really need to be feared' (2009, p.216; see also: Klaus, 2012). *Harry Potter* even extends this reversal to sea monsters: at Hogwarts the giant squid – the marine creature that inspired the dreaded ship-sinking Kraken of legend – turns out to be rather kindly. Rather than,

Kraken-like, sinking the fleet of little boats as they sail across the lake, it pops little Dennis Creevey back in his craft when he falls out (Colbert, 2007, p.110).

Another example of the way in which *Harry Potter* both draws on, and subverts, folk-tale traditions can be seen in its use of traditional number symbolism. 'The Tale of the Three Brothers' is *Harry Potter*'s most explicit engagement with the fairy-tale form and its narrative, as with many folk tales, revolves around the number three (three brothers, three gifts, three responses to death). Another traditionally significant number (seven) also recurs throughout the series. There are seven floors in Hogwarts, seven Weasleys, seven tasks to reach the philosopher's stone (one of which involves seven bottles of potion), seven secret passages out of Hogwarts, Harry pays seven galleons for his wand, Dumbledore puts out seven lights on Privet Drive, Harry is born in the seventh month, and Voldemort tries and fails to kill Harry seven times. When Rowling first wrote a list 'of all the subjects to be studied[,] I knew there had to be seven' (2002a). Harry's wife-to-be is the seventh child: 'there's that old tradition of the seventh daughter of a seventh daughter and a seventh son of a seventh son, so that's why she's the seventh, because she is a gifted witch' (Rowling, 2005c). In *Half-Blood Prince* the reader learns both that seven is 'the most powerfully magical number' (Chap 23, p.466) and that Voldemort has split his soul into seven parts.[6] The constant repetition of seven throughout the series leads up to seventh novel of the series, in which Harry must destroy this seven-part soul. And the dedication to *Deathly Hallows* – like both the series itself and Voldemort's soul – is '*split seven ways.*'

This seven-part aspect of Voldemort's soul is reiterated in the opening scenes of *Deathly Hallows*. When seven Harrys are created by using Polyjuice Potion, Moody thinks that the plan will work because '"even You-Know-Who can't split himself into seven"' (Chap 4, p.47) – and Harry and Hermione share a knowing glance. The reader thinks that they are just being reminded of something they already know and having the satisfying parallel of a seven-book series and a soul split into seven parts, pointed out to them. But yet another trick is being played on the reader here. In the subtlest of hints, the seven-part dedication (which is an explicit allusion to Voldemort's Horcruxes) takes the shape of Harry's lightning-scar: the seventh Horcrux and the *eighth* part of Voldemort's soul. The folktale-style repetition of a talismanic number throughout the series actually serves to keep hidden from the reader – as Dumbledore keeps hidden from Harry – that Voldemort's soul has been split into eight.

The number seven turns up in one of the oldest fairy tales in existence, an ancient Egyptian story whose title bears a striking resemblance to the fairy tale in *Deathly Hallows*: 'The Tale of the Two Brothers'. The ancient nature of this tale is evident through its language, for it is written in Egyptian hieroglyphs. This appearance of ancient wisdom is likewise conferred on the 'Tale of the Three Brothers' through its antique, difficult to decipher script (in this case, runes). 'The Tale of the Two Brothers' may also have influenced the idea of Horcruxes within *Harry Potter*. Tolkien writes about this ancient Egyptian fairy tale in his 'On Fairy-Stories', an essay Rowling is likely to have read (it also

contains a reference to Michael Drayton's fairy knight Pigwiggen, the probable
source for Pigwidgeon's name [Tolkien, 1997, p.122]). Tolkien notes in this
essay that the 'Tale of the Two Brothers' is an early example of the 'ancient
and very widespread folk-lore notion, which does occur in fairy-stories; the
notion that the life or strength of a man or creature may reside in some other
place or thing' (Tolkien, 1997, p.118). In 'The Tale of the Two Brothers' the
hero tells his brother that he will 'enchant my heart, and I shall place it upon
the top of the flower of the cedar. Now the cedar will be cut down and my
heart will fall to the ground, and though shalt come to seek for it, even though
thou pass seven years in seeking it, but when thou hast found it put it in a vase
of cold water, and in very truth I shall live' (Wallis Budge, 1896, p.xxi). This
earliest of fairy tales encodes the nucleus of Harry's journey: a seven-year quest
after something that looks very much like a Horcrux.[7]

'The Pardoner's Tale' and 'The Tale of the Three Brothers'

Chaucer's 'Pardoner's Tale', like Rowling's 'Tale of the Three Brothers', is
likewise a conscious response to folk-tale traditions. Both stories relate the history of three brothers: 'each of us will become the others' brother . . . these
three swore together to each live and die for the other' ('and ech of us bicomen
otheres brother/. . . Togidres han thise thre hir trouthes plight/ To lyve and
dyen ech of hem for oother' [ll.698, 702–3]). In Rowling they are real brothers,
in Chaucer 'sworn brothers' – whose promise 'to live and die for each other'
turns out to be rather more accurate than they had intended. In both stories
the brothers meet Death in a personified form – rather to Harry's confusion:
'"Sorry," interjected Harry, "but *Death* spoke to them?"' (Chap 21, p.330).
'The Pardoner's Tale', likewise, personifies Death. At the beginning of the story
the sworn brothers hear of 'an underhand thief called Death' ('a privee theef
men clepeth Deeth' [l.389]). They set out to find and kill him, oblivious to the
rather obvious problems connected with such an enterprise.

There is also a mysterious person whom they meet on the way, an old man
who directs them to Death: 'now, sirs, he said, if you are so keen to find Death,
turn up this crooked path for in that grove I left him, by my faith, under a tree
and there he will be still' ('now, sires,' quod he, 'if that ye be so leef/ To fynde
Deeth, turns up this croked wey,/ For in that grove I lafte hym, by my fey,/
Under a tree, and there he wole abyde' [ll.474–7]). The identity of this man is
one of the puzzles of Chaucer's tale. Chaucer's Old Man is more ominous, as
well as much more aged, than he is in other versions of the folk tale, and this
has led to the tradition of reading him as a messenger from Death or perhaps
Death himself. This interpretation imparts an added frisson to the tale and it
seems to be the reading that has influenced Rowling. In *Harry Potter*'s version
of the fable the three brothers do indeed meet and converse with Death, as
Chaucer's three brothers do with the Old Man. (And in a pleasing circularity
Rowling has named as her favourite fan theory the idea that Dumbledore –
another old man – takes the role of Death in 'The Tale of the Three Brothers'.

Like Death, he gives Harry the invisibility cloak and greets him as an old friend at his death: 'Dumbledore as death. It is a beautiful theory and it fits' [Twitter, 21 Aug 2015]).

In Chaucer the three sworn brothers meet the Old Man at the very moment they are crossing a stile ('right as they wolde han troden over a stile' [l.712]). In *Deathly Hallows* the three brothers meet Death on a bridge – *Harry Potter*'s version of Chaucer's stile, and one of the many times that the series explores the potency of 'in-between' (or 'liminal') places. Liminal spaces are traditionally important in works about magic or the uncanny, such as in the film *The Exorcist* (1974) in which the first meeting with the exorcist takes place on a bridge. Bridges and stiles are natural settings for the meeting of two worlds. *Harry Potter* has many such physical embodiments of this concept of liminal space; the most important and memorable is Platform 9¾, at King's Cross Station. *Deathly Hallows* plays with this by making King's Cross Station into a limbo between life and death, reality and imagination. Rowling has explained how in the 'King's Cross' chapter of *Deathly Hallows* 'Harry entered a kind of limbo between life and death' and notes that this links with the way in which King's Cross is a liminal space throughout the novels: 'it has been established in the books as the gateway between two worlds, and Harry would associate it with moving on between two worlds' (2007f). Like King's Cross in *Deathly Hallows*, both the bridge in the 'Tale of the Three Brothers' and Chaucer's stile are physical symbols for the division between life and death. Chaucer's Old Man offers the brothers a way back, but in Chaucer – unlike in *Harry Potter* – none of the brothers takes it.

The parting words of the Old Man in Chaucer's tale are, 'God, who redeemed mankind, save you and amend your life' ('God save yow, that boghte agayn mankynde,/ And yow amende!' [ll.766–7]). Redeem literally means 'to buy back' and the literalisation of this financial metaphor in Chaucer's phrasing – 'boghte agayne mankynde' – encourages the reader to notice that the grace of God stands in exact opposition to the pile of gold. The road to redemption, however, is studiously avoided by all three of the brothers in Chaucer's tale in their search for gold. It is, nonetheless, taken by Ignotus Peverell in *Deathly Hallows'* reworking of Chaucer's story, and by his future descendant, Harry Potter.

The Pardoner and his Tale

Chaucer's folk tale is a particularly complex and literary version of the genre, a sophistication embodied by the relationship between the tale and its teller. The tension between the immorality of the speaker and the morality of his tale is made explicit when the Pardoner claims that, though he is a wicked man, he can tell a moral tale ('for though myself be a ful vicious man,/ A moral tale yet I yow telle kan' [ll.459–60]). As the Pardoner is an unreliable narrator, this assertion (like everything he tells his listeners) is open to question.

Pardoners in Chaucer's time were itinerant preachers who made money by selling 'indulgences': pieces of paper, supposedly blessed by the Pope, which promised those who bought them time off Purgatory. In effect, Pardoners offered forgiveness in return for money. As a result, Pardoners were generally viewed as grasping and unscrupulous, and Chaucer's Pardoner is the classic example of the type. His tale is presented in the form of a sermon and – like a traditional sermon – it has a 'text': the name for the passage from scripture on which a sermon is based. The text of the Pardoner's sermon is *radix malorum est Cupiditas* ('greed is the root of all evil' [1 Timothy 6.10]). But this biblical passage is not only the 'text' of the Pardoner's sermon; it is also the epigraph that Chaucer places over the whole of the Pardoner's Prologue and Tale: '*Radix malorum est Cupiditas*' (l.328). By using the same 'text' as his unreliable narrator Chaucer is playing a complex narrative game. The Pardoner hypo-critically preaches that greed is the root of all evil in order to part his listeners from their gold. Yet this is also the message that is conveyed by Chaucer's 'Pardoner's Tale' itself. By wrapping up the Pardoner's tale in an ironic pack-aging Chaucer sweetens the moral pill. The Pardoner's outrageous hypocrisy renders that moral entertaining as well as raising a question as to the extent to which 'a ful vicious man' really can tell 'a moral tale' without the moral becoming corrupted.

This narrative framing, and tension between the worth of the tale and the moral ambiguity of its teller, is also important in *Harry Potter*. 'The Tale of the Three Brothers' has been left as a clue for Hermione by Dumbledore, but the person who interprets it for the trio is Xenophilius Lovegood. Up to this point in the series, Xenophilius (meaning 'lover of the strange') has been presented as a charmingly batty character. He is chosen to explain the meaning behind the 'Tale of the Three Brothers' partly because his alternative ideas about the existence of Crumple-Horned Snorkacks, or the advisability of declaiming in Mermish during other people's weddings, mean that the exist-ence of the Hallows is likely to be doubted by the listener. And yet, he will be proved right. In this scene, however, Xenophilius is not only correctly inter-preting a highly moral tale but also (just like the Pardoner) acting in a manner that directly contradicts the moral of the story. The Pardoner preaches a tale about the evils of greed in order to rob people and Xenophilius interprets a tale about the need to accept mortality after he has capitulated to the Death Eaters. In one of *Harry Potter*'s most chilling moments the reader gradually realises that Xenophilius' act of literary criticism is actually intended to keep the trio in conversation so that they can be captured and killed. Xenophilius, like the Pardoner, fails to live out the moral of the story he tells.

The parting words of the Old Man within Chaucer's tale – of God who 'boghte agayn mankynde' – echo in the story's narrative frame. As the myste-riously appearing gold of the tale stands in opposition to Christ's freely given redemption, so the Pardoner eventually acknowledges that the 'indulgences' he sells are worthless beside the true pardon that is in Christ: 'and Jesus Christ who is the healer of our souls, grant that you receive his pardon, for, to be honest with you, his pardon is best' ('and Jhesu Crist, that is oure soules leche,/ So graunte yow his pardoun to receyve./ For that is best; I wol yow nat deceyve' [ll.916–9]). The narrative opens up the idea that the Pardoner, armed with the knowledge that his pardons are worthless in comparison to true grace, may yet himself be redeemed (and after a heated exchange with the Host, their differences are finally reconciled with a kiss of peace).

Harry Potter brings this reconciliation (which occurs in the narrative frame of Chaucer's tale) into the tale itself. Chaucer's austere ending – in which all three brothers die – is replaced by a hopeful one, in which the youngest brother outwits Death. The wily yet pure Ignotus Peverell inverts the storyline of Chaucer's more uncompromising tale. Ignotus is able to put into practice the moral of 'The Tale of the Three Brothers' and live without fear of death. While in Chaucer it is the sworn brothers who set out to search for Death – 'I shal hym seke, by wey and eek by street' (l.408) – in the 'Tale of the Three Brothers' it is Death who is left searching fruitlessly for the youngest brother.

The exchange between the Pardoner and the Host at the end of the 'Pardoner's Tale' draws attention to the way that this text, like all Chaucer's Canterbury tales, is a narrative that is enfolded within another. The speaker of each of these stories-within-a-story is part of a larger pilgrimage narrative, as each of the characters journeys towards Canterbury, and the stories they tell reveal something of their own character and, perhaps, something about the journey they are taking. Harry, Ron and Hermione reveal something about their own characters, and their understanding of the quest on which they have embarked, by their own interpretations of *Harry Potter*'s story-within-a-story. All draw a different conclusion from the tale:

> 'It's just a morality tale, it's obvious which gift is best, which one you'd choose –'
> The three of them spoke at the same time; Hermione said, 'the Cloak,' Ron said, 'the wand,' and Harry said, 'the stone.'
> They looked at each other, half-surprised, half-amused.
>
> (Chap 21, p.336)

These differing acts of interpretation reflect on Harry, Ron and Hermione's characters: 'what the Hallows are and what they represent reveals a lot about the people who seek them, want to use them, and being drawn to a particular hallow tells you something about the kind of person you are' (Rowling, 2012f). But these differing responses also reflect back on the capacious ability of literature to contain and allow multiple acts of interpretation.

This chapter's consideration of the medieval underpinning of the Deathly Hallows also opens up a different interpretative aspect of the series. All the stories considered here have a Christian aspect. There are explicit Christian references in the Judas myths and the Pardoner's story, both of which are imaginative responses to biblical texts. *Gawain* is, likewise, set in an explicitly Christian context of Christmas masses and prayers to the Virgin Mary, but seems (with its Green Chapel, holly branch and return from death) to be suffused with further layers of evocative, if unexplained, theological meaning (Hatt, 2015).

The next chapter will give the biographical evidence for Rowling's own faith and look more fully at the influence of Christianity, and its narrative structures, on *Harry Potter*. The series personifies the struggle between good and evil as a conflict between a Satanic villain and hero who has (as Rowling has acknowledged) 'certain messiah traits' (2007i). Christian ideas about the battle between good and evil are shaped by the two direct confrontations between Jesus and Satan in the Christian story: the Temptation in the Desert and the Harrowing of Hell. Chapter 4 argues for the influence of these episodes – and the way they are played out in texts such as medieval mystery plays and Milton's epics – on *Harry Potter*.

Notes

1 Hermione - the only female character with the same level of narrative importance as Harry, Ron, Dumbledore, Hagrid, Voldemort or Snape – spends a quarter of *Chamber* Petrified, so *Chamber* is an even more male-dominated text than the other novels of the series.

2 For the sexual aspect of snakes in *Harry Potter*, and the snake as an emblem of the 'dangers and seductions of language' see Wolosky, 2010, p.32.

3 On *Pottermore* Rowling attempts comedy even in relation to the beheadings of the French Revolution (2015b).

4 Rowling has referenced Green Men in interview (2006c).

5 It is perhaps an echo of this poisoned wine when the eldest brother in *Harry Potter* dies while he is drunk.

6 The symbolic importance of seven is suggested by Rowling's strikingly (and unusually) hesitant answer to the prescient interview question in 1999: 'why seven?' (1999e). The films picked up on the importance of this number by giving Harry the number seven Quidditch jersey in *Azkaban* and *Half-Blood Prince*.

7 As Wolosky notes, the etymology of Horcrux points to 'something crucial (the crux)', which is 'projected outside (from the French *dehors*)' (2010, p.10).

4   The Temptation in the Desert and the Harrowing of Hell

Harry Potter, Mystery Plays and Milton

'Um. I don't think they're that secular.' (Rowling, 2005f)

Rowling has long been drawn to churches, and they have provided the source for a number of her names. She has noted that one of her character's names was taken from the visitor's book at St Luke's (her childhood church) and another from an Edinburgh church's memorial (2012f, 2007l). Edinburgh's famous Greyfriars Kirkyard (next to the Elephant House café where Rowling often wrote) contains the tombstone of Thomas Riddell.[1] It also seems likely that Rowling was inspired by the name of Edinburgh's Lockhart Memorial Church (formally known as St Mungo's). This chapter argues that *Harry Potter* is also inspired by the Church in more fundamental ways. As a child Rowling cleaned St Luke's and was baptised there at her own request, aged eleven (Rowling, 2007l) – the age she would later choose for full entry into the Wizarding world.

An explicitly Christian interpretation of *Harry Potter* might seem surprising given the negative reaction the series has provoked in some Christian circles but, as critics such as Connie Neal, Greg Garrett and John Granger have ably shown, the Christian framework is more germane to *Harry Potter* than we might initially expect (Neal, 2008; Garrett, 2010; Granger, 2008a). Rowling, a practising Christian, has expressed her own frustration at the way this aspect of the series has been ignored – noting that 'extremist religious folk have missed the point so spectacularly' (2001d) and that 'there was a Christian commentator who said that *Harry Potter* had been the Christian church's biggest missed opportunity. And I thought, there's someone who actually has their eyes open' (2008c).

As a child Rowling sought out Christianity for herself and as an adult she has once again become a practising Christian, attending an Episcopalian church in Edinburgh (Rowling, 2012a). In one interview (2007i) she described her religious journey in some depth:

> I was officially raised in the Church of England, but I was actually more of a freak in my family. We didn't talk about religion in our home. My father didn't believe in anything, neither did my sister. My mother would

incidentally visit the church, but mostly during Christmas. And I was immensely curious. From when I was 13, 14, I went to church alone. I found it very interesting what was being said there, and I believed in it. When I went to university, I became more critical. I got more annoyed with the smugness of religious people and I went to church less and less. Now I'm at the point where I started: yes, I believe. And yes, I go to the church. A protestant church here in Edinburgh.

The importance of her own faith (and her own doubt) to the plot of *Harry Potter* is something that Rowling has openly acknowledged since the completion of the series. She has said that while, for her, the religious parallels of the novels had always been 'obvious', 'I never wanted to talk too openly about it because I thought it might show people who just wanted the story where we were going' (2007g; see also 2000m, 2007d).

Rowling has dropped strong hints about the relevance of Christianity to *Harry Potter* in interviews, but she has also left a major clue within the novels themselves by choosing a piece of explicitly Christian writing as an epigraph to the final novel:

Death is but crossing the world, as friends do the seas; they live in one another still. For they must needs be present, that love and live in that which is omnipresent. In this divine glass they see face to face; and their converse is free, as well as pure. This is the comfort of friends, that though they may be said to die, yet their friendship and society are, in the best sense, ever present, because immortal.

This is a passage from *More Fruits of Solitude* (Penn, 1718, pp.48–9) – a work of Christian spirituality by the Quaker William Penn (the founder of Pennsylvania). Rowling has described how deeply this quotation speaks to her: 'I really enjoyed choosing those two quotations because one is pagan, of course, and one is from a Christian tradition . . . . I'd known it was going to be those two passages since *Chamber* was published. I always knew [that] if I could use them at the beginning of book seven then I'd cued up the ending perfectly. If they were relevant, then I went where I needed to go. They just say it all to me, they really do' (2007g).

Deathly Hallows contains more explicitly Christian imagery than earlier books. It describes the residents of Godric's Hollow going to Midnight Mass on Christmas Eve; Harry marks the spot where he buries Mad-Eye's eye with a cross and the tombstones Harry reads in Godric's Hollow quote from the King James translation of the bible: '*Where your treasure is, there will your heart be also*' (Chap 16, p.266; Luke 12.34, Matthew 6.21); '*The last enemy that shall be destroyed is death*' (Chap 16, p.268; 1 Corinthians 15:26). Rowling has placed great emphasis on these two quotations (which are the only direct biblical quotations in *Harry Potter*) saying that 'they almost epitomise the whole series' (2007g).

Hermione gives a traditional interpretation for the passage from 1 Corinthians 15.26 on Lily and James's tombstone – '*The last enemy that shall be destroyed is death*' – explaining that it refers to life after death. The reader is left, however, to interpret the biblical reference on the Dumbledore family tombstone without assistance: '*Where your treasure is, there will your heart be also.*' It is a quotation drawn from Jesus' instructions to his followers to 'sell that ye have, and give alms; provide yourselves bags which wax not old, a treasure in the heavens that faileth not, where no thief approacheth, neither moth corrupteth. For where your treasure is, there will your heart be also' (Luke 12.33–4; see also: Matthew 6.21). The underlying meaning of these words is that true 'treasure' is seeking the good of others rather seeking gain for oneself. Dumbledore's choice of this quotation symbolises his regret at seeking the wrong kind of 'treasure:' he has neglected his sister in his obsession with the Hallows.[2] As has been explored in the previous chapter, Rowling puts 'dangerous sparkling objects' (2013c) at the heart of *Harry Potter* and the choice her hero needs to make in the final book is a decision between different types of 'treasure': the quest to unite the Hallows or the quest to destroy the Horcruxes. The quotation on the Dumbledore family tomb gives a specifically Christian colouring to this choice. Harry's final decision to seek the good of all by destroying the Horcruxes, rather than reuniting the Hallows that will make him powerful, follows the choice that Jesus advocates: 'a treasure in the heavens that faileth not, where no thief approacheth, neither moth corrupteth.' Unlike the Elder Wand (which is indeed stolen by a thief) Harry's 'treasure' is incorruptible.

THE TEMPTATION AND THE HARROWING

Rowling has used biblical quotation in political argument on Twitter (29 Jan 2017) and has also given an explicitly Christian answer when naming her favourite painting: Caravaggio's *Supper at Emmaus* (which is in the National Gallery in London). The subject of this painting – the disciples' astonished realisation of who the man they have met on the Emmaus road really is – is perfectly encapsulated by Caravaggio's realism. Caravaggio manages to make reality miraculous to the viewer in the way that he paints the moment. This painting is a revealing choice for Rowling not only because it is such a theological painting but also because its theology is what she likes about it. She describes its subject as 'when Jesus reveals himself to the disciples having risen from the dead. I love it. Jesus looks very likeable – soft and rounded – and the painting captures the exact moment when the disciples realise who this man is, blessing their bread' (Fraser, 2001, pp. 30–31).

In this biblical story the disciples fail to recognise the resurrected Jesus when they meet him on the road from Jerusalem to Emmaus, and only realise who he is as he blesses the bread at their meal. The most obviously striking aspect of this picture is Caravaggio's facility with perspective: the way that the arms of Jesus and the disciples seem to break out of the flat canvas. Rowling draws attention to a different, but related, aspect of the painting – the humanity of

Caravaggio's Jesus: he looks 'very likeable – soft and rounded'. Caravaggio's skill in realism – his dexterity with perspective and his unusually realistic depiction of Jesus – is used to particularly brilliant effect in this painting because it dovetails perfectly with the theology of the Emmaus story. The disciples do not recognise Jesus before he breaks bread because he is a real man: not a ghost or a 'fake', but a normal man you might meet on the road, a man with whom you might become friends and share a meal. Rowling's favourite painting is a depiction of the mystery of the Incarnation: that Jesus is at once true God and true man.

Harry Potter also has a very human and 'likeable' hero, who, after his death in *Deathly Hallows*, is revealed to be something more. Harry's sacrificial death and return to life come to the reader as a startling discovery of theological meaning. Harry is not an allegory of Christ but because (to Christian thinking) the Incarnation transforms humanity, it enables human beings to be Christ-like. As Gerard Manley Hopkins put it in his poem 'That Nature is a Heraclitean Fire and of the comfort of the Resurrection': 'I am all at once what Christ is, since he was what I am' (see Groves, 2012, pp.129–34). In any Christian fable the hero, because he embodies goodness, is going to reflect Christ on a narrative level. Rowling has acknowledged her hero's embodiment of goodness – 'he's the hero. Harry is just good' (2007i) – but in bringing Harry back to life, after his self-sacrificial death, *Harry Potter* gives this a more pointed application. The readers of *Deathly Hallows*, like the disciples in Caravaggio's painting, suddenly have a theological meaning revealed to them of which they were previously unaware.

Rowling is an author who loves to spring surprises on her readers and she instinctively responds to the element of revelation in the Christian story. The Resurrection astounds Christ's followers in Rowling's favourite painting, and *Harry Potter* responds to a reading of salvation history, which puts the idea of surprise at its heart. This traditional and influential interpretation is known as the 'guiler beguiled' theory (Aulen, 1931): it suggests that through the Incarnation God tricks or 'beguiles' the devil. The devil is the arch-trickster – who tricked Man with the apple in Eden – and in the 'guiler beguiled' model God beats him at his own game with the ultimate 'trick', or paradox of the God–man Jesus. *Piers Plowman* imagines Jesus as a knight who enters a joust dressed in the lowly armour of humanity to hide the true nobility of his nature: 'Jesus, because of his nobility, will joust in Piers Plowman's armour, in his helmet and mail coat, "human nature" in order that Christ will not be known to be absolute God' ('this Jesus of his gentries wol juste in Piers armes,/ In his helm and his haubergeon, *humana natura./* That Crist be noght biknowe here for *consummatus Deus*' [Passus 18.22]).

The Bible explains that Jesus unites the human and the divine: 'who, being in the form of God, thought it not robbery to be equal with God but made himself of no reputation, and took upon him the form of a servant, and was made in the likeness of men: and being found in fashion as a man, he humbled himself, and became obedient unto death, even the death of the cross' (Philippians 2.6–8).

In the 'guiler beguiled' reading, the Incarnation is a mystery that the devil cannot understand. His power-hungry nature cannot comprehend how God could have chosen to become less powerful, and his loveless heart cannot understand the divine outpouring of love for mankind that the Incarnation expresses. As the devil says when he meets Christ at the Harrowing of Hell in *The Gospel of Nicodemus* (a fourth-century Apocryphal Gospel): 'who art thou that art so great and so small, both humble and exalted, both soldier and commander, a marvellous warrior in the shape of a bondsman?' (James, 1924 [c.350]). As Satan does not understand what has happened at the Incarnation he thinks that Jesus is an ordinary, sinful man and hence assumes that he can claim his soul. But because Jesus is sinless this is an abuse of his power (the devil only has dominion over sinners) and because the devil has over-reached his jurisdiction he forfeits his rights over the souls of sinful mankind.

This 'guiler beguiled' interpretation focuses on the two moments when Jesus and Satan come face to face: the Temptation in the Desert (the only direct, biblical, confrontation between Christ and the devil) and the Harrowing of Hell. In the Temptation in the Desert, the devil closely questions Jesus to try to penetrate the secret of his true nature. In the Harrowing (literally 'ploughing up') of Hell, which is mentioned in the Apostles' Creed although not explicitly in the Bible itself, Jesus astounds the devil by entering hell after his death, defeating the powers of darkness and revealing that he has been God all along. The underlying narrative that connects the Temptation in the Desert to the Harrowing of Hell is that of Satan's inability to understand the power of love. Satan has fundamentally misunderstood the Incarnation – God's choice to give himself in love to mankind – and it is this incapacity to understand the power of love that destroys him. This is, of course, a fate he shares with Voldemort, whose demise is likewise brought about by love, and his inability to comprehend it. Through his own malice and ignorance Voldemort, like the devil, seeks his adversary's death only to discover that it is his own power he has unwittingly destroyed. Harry, like Jesus, has a *'power the Dark Lord knows not'* (*Phoenix*, Chap 37, p.743).

Harry Potter personifies the cosmic struggle between good and evil as a conflict between two people: the 'underlying theme' of the series, as Rowling has said, is 'Harry faces Voldemort' (2005g). In this personification the series draws on Christianity's embodiment of the battle between good and evil as the conflict between Jesus and the devil. The next section, therefore, establishes the ways in which *Harry Potter* links its hero with Jesus, and its villain with the devil (and Milton's Satan in particular[3]), before considering the Temptation and the Harrowing in more detail.

'CERTAIN MESSIAH TRAITS'

Harry Potter and the gospel narratives tell similar stories of their hero's early life: a baby is the subject of prophecy, miraculously survives the murderous attack this prophecy provokes, escapes into hiding and returns again to view as a pre-teen discovering his uniquely special identity (see Chapter 5 for a further discussion of these parallels). After the initial chapter of *Philosopher's Stone*, which describes Harry's babyhood, Harry returns to the narrative (aged eleven) and discovers his extraordinary destiny. Likewise, the gospels do not give any information about Jesus' life between the events of his nativity and the moment when (aged twelve) he expresses his understanding of his true nature. Jesus leaves his parents to go and teach in the Temple in Jerusalem. After Mary and Joseph have sought for him for three days they find him confounding the scholars in the Temple with his biblical knowledge. When his parents rebuke him for his disappearance he hints at his comprehension of his higher calling: 'wist ye not that I must be about my Father's business?' (Luke 2.49).

Harry, like Jesus, exhibits a further understanding of his mission in adulthood. *Deathly Hallows* transforms Harry from a boy-hero into an adult with a painful, self-sacrificial, calling. The reader of the gospels, likewise, gains a new understanding of who Jesus is and what he will do, when he becomes an adult. Jesus goes to John the Baptist to be baptised in the River Jordan and John tells the crowds 'behold the lamb of God' (John 1.29). John the Baptist had himself been mistaken for the messiah, and this proclamation of Jesus as the 'lamb of God' states that here is the true messiah, as well as hinting at the sacrificial role Jesus will fulfil (when, like a lamb, he is killed at Passover).

Deathly Hallows has a subtle allusion to John the Baptist's proclamation of Jesus, suggesting that this is the novel in which Harry will take up his new mantle.[4] Like Jesus, Harry has followers and friends who believe that he is the 'Chosen One' (*Half-Blood Prince*, Chap 3, p.43). In *Deathly Hallows*, while Harry suffers in the wilderness with no clear sense of how he can fulfil his mission, these faithful friends and followers have banded together to create *Potterwatch* – a radiobroadcast run by Lee Jordan. This is surprising given Jordan's relatively small role in the series up to this point, but it works perfectly in symbolic terms. Many of the people on *Potterwatch* take code-names that pun on their real name (Remus Lupin is 'Romulus', Kingsley Shacklebolt is 'Royal') and Lee Jordan's alias is 'River' (Chap 22, p.356). The River Jordan is a potent symbol in Jewish and Christian tradition: in particular it is the river that needs to be crossed to reach the Promised Land and the place where Jesus is baptised. River/Jordan, recognising Harry as the 'Chosen One', recalls John the Baptist, who, as he stands by the River Jordan, declares that Jesus is the messiah – a name that means the anointed (or 'chosen') one.

The 'messiah traits' that have been hinted at earlier in the series, however, suddenly become clear in Harry's death (Granger, 2009, p.147). *Harry Potter* draws on the Christian emphasis on Jesus' walk to death – the *Via Dolorosa*, which is liturgically remembered and re-enacted in the Stations of the Cross during Lent – in its concentration on Harry's final walk to death.[5] *Deathly Hallows* dedicates an entire chapter to this short journey and it is a chapter that is the culmination of the series, a chapter that Rowling 'waited seventeen years' (2008b) to write. Rowling describes this as the most moving passage in *Harry Potter*, a climactic part of the story she had long known was coming and one that had a therapeutic emotional force for her: 'it was the culmination of 17 years' work and the most cathartic piece of writing of my life' (Twitter, 17 June 2015; see also 2007e). Like the *Via Dolorosa*, Harry's long walk to a death that he is painfully, but willingly, encountering is punctuated by encounters with those he loves. Both Harry and Jesus meet their mother, and they also meet friends. Neville, like Simon Cyrene who takes Jesus' cross on the *Via Dolorosa*, willingly shoulders part of Harry's burden (the destruction of the final Horcrux) as Harry walks to his death.

While it is not clear within the series that Harry, too, will die at the end of his *Via Dolorosa*, it is one viable interpretation of what happens after Voldemort hits him with the killing curse. Harry's 'death' has the same effect on Voldemort's power – his inability to hurt those whom Harry died to save – as Lily's death did: 'I've done what my mother did. They're protected from you' (*Deathly Hallows*, Chap 36, p.591). It also makes sense in terms of Horcrux mythology within the novels. Rowling has repeatedly emphasised that the part of Voldemort's soul that Harry carries cannot be destroyed unless its carrier dies; which is why this piece of soul was not destroyed when Harry is stabbed with a basilisk fang in *Chamber*: 'he has to *die* to get rid of that piece of soul' (2007k; see also Twitter, 11 Feb 2016). The corollary of this is that when the Horcrux *is* destroyed, Harry must have died.

After he is hit by the killing curse Harry enters 'a kind of limbo between life and death' (Rowling, 2007f) and the name of this limbo – 'King's Cross' – is a hint about the Christian aspect of *Harry Potter*. King's Cross Station has been important throughout the series, but in *Deathly Hallows* the Christian pun within its name becomes newly audible. (As Rowling coolly noted when questioned as to why she chose King's Cross as the location of this limbo, 'the name works rather well' [2007f].[6]) After his death, Harry's body is carried out of the forest by Hagrid. This image of Hagrid carrying Harry is significant to Rowling: 'I always knew, and this is from really early on, that I was working towards the point where Hagrid carried Harry, alive but supposedly dead, out of the forest, always. . . I always cleaved to this mental image of Hagrid being the one carrying Harry out, and that was so perfect for me' (2012g). This 'perfect' image recalls the *Pietà*: the iconography of Jesus' dead body carried by his mother (famously depicted in Michelangelo's *Pietà* statue in St Peter's, Rome). In interview Rowling speaks of Hagrid as a father-figure to Harry (2012g), but in fact she has written a stereotypically *maternal* role for Hagrid (Prinzi, 2009, p.275). As Annette Wannamaker notes, 'Hagrid is both manly and motherly' (2008, p.137). He has a blind, maternal love for the 'interestin' creatures' that he nurtures and croons over: he reads stories to Aragog when he is poorly, packs a teddy bear for Norbert and explicitly refers to himself as Norbert's 'Mummy' (*Philosopher's Stone*, Chap 14, p.175). Because Hagrid is a vast, hard-drinking, bearded, half-giant Rowling can depict him knitting and bustling around his kitchen wearing a flowery apron and providing tea, sympathy, baked goods and a safe, caring haven for Harry without the maternal aspects of his love appearing clichéd. The echo of the *Pietà* as Hagrid carries

Harry's apparently lifeless body forms the apogee of Hagrid's mothering role as well as providing another Christic echo for Harry's death.

When Jesus returns from the dead he has destroyed the traditional barriers between people: 'there is neither Jew nor Greek, there is neither bond nor free, there is neither male nor female: for ye are all one in Christ Jesus' (Galatians 3.28). There is an echo of this reconciliation in the newly unified world of Hogwarts, when after Harry's victory over Voldemort 'nobody was sitting according to house any more: all were jumbled together, teachers and pupils, ghosts and parents, centaurs and house-elves' (*Deathly Hallows*, Chap 6, p.597). Harry is the saviour of the Wizarding world, a status noted (if also undercut) when Hermione nervously refers to Harry's '"*saving-people thing*"' (*Phoenix*, Chap 32, p.646). But the final book is less equivocal: Harry is 'their leader and symbol, their saviour and their guide' (*Deathly Hallows*, Chap 36, p.596). As Rowling acknowledged after the publication of *Deathly Hallows*, Harry 'does have certain messiah traits. I chose that on purpose' (2007i).

While Harry's Christ-like characteristics are only fully revealed in the final novel, Voldemort is clearly linked with Satan throughout *Harry Potter*. Voldemort is not an allegory of Satan, any more than Harry is an allegory of Jesus, but the moral allegiances of both are signalled by these allusions.

VOLDEMORT AND DIVINE PARODY

Augustine of Hippo, one of the most influential Christian thinkers, has argued that evil has no positive existence; that it is, rather, an absence of good: 'what, after all, is anything we call evil except the privation of good?' (1955 [421], p.342). Rowling has commented that, for her, likewise '"evil" is something that exists in the negative – it's the absence of the empathy and moral code that enables acts of kindness and love.'[7] This comment suggests that Rowling has been influenced by Augustine's famous formulation of evil as something that 'has no being' (1955 [c.397–8], p.69); it is 'something that exists in the negative.' This idea of evil as something without a positive existence derives in part from God's revelation of himself as that which *is*: 'I am that I am' (Exodus 3.14). The 1611 King James Bible (the translation used in the two biblical quotations within *Harry Potter*) prints this phrase in capitals: 'and God said unto Moses, I AM THAT I AM.' God declares that he is what is and, Augustine argues, it follows therefore that evil is what is not. In response to Augustine's insight, in much Christian literature evil 'exists only as parody' (Fichter, 1982, p.59). In Milton's *Paradise Lost*, for example, Satan's relationship with Sin and Death is a parodic version of the relationship between the Father, Son and Holy Spirit. Satan rapes his daughter Sin, who then gives birth to Death, and the unholy, incestuous closeness of this trio is intended as a shocking parody of the love of the Trinity. Shakespeare's Iago likewise declares 'I am not that I am' (*Othello*, 1.1.65): a direct parody of God's 'I am that I am.' Shakespeare gives his most evil character a self-definition that is the inversion of God's own identification of himself.

Voldemort's devilish nature, like Iago's, is expressed through his parody of the divine 'I am.' In a magnificently creepy moment Tom Riddle reveals himself to Harry:

> 'Why do you care how I escaped?' said Harry slowly. 'Voldemort was after your time.'
>
> 'Voldemort,' said Riddle softly, 'is my past, present and future, Harry Potter . . .'.
>
> (*Chamber*, Chap 17, p.231)

Voldemort's defining feature is his longing for immortality. In this passage he expresses his belief that he has always been Lord Voldemort in words that imply that the Dark Lord – like the Lord – is eternal. Riddle's grand claim that Lord Voldemort is 'my past, present and future' recalls Jesus' own declaration of eternal existence: 'before Abraham was, I am' (John 8.58). The diary-Riddle is fifty years old so how, Harry asks, could it know about something that happened eleven years ago? Jesus, likewise, is responding to a questioner who is sceptical that he could know about another time: 'thou art not yet fifty years old, and hast thou seen Abraham? Jesus said unto them, Verily, verily, I say unto you, Before Abraham was, I am.' Jesus responds to those who doubt his knowledge of another time with an answer that, by asserting his existence as an eternal present ('I am' not 'I was') stresses his divine nature. Jesus identifies himself with the divine present of Exodus, the 'I am' that is God's name: 'Before Abraham was, *I am*.' It is an identification that Voldemort blasphemously echoes, for the divine 'I am' is parodically present in Tom Riddle's own name for himself. The anagram of Tom Marvolo Riddle from which Voldemort creates his name lays claim to the divine, eternal 'I am': 'I AM LORD VOLDEMORT' (*Chamber*, Chap 17, p.231).

TOM MARVOLO RIDDLE: MAD TOM OR EVIL LORD?

One of Voldemort's most clearly satanic aspects is his affinity with snakes. He places part of his soul within Nagini, he is able to control the Basilisk (the king of serpents) and he has inherited Slytherin's gift of being able to talk to snakes. Rowling has invented the idea of a Parselmouth but, as Ian Parker has noted, the idea feels ancient (Rowling, 2012d). One reason for this is that Parselmouth is an old word (originally describing a person with a cleft palate [Rowling, 2000n]) but another is that conversing with snakes comes from an old story: the Book of Genesis. In Genesis Satan enters the snake in order to tempt mankind and it is as a snake that he persuades Eve to eat the fatal apple. Eden, like the world of *Harry Potter*, is not generally inhabited by talking animals and in both almost the only animal that can speak with humans is the snake. Talking snakes, and talking to snakes, therefore, has a specifically satanic resonance.

Voldemort (like Satan in the garden of Eden) possesses snakes, both when he makes Nagini into a Horcrux and prior to his rebirth when he '"inhabited animals – snakes, of course, being my preference"' (*Goblet*, Chap 33, p.567). There is also another close link between Voldemort and the serpent of Genesis. The snake begins the Genesis story walking on its feet and ends it being cursed with having to crawl on its belly: 'and the LORD God said unto the serpent, Because thou hast done this, thou art cursed above all cattle, and above every beast of the field; upon thy belly shalt thou go' (3.14). The footed snake at the beginning of Genesis is recalled the first time the reader meets He-Who-Must-Not-Be-Named. When Harry stumbles upon Quirrell/Voldemort drinking unicorn's blood in the Forbidden Forest, he makes a 'slithering' sound like a snake but he also has feet ('it got to its feet', *Philosopher's Stone*, Chap 15, p.184). This combination is reiterated three pages later when this hooded figure makes 'a slithering sound' while 'crawling across the ground like some stalking beast' (p.187). This simultaneous stalking and slithering recalls the strange footed snake in the biblical story of mankind's Fall: the snake inhabited by Satan.

Milton's epic *Paradise Lost* is a rewriting of the Genesis story and in Milton's version Satan is even more closely identified with the snake than he is in the Bible. While in the Bible Satan briefly takes the form of a snake, in *Paradise Lost* Satan actually becomes a snake at the end of the poem. Voldemort, likewise, turns into a snake over the course of *Harry Potter* as his moral degeneracy is spelt out in a physical degradation in which he seems "'to grow less human with the passing years"' (*Half-Blood Prince*, Chap 23, p.469). Over the course of the novels Voldemort is described in progressively snakier terms. When Harry listens to Voldemort in the Shrieking Shack he can no longer distinguish between the sound of Nagini and her master: 'Harry imagined he could hear the snake hissing slightly as it coiled and uncoiled, or was it Voldemort's sibilant sigh lingering on the air?' (*Deathly Hallows*, Chap 32, p.525). Voldemort is no longer described as being 'snake-like' but as a snake: his voice is a 'soft snake's hiss', and he mocks the saving power of love with 'his snake's face jeering' (*Deathly Hallows*, Chap 36, pp.585, 592).

The reader follows Riddle's descent into his evil snake-like form over the course of the novels through the gradual flattening of his face, the increased hissing of his voice and the gradual reddening of his eyes. As Harry watches Tom Riddle in the Pensieve as he begins his descent into Horcrux-creation, desiring Hepzibah Smith's possessions and intending to kill her to gain them, Harry thinks that he catches a gleam of red in Riddle's eyes. Ten years later – as Riddle asks for a job at Hogwarts – this fleeting ruddiness has turned into eyes that look blood-stained and once Riddle has fully inhabited his Voldemort persona his eyes are pure scarlet. And Milton's Satan, likewise, has eyes that gleam red.[8]

Milton's Satan, like Voldemort, becomes imprisoned within the snaky form that is the physical expression of his sin. In *Paradise Lost* Satan decides to leave hell and travel to Eden to tempt Adam and Eve. Taking the form of a snake he persuades Eve to eat the apple and then returns to hell to gloat to the other devils of his triumph. He waits for hell to resound with the applause of his followers – only to find that they have all been transformed into snakes:

So having said, a while he stood, expecting
Their universal shout and high applause
To fill his ear, when contrary he hears
On all sides, from innumerable tongues
A dismal universal hiss, the sound
Of public scorn; he wondered, but not long
Had leisure, wondering at himself now more;
His visage drawn he felt to sharp and spare,
His arms clung to his ribs, his legs entwining
Each other, till supplanted down he fell
A monstrous serpent on his belly prone.
                    (2007 [1667], Book 10, ll.504–514)

Milton stages Satan's triumph here as if it were happening in a theatre – Satan is an actor waiting to hear applause at the end of the play but hears instead derisive hissing (the only sound a snake can make as well as the sound of a discontented audience). And Satan is even forced to add his own censure: he 'would have spoke,/ But hiss for hiss returned' (ll.517–8). The declaration of Satan's greatest triumph turns out to be the moment he is overthrown.

Voldemort, like Satan, is fond of the theatrical gesture. But when Voldemort gathers his Death Eaters to witness his triumph over Harry, things, likewise, do not go to plan. In *Goblet* Voldemort expects his Death Eaters to laugh derisively at Harry as they duel but the appreciative laughter with which they begin is first silenced and then transformed into anxious yelling. Similarly the crowd of Death Eaters gathered to witness Voldemort's final triumph over Harry do not make the anticipated noise: 'he had expected to hear cheers of triumph and jubilation at his death, but instead hurried footsteps, whispers, and solicitous murmurs filled the air' (*Deathly Hallows*, Chap 36, p.580). As Milton does in *Paradise Lost*, *Harry Potter* stages its villain's failure with a soundscape in which murmurs or hisses replace the expected shouts of jubilation.

The passage above in which Milton's Satan turns into a snake is a bravura piece of writing. Milton makes his poetic form enact the transformation that Satan undergoes. The cutting down of Satan's person happens within the grammar of the poetry itself as Milton turns adjectives into verbs. 'Sharp' and 'spare' are usually adjectives – words that are followed by other words ('sharp cheekbones', 'spare form') – but the expected nouns do not materialise. Satan is pulled up short, and so is the reader. As Ricks puts it, 'it is characteristic of art to find energy and delight in an enacting of that which it is saying' (2002, p.9). Satan's form withdraws into himself and the reader likewise finds their expectations foreshortened. The flattening of Satan's features into a flat snake's face like Voldemort's is enacted within the verse by the dropping away of expected nouns as adjectives transform into verbs: 'his visage drawn he felt to sharp and spare.'

This transformation of Satan and his devils into snakes is Milton's unique addition to the biblical story, although the reader has been prepared for it by subtle hints earlier in his poem. When the devils gather in Book One, for example, they make a hissing noise, swarming together 'with the hiss of rustling wings' (l.768). The sinful plots they hatch at the beginning of *Paradise Lost* result in the transformation of this 'hiss of rustling wings' into their helpless hisses at the end of the poem: 'the applause they meant,/ Turned to exploding hiss, triumph to shame/ Cast on themselves from their own mouths' (Book 10, ll.545–7). *Harry Potter* echoes Milton's poetic manoeuvre here, as it, too, leaves a clue as to where dehumanising sin is leading Voldemort. The eventual transformation of Voldemort's voice into a 'soft snake's hiss' is intimated in the way Tom Riddle's voice is transformed by anger early in the series: '"Dumbledore's been driven out of this castle by the mere *memory* of me!" he hissed' (*Chamber*, Chap 10, p.232).

MILTON'S HIPPOGRIFF

Something else Voldemort and Milton's Satan share is their ability to fly. In *Paradise Regained* (Milton's sequel to *Paradise Lost*) Satan flies Jesus up to the highest tower of the Temple: 'he caught him up, and without wing/ Of hippogrif bore through the air sublime' (1997 [1671], Book 4, ll.541–2). Milton describes Satan's capacity to fly with the odd phrase 'without wing/ Of hippogrif' and *Harry Potter*, likewise, twice notes that Voldemort remains airborne 'without need of broomstick or thestral' (*Deathly Hallows*, Chap 17, p.278; Chap 4, p.56). Voldemort's ability to fly is stressed as something extraordinary (even though all wizards can fly on broomsticks) and the news that he can fly is breathlessly repeated three times in quick succession at the beginning of *Deathly Hallows* (Chap 4, pp.56, 65, 70). It seems possible that this ability is so strongly emphasised because it is a Satanic characteristic.

Milton mentions a hippogriff when Jesus is carried up to the highest pinnacle of the Temple, and the most important plot-function of the Hippogriff in *Harry Potter* is to carry Harry and Hermione to free Sirius from the top of a high tower. Hippogriffs – a legendary offspring of griffins and horses – were first so-named by the Italian poet Ariosto in the sixteenth century and in his epic *Orlando Furioso*, suitably enough, the hippogriff makes its first appearance being ridden by a wizard (2009 [1532], Canto 4, verses 18–9). Milton's comment that Satan can fly 'without wing/ Of hippogrif' is an *hommage* to Ariosto's poem. But is it also Milton's conscious statement of the difference of his own style from Ariosto's. Milton is not writing a flamboyant epic romance resembling Ariosto's – full of knights, ladies and fantastical beasts – but something that takes itself more seriously. Milton's epics hold up Christian obedience as the highest epic virtue and in keeping with this sober vein Milton mentions Ariosto's fantastical hippogriff only to stress that it was *not* present ('*without* wing/ Of hippogrif').

THE TEMPTATION IN THE DESERT

There is, however, yet another reason that Milton refers to hippogriffs in *Paradise Regained*. The hippogriff – the union of land-dwelling horse and sky-dwelling griffin – is conventionally understood to symbolise the Incarnation (Sax, 2013, p.195).[9] Milton mentions the hippogriff in *Paradise Regained* because this poem is a retelling of the temptation of Jesus by the devil in the wilderness, a story that centres on the relationship between Christ's divine and human natures.

> And Jesus being full of the Holy Ghost returned from Jordan, and was led by the Spirit into the wilderness, Being forty days tempted of the devil. And in those days he did eat nothing: and when they were ended, he afterward hungered. And the devil said unto him, If thou be the Son of God, command this stone that it be made bread. And Jesus answered him, saying, It is written, That man shall not live by bread alone, but by every word of God.
>
> And the devil, taking him up into an high mountain, shewed unto him all the kingdoms of the world in a moment of time. And the devil said unto him, All this power will I give thee, and the glory of them: for that is delivered unto me; and to whomsoever I will I give it. If thou therefore wilt worship me, all shall be thine. And Jesus answered and said unto him, Get thee behind me, Satan: for it is written, Thou shalt worship the Lord thy God, and him only shalt thou serve.
>
> And he brought him to Jerusalem, and set him on a pinnacle of the temple, and said unto him, If thou be the Son of God, cast thyself down from hence: For it is written, He shall give his angels charge over thee, to keep thee: And in *their* hands they shall bear thee up, lest at any time thou dash thy foot against a stone.
>
> And Jesus answering said unto him, It is said, Thou shalt not tempt the Lord thy God.
>
> And when the devil had ended all the temptation, he departed from him for a season.
>
> (Luke 4.1–13; see also Matthew 4.1–11)

Jesus defeats Satan by quoting scripture ('it is written. . .') to sidestep each of the devil's temptations. It is by holding fast to his faith in God, expressed in his unfaltering confidence in his word, that he defeats the devil. The scene in *Harry Potter* that most clearly recalls the Temptation in the Desert is Harry's conversation with Tom Riddle in the Chamber of Secrets. In this scene Harry is taunted by Riddle but expresses his unwavering belief in Dumbledore, firmly declaring to Riddle's fury that Dumbledore is "'the greatest wizard in the world'" (*Chamber*, Chap 17, p.232). This is Harry's strongest expression of faith in Dumbledore in the series. As a result of this loyalty Harry is sent the two things he needs to triumph: the Sorting Hat and Fawkes. Harry's expression of his faith in Dumbledore enables his victory over the satanic Riddle (Chap 18, p.244).

In the Temptation in the Desert the devil offers Jesus obvious temptations of food, power and glory but, as Christian interpreters have long argued, there is also a more subtle, underlying temptation for Jesus to withstand. In this reading, the repeated question 'if thou be the Son of God' lies at the heart of the scene. The devil is trying to penetrate the mystery of who Jesus really is and the temptation Jesus must withstand is that of revealing his true nature by demonstrating his divine power.

The Temptation in the Desert has traditionally been read as a scene about the confusion and anxiety the devil experiences because Jesus has committed no sin: might he be something more than human? In *Paradise Regained* Satan explains that ever since he has heard the prophecy of Jesus' birth he has been closely observing him, and wants to talk with him because:

I thought thee worth my nearer view
And narrower scrutiny, that I might learn
In what degree or meaning thou art called
The Son of God, which bears no single sense...
              I collect
Thou art to be my fatal enemy.
Good reason, then, if I beforehand seek
To understand my adversary, who
And what he is; his wisdom, power, intent.
              (Book 4, ll.510–28)

As Milton's Satan explains here 'Son of God' is an equivocal phrase: does it just mean a holy man, someone who does God's will, or does it mean God's literal son? The devil's repeated question – 'if thou be the Son of God' – is an attempt to get Jesus to reveal the precise meaning of this phrase. When Jesus does not turn rocks into bread nor leap from the Temple roof uninjured the devil becomes confident that he is merely human, and hence can be killed with impunity.

In some depictions of the Temptation in the Desert the devil probes Jesus' identity while disguised (sometimes dressed as a friar, as he is in John Bale's early Reformation play *The Temptacyon of Our Lorde and Saver Jesus Christ by Sathan in the Desart* [Bale, 1986 (1538), ll.74–5]). In the encounter in the Chamber of Secrets Voldemort likewise takes the form of Tom Riddle to increase the chance that Harry might reveal the secret of his power. (There is a little slip of the mask when Riddle questions Harry, however, for Harry catches an 'odd red gleam' [*Chamber*, Chap 17, p.231] in his eyes. This is the first appearance of the red eyes that symbolise Riddle's descent into evil. As mentioned above they are a satanic marker and it is therefore especially telling that they first appear at this moment.) Shocked and terrified by what happened when he tried to kill Harry as a baby, Voldemort decides to question Harry as to his true identity, before again trying to eliminate him. Might he (as is rumoured) be a powerful dark wizard, disguised as an ordinary boy? After drawing Harry away to a deserted space, he starts an apparently friendly conversation with Harry in which he asks: "'how is it that a baby with no extraordinary magical talent managed to defeat the greatest wizard of all time?'" (*Chamber*, Chap 17, p.231).

Satan in *Paradise Regained*, as in the mystery plays and *Piers Plowman*, engages Jesus in conversation in the desert because he, like Voldemort, is desperate to find out the true origin of his adversary's power. Why was he not able to kill him when he was a baby? Might it be dangerous to himself to try to kill him again now? In the York mystery play of the temptation Diabolus states that he will go and talk to Jesus 'in order that it can be known and understood if Godhead is hidden in him' ('for so it schall be knowen and kidde,/ If Godhed be in hym hidde' [Beadle, 1982 (c.1470), play 22, ll.49–50]). But, as in *Piers Plowman*, he leaves baffled: 'I assailed him with temptations, and asked him whether he was God or God's son, but he didn't give me a clear answer' ('I have assailed hym with synne, and some tyme I asked/ Wher he were God or Goddes sone – he gaf me short answere' [Langland, 1995 (c.1370–90), Passus 18, ll.296–7]). Due to Jesus' refusal to engage with the temptations, the devil departs no wiser than he came: 'I cannot tell what he is; I cannot make any headway as to whether he is God or man' ('what that he is I kannot se;/ Whethyr God or man, what that he be/ I kannot telle in no degré' [Spector, 1991 (c.1425–75), play 23, ll.192–4]). Jesus' identity as God *and* man – rather than 'God or man' – is the trump card that Satan does not even know is in the pack.

Jesus' refusal to display his power convinces the devil that he must be weak, but the very fact that he does not give into temptation should itself have given the devil pause. In *Paradise Regained* Satan notes to his chagrin that Jesus is 'proof against all temptation . . . [of] honours, riches, kingdoms, glory' (Book 4, ll.533–6) but, like Voldemort, he fails to recognise this as proof of his adversary's strength. Voldemort, like Satan, should have grown suspicious after his early failure to tempt Harry with the power, riches and eternal life offered by the Philosopher's Stone: '"Voldemort should have known then what he was dealing with, but he did not!"' (*Half-Blood Prince*, Chap 23, p.478).

In both the Temptation in the Desert and *Harry Potter* the embodiment of evil fails to recognise their enemy's supremacy because of an inability to comprehend the power of love. Voldemort questions Harry, saying '"twice – in *your* past, in *my* future – we have met. And twice I failed to kill you. *How did you survive?*"' (*Chamber*, Chap 17, p.233). When he learns that Harry has defeated him through love – through the protection that his mother's love conferred on him – Voldemort thinks he has nothing to fear. If Harry was saved by love he cannot be particularly powerful, and Voldemort dismisses him as a negligible danger. Voldemort, like Satan, fatally underestimates the power that will be his downfall.

CHRISTUS VICTOR AND THE HARROWING OF HELL

The 'guiler beguiled' interpretation reads the Temptation in the Desert as evidence that the devil is bamboozled by Christ's double-nature as God and Man. It is for this reason that, at precisely the moment in *Paradise Regained* when Satan is expressing his non-comprehension of the Incarnation ('in what degree or meaning thou art called/ The Son of God') that Milton mentions the hippogriff: 'So saying he caught him up, and without wing/ Of hippogrif bore through the air sublime.' The hippogriff, uniting as it does creatures of land and air, earth and heaven, embodies the union of humanity and divinity present in the Incarnation, a union that Satan has no hope of understanding.

Rowling has noted that she took her Hippogriff research seriously (2005g). It seems likely, therefore, that she is aware of its traditional religious symbolism. There may even be a joke about Harry's 'saviour' status in the gossip doing the rounds in *Half-Blood Prince* that Harry has a hippogriff tattooed on his chest. Ginny's response to this is to tell Romilda Vane that the tattoo is a Hungarian Horntail ('"much more Macho"' [Chap 25, p.500]), which is a sweet semi-acknowledgement that Harry is not in fact very macho. In the Temptation in the Desert Jesus defeats the devil verbally: he triumphs not through martial prowess but through purity of heart and superior understanding of the scriptures. Neither purity nor learning have much to do with being macho and the Temptation in the Desert, like much of the New Testament, presents a messiah who does not precisely fulfil traditional masculine stereotypes. The Jews at the time of Christ appear to have been awaiting a martial messiah who would throw off the Roman oppressor. The echo of this desire reverberates through the gospels as Jesus' followers have to learn that he is not going to be the military leader they had expected. When soldiers come to arrest Jesus, Peter fights back and cuts off the ear of one of those who has come to arrest him, but Jesus – like Harry (who merely attempts to disarm Snape after he has cut off George's ear) – refuses to retaliate. Lupin argues with Harry over his continued use of the Disarming spell and, like some of Jesus' followers, cannot accept that, even when threatened with death, Harry is still advocating non-violence.

Christ's choice to suffer rather than fight is a truly radical inversion of the idea of what a hero should be. The Western culture of masculinity (bred on classical martial heroes) has long struggled with the inversion of traditional heroism embodied by the Passion. Jesus' challenge is to forgive one's enemies rather than defeat them – a challenge he lays down as he forgives even those who fix him to the cross. This is the Christian inversion of what true heroism, true manliness is, and an echo of it is found in Harry's final words to Voldemort. To Voldemort's astonishment, Harry admonishes him to seek manliness in repentance: 'be a man . . . try . . . try for some remorse' (*Deathly Hallows*, Chap 36, p.594).[10] *Harry Potter* follows in the footsteps of Christian heroism by making repentance rather than victory the heroic ideal; it is remorse that makes you 'a man'.

Taken together, the two crucial scenes of the 'guiler beguiled' interpretation of salvation – the Temptation in the Desert and the Harrowing of Hell (discussed below) – are witness to a tension between Christianity's rejection of martial masculinity and the tenacity of that model within Western culture. While it is clear from the Bible that there is nothing martial about Christ's victory over Satan in the Temptation in the Desert, writers have often chosen to depict this verbal tussle as if it were a martial combat. Lancelot Andrewes (a seventeenth-century clergyman and one of England's greatest preachers) imagines the Temptation in the Desert as a joust in which Jesus is God's 'Champion' (1592, A3r) (as he is likewise in some poems about the Harrowing [Gray, 1992, p.38]). A Champion is a knight who defends the honour of another, as Jesus at the Temptation defends God's word from the devil's attempts to twist its meaning. Riddle, likewise, mockingly describes Harry as Dumbledore's champion (*Chamber*, Chap 17, p.233). In both narratives, this early encounter in which the evil character underestimates the strength of the good, predicts the outcome of their final battle.

Christian epics such as Milton's *Paradise Lost* (in which readers have long felt that Satan, rather than Christ, is the hero[11]) show how difficult it is to write a convincingly heroic hero who rejects violence. It is, however, a challenge to which *Harry Potter* rises to an impressive degree. In *Azkaban*, for example, the expected murderous climax towards which the novel appears to be building is replaced by Harry's decision to spare the man who betrayed his parents. Harry also remains steadfast in his use of his 'signature move' (*Deathly Hallows*, Chap 5, p.64) – his non-violent Disarming spell – when he faces Voldemort in the duels at the end of *Goblet* and *Deathly Hallows*.[12]

In *Deathly Hallows* Harry passively submits to a sacrificial death. Nonetheless, the heroism of self-sacrifice alone is clearly felt by Rowling to be just a little anti-climactic. The readers of *Harry Potter*, therefore, like the audience of the medieval mystery plays in which Jesus' death is followed by his Harrowing of Hell, watch their hero die a perfect, obedient death in which he sacrifices himself unresistingly for the good of the others; but they also get to see their hero rise from the dead and have one final, victorious duel with his enemy. Christ-as-knight (*Christus Victor*) breaks into hell, defeats the devil and saves all the souls within it; and at the end of *Harry Potter* Harry defeats Voldemort in a chivalric final single combat in the Great Hall, freeing all from the Dark Lord's power.

The Harrowing of Hell is a part of the salvation story that allows writers and artists to depict Christ as a glorious victor 'fierce in battle and worthy to win honour' ('full fers in fight/ Worthi to wyn honoure' [Stevens and Cawley, 1994 (c.1450), play 25, ll.139–40]). It portrays Christ as a physically dominant hero who vanquishes Satan not only through obedient, self-sacrificial love at his Passion, or through his integrity and unrivalled scriptural knowledge in the Temptation in the Desert, but also through physical prowess. Martin Luther wrote of how the Harrowing was traditionally depicted in the early sixteenth century, with Jesus as a conquering hero dressed in 'a cape and with banners in his hand as he makes his descent and stalks and assaults the devil, as he storms hell and rescues his own people from it' (2001 [1533], p.246). Medieval illustrations and wall paintings, likewise, depict the Harrowing as the martial and chivalric climax of the salvation story, with Christ pinioning Satan with his cross-staff as if it were a spear and crushing him under the gates of hell. Christ is revealed as a glorious knight ('so douhti a knyht' [Gray, 1992, p.38]) and the York playwright exults that 'great is your might' ('mekill is thi myght' [Beadle,

1982 (c.1470), play 37, l.349]). Christ encounters the devil and routs him in his hellish citadel: 'he has overcome the strength of death and broken down hell's doors with his foot' ('the strength of the deth hadde overcome;/ Helle dore he brake with his fot' [Gray, 1992, p.36]).

Another crucial aspect of the imagery of the Harrowing is the light that breaks in on hell as Jesus enters it (this light imagery is central to two of the most famous depictions of the harrowing, an engraving by Durer and a Giotto fresco). The *Gospel of Nicodemus* describes how at the Harrowing 'on a sudden there came a golden heat of the sun and a purple and royal light shining upon us' (James, 1924 [c.350]). Light symbolism is used likewise when Harry defeats Voldemort at the precise moment that light breaks in on the Great Hall: 'a red-gold glow burst suddenly across the enchanted sky above them, as an edge of dazzling sun appeared over the sill of the nearest window' (*Deathly Hallows*, Chap 36, p.595). In both stories the arrival of light symbolises the triumph of love.

In the York plays, the captive soul of Isaiah speaks of 'a glorious gleam that gladdens us and gives us hope that our release is coming' ('a glorious gleme to make vs gladde,/ Wherefore I hope oure helpe is nere' [Beadle, 1982 (c.1470), play 37, ll.42–3]). This is an allusion to Isaiah's famous prophecy that 'the people that walked in darkness have seen a great light: they that dwell in the land of the shadow of death, upon them hath the light shined' (9.2). This reference to Isaiah is part of the way that the Harrowing joins in the biblical presentation of the triumph of God's love as the triumph of the light: 'and the light shineth in darkness; and the darkness comprehended it not' (John 1.5). This ascendancy of love, expressed as light breaking in on darkness, is given narrative expression in the Harrowing of Hell. It is likewise the narrative of Harry's defeat of Voldemort as a spectacular dawn breaks in upon the Great Hall, as 'a red-gold glow burst suddenly across the enchanted sky above them.'

THE POWER THE DARK LORD KNOWS NOT

The Harrowing is paired with the Temptation in the Desert because it is the moment when the question posed by the devil at the Temptation (who are you?) is answered. It is the dramatic climax of the 'guiler beguiled' model of salvation because it is when Jesus reveals his divinity and finally explains to the devil what has really been going on: 'I, who am the Lord of heaven, in the likeness of an ordinary man have graciously matched your trickery – I have used guile against guile' ('I in liknesse of a leode, that Lord am of hevene,/ Graciousliche thi gile have quyt – go gile ayein gile!' [Langland, 1995 (c.1370–90), Passus 18, ll.357–8]).

In the medieval Harrowing plays Christ explains that the reason that God has tricked the devil in this way is 'the deep love I had for the soul of mankind' ('for hartely loue I hadde/ Vnto mannis soule' [Beadle, 1982 (c.1470), play 37, ll.244–6]). It is 'for love of mankind I suffered death, and for love of mankind I have risen up red with blood' ('For mannys loue I tholyd dede,/ And for mannys loue I am rysyn up rede' [Spector, 1991 (c.1425–75), play 35, ll.81–2]).

The 'guiler beguiled' plot works because the devil is unable to comprehend love and in *Harry Potter*, likewise, the 'power the Dark Lord knows not' is, of course, love. In the final duel with Voldemort, as at the Harrowing, it is finally explained to the Dark Lord what has been really going on. Harry explains that his sacrificial death has fatally wounded Voldemort's power; that Dumbledore intended for Snape to kill him and that Snape has been working against Voldemort all this time. The underlying motivation for all three actions is love: Harry and Dumbledore have died to save those they love and Snape has risked his life because of his love for Lily. Voldemort, like the devil, is defeated because he does not understand love's power for, as one medieval poem summarises the salvation story, 'love has ended the strong fight' (Gray, 1992, p.46).

Self-sacrificial death has immense power in the world of *Harry Potter* – Lily's, Dumbledore's and finally Harry's deaths all provide protection for the people they love. One astute questioner noticed the power of voluntary death in *Harry Potter* in 2005 when they asked Rowling why Voldemort offered Lily so many chances to live. Rowling replied: 'can't tell you. But he did offer, you're absolutely right. Don't you want to ask me why James's death didn't protect Lily and Harry? There's your answer, you've just answered your own question, because she could have lived and chose to die. James was going to be killed anyway . . . . [Lily] did very consciously lay down her life. She had a clear choice' (2005b). In a later interview Rowling explicitly links this idea of choice with Harry's death: 'there has to be space, to make Harry truly heroic, for free will. It has to be his choice. The whole thing's his choice. He *chooses* to sacrifice himself, just as Lily chose to sacrifice herself. He *chooses* to pull himself back to life. And that's his own will and courage. So ultimately, those things, all of them were more important than the magic' (2007k). Harry, likewise, explicitly links the *voluntary* nature of his sacrifice, and its resulting power, with Lily's death for him (*Deathly Hallows*, Chap 36, p.591). In making the voluntary, chosen nature of Harry's sacrifice crucial, *Harry Potter* has 'Christianised' Harry's death beyond what the plot-mechanics demanded. Harry may have returned to life for magical reasons – to do with Horcruxes, Voldemort's taking Lily's blood or Harry becoming Master of Death (having unwittingly united the Hallows) – but all these reasons would have continued to operate if Harry had fought Voldemort rather than facing him unarmed. Dumbledore, nonetheless, insists that Harry's self-sacrificial love, his choice to die, is crucial:

'I didn't defend myself! I meant to let him kill me!'
'And that,' said Dumbledore, 'will, I think, have made all the difference.'
(*Deathly Hallows*, Chap 35, p.567)

Harry Potter has made love – Harry's love for his friends and decision to die for them – the power that will defeat Voldemort: 'greater love hath no man than this, that a man lay down his life for his friends' (John 15.13). In making Harry's self-sacrificial decision to die for others crucial to his return from the dead *Harry Potter* links Harry's fate explicitly with the Christian story.

Dumbledore's explanations to Harry about the power of love, and the importance of Voldemort's inability to understand this power, are one of the circular connections between the first and last novels of the series (discussed in more detail in Chapter 8). In the opening novel Dumbledore explains "'your mother died to save you. If there is one thing Voldemort cannot understand, it is love'" (Chap 17, p.216). In the final book this explanation returns: "'that which Voldemort does not value, he takes no trouble to comprehend'" (Chap 35 p.568). In the first novel Voldemort cannot 'understand' love; in the final one he cannot 'comprehend' it. Voldemort's final failure to 'comprehend' love echoes the beginning of John's gospel, mentioned above: 'the light shineth in darkness; and the darkness comprehended it not.' 'Comprehend' means 'to grasp with the mind, conceive fully or adequately, understand' but also to 'seize, grasp, lay hold of, catch . . . contain.' The darkness at the beginning of John's gospel cannot 'comprehend' the light: it cannot understand it, but it also cannot 'contain' or 'seize' it; the darkness has no power over the light. Voldemort's inability to comprehend love means, likewise, that it has power to defeat him.

Notes

1 Tom Riddle (Snr)'s tombstone turns up in *Goblet* and it is noticeable that the historical Thomas Riddell, like Rowling's Tom Riddle, also had a son named after him. The poet William McGonagall is buried in this churchyard too.

2 It is not certain that Albus, rather than Aberforth, chose this quotation, but it is what Harry assumes and it seems probable, particularly since Rowling has said that Dumbledore believes in God (Fraser, 2014).

3 For more on the connections of Voldemort with Milton's Satan, see Lurie, 1999, p.6; Wolosky, 2010, pp.113–4.

4 Rowling is interested in the status of those who – like John the Baptist and Neville Longbottom – are almost-but-not-quite the hero. In one interview, commenting on Dumbledore's inability to unite the Hallows, she noted the universality of this narrative idea, calling Dumbledore 'John the Baptist to Harry's Christ' (2013d).

5 The Stations of the Cross are fairly unusual in Anglican liturgy, but it is quite possible that Rowling has encountered them, especially as she attends an Episcopalian church (Rowling, 2012a).

6 Rowling has also written that her original choice of King's Cross Station as 'the portal that would take Harry to Hogwarts' was due in part to its having 'such an evocative and symbolic name' (2012–14).

7 This is not a verbatim quote, but a report by an audience member of Rowling's words during her talk entitled 'Morality and Mortality in Harry Potter' (10 February 2014) (Joseph, 2014).

8 *Half-Blood Prince*, Chap 20, pp.408, 410, 413; *Philosopher's Stone*, Chap 17, p.212; *Deathly Hallows*, Chap 36, p.593. Milton describes Satan's eyes as 'carbuncles' (Book 9, l.500), a red semi-precious stone.

9 Despite the clear etymology of the name 'Hippogriff' – a horse ('*hippo*') united with a griffin ('griff') – *Harry Potter*'s Hippogriffs are not created from the traditional union of horse and griffin but from a simpler, arguably even more symbolic, union of earth and air (horse and eagle).

10 Remorse would undo the dehumanisation that Voldemort has wrought himself through Horcrux-creation. Hermione explains earlier in the novel that it is only remorse that can reverse the process of making a Horcrux (Chap 6, p.89).

11 William Blake famously said that Milton was 'of the Devils party without knowing it.' For an effective riposte to this view, see Fish (1997 [1967]).

12 In the Harrowing of Hell, likewise, Christ does not attempt to kill Satan but 'disarmed' him: Thomas Bilson, *The effect of certaine Sermons touching The Full redemption of mankind by the death and bloud of Christ Jesus* (London, 1599), A4r.

5 Comedy, tragicomedy and Shakespearean influence in *Harry Potter*

Harry Potter makes its readers laugh, and comedy is an essential part of how it handles its serious themes. At the climax of *Deathly Hallows* – after all the loss and self-sacrifice, after Harry faces death, glimpses the afterlife and defeats Voldemort in the grand final battle – comedy returns with Peeves' victory song about how all should enjoy themselves now that 'Voldy' has gone 'mouldy'. '"Really gives a feeling for the scope and tragedy of the thing, doesn't it?" said Ron, pushing open a door to let Harry and Hermione through' (Chap 36, p.598). Ron's action of opening the door here neatly expresses the way that his characteristic humour eases the transition from the excitement and peril of battle to the quiet contentment of the novel's conclusion.

Harry Potter is a joyous riot of genres and it mixes low-status genres – 'pulp fiction . . . horror stories, detective fiction, the school story . . . sports story, and series books' (Alton, 2003, p.141) – with eternal literary themes: 'life and death and evil and goodness and the nature of loyalty' (Rowling, 2007d). Rowling has spoken of the series as being 'largely about death' (2006a) and the death-toll of much-loved characters (Sirius, Dumbledore, Cedric, Hedwig, Moody, Fred, Lupin, Tonks, Colin Creevey, Snape and Dobby) is truly striking for a series ostensibly aimed at children. The body-count at the end of the Battle of Hogwarts resembles a bloody Jacobean revenge tragedy where most of the major characters lie dead upon the stage. But while Rowling has spoken of the subject of *Harry Potter* as 'love, loss, separation, death' (2008a) and has adopted the phrase 'morality and mortality' (2012i) as a shorthand for her central themes, *Harry Potter* balances this seriousness with large doses of humour.

Rowling has spoken of how 'British comedy is an obsession of mine. I love Monty Python' (2000k), and the influence of Python's anarchic humour is clear throughout *Harry Potter*. A chocolate from Python's Whizzo Quality Assortment – the Cockroach Cluster – is sold in Honeydukes, and Wizarding Chocolate Frogs, likewise, appear to have been inspired by Python's Crunchy Frog. The exchange in *Phoenix* when Ron asks what Hermione can possibly see in older, famous, international-Quidditch-star Krum strongly recalls the 'what have the Romans done for us?' skit in *Life of Brian*; and 'The House-Elf Liberation Front' title of this chapter likewise appears to echo *Life of Brian*'s 'Judean People's Front'. Nancy Solon Villaluz has pointed out an arresting

Python parallel in the way that the series opens by introducing the reader not to its hero, but to the 'perfectly normal' Dursleys, who are 'the last people you'd expect to be involved in anything strange or mysterious.' In the Python episode 'You're no fun anymore', 'it was a day like any other and Mr and Mrs Samuel Brainsample were a perfectly ordinary couple, leading perfectly ordinary lives – the sort of people to whom nothing extraordinary ever happened, and not the kind of people to be the centre of one of the most astounding incidents in the history of mankind . . . . So let's forget about them and follow instead the destiny of this man . . . Harold Potter' (quoted in Villaluz, 2008, p.180).

While *Harry Potter* is punctuated with Python-style irreverence, the greatest practitioner of the mixed mode of comedy and tragedy – of profound emotion punctuated with laughter – is Shakespeare. Shakespeare famously puts a joke-cracking gravedigger in *Hamlet* and a Fool as companion to the king in *King Lear*. Cleopatra takes delivery of the asp with which she will commit suicide from a clownish countryman who warns her 'his biting is immortal; those that do die of it do seldom or never recover' (*Antony and Cleopatra*, 5.2.241–2). The comedy such characters provide is not divorced from, but intimately connected to, the tragic fate of the protagonists (Snyder, 1979). The clown's mistake – saying 'immortal' when he means 'mortal' – links directly to what Cleopatra hopes to achieve through her death. Cleopatra intends to be remembered for ever by killing herself: 'give me my robe. Put on my crown. I have/ Immortal longings in me' (5.2.275–6). The repetition of the clown's 'immortal' in Cleopatra's words is remarkable. Few writers would dare to use a word seriously mere lines after it has been used for a comic purpose but Shakespeare is justifiably confident of his ability to make the earlier laughter strengthen, not destabilise, the pathos and power of Cleopatra's death.

Rowling loves Shakespeare's plays (2012e) and there are direct allusions to his comedies in her work (she has named Luna's future son, Lysander, for example, after a character in *A Midsummer Night's Dream* [2007l]). In the 2001 Comic Relief book *Fantastic Beasts and Where to Find Them* the description of the Mooncalf suggests that Rowling is remembering a classic scene of Shakespearean slap-stick. Rowling's Mooncalf (which also makes a brief appearance in the 2016 film) has a body that 'is smooth and pale grey, it has bulging round eyes on top of its head and four spindly legs with enormous flat feet. Mooncalves perform complicated dances on their hind legs in isolated areas in the moonlight' (Scamander [Rowling], 2001, p.29). 'Mooncalf' is a very rare word in modern English, but it does turn up five times in *The Tempest*. In Act 2, scene 2 Caliban, thinking Trinculo is a tormenting spirit, hides from him under his gabardine (a type of large, baggy coat). The clownish Trinculo arrives and decides to shelter under this coat too and then gets a fright when it starts to move. Trinculo's friend Stephano turns up next and is confronted by the sight of these two struggling under a coat and mistakes them for 'some monster of the isle with four legs', which he calls a 'mooncalf' (2.2.65, 105). In performance this is a scene of classic physical comedy as the 'moon-calf' dances round the stage as Caliban and Trinculo attempt to escape from each other while being chased by Stephano. The comic 'dance' of Shakespeare's 'moon-calf' (created from a gabardine and two sets of legs) appears to lie behind Rowling's 'Mooncalf' with its smooth grey body, 'four spindly legs' and 'complicated dances . . . in isolated areas in the moonlight.'

This chapter argues that *Harry Potter* follows in Shakespeare's footsteps in using comedy to interrogate more serious themes. Luna Lovegood, for example, is both one of *Harry Potter*'s most humorous characters and one of its more profound. Luna holds comic beliefs about things such as Fudge's Umgubular Slashkilter and the Rotfang conspiracy but the affection such quirkiness inspires ('really, it had been worth bringing Luna just for this' [*Half-Blood Prince*, Chap 15, p.299]) renders both Harry and the reader more responsive to her insights. Luna is a character of great integrity who has a 'knack of speaking uncomfortable truths' (*Half-Blood Prince*, Chap 15, p.291), an intuitive understanding of death and a faithful optimism that brings comfort to those in need (see Chapter 8).

Harry Potter also uses Shakespearean allusion itself in both comic and serious ways. As will be discussed in this chapter, for example, while the hairy band the Weird Sisters forge a comic connection with *Macbeth* in *Goblet*, the prophecy in the following novel responds to *Macbeth*'s interrogation of the relationship between fate and freewill. Another Shakespearean tragedy – *Hamlet* – is also drawn on in ways that are both serious and playful. In *Hamlet* a situation of undefined menace is created at the very outset of the play as two guards meet at the stroke of midnight:

> *Barnardo.* Who's there?
>
> *Francisco.* Nay, answer me. Stand and unfold yourself.
>
> (1.1.1–2)

The atmosphere of this scene is echoed in the opening of *Deathly Hallows* when two men meet in the darkness and anxiously face each other, wands drawn, before realising that they are on the same side (Chap 1, p.9). Both encounters involve two men who are meeting by appointment, and in both texts they arrive at the exact time they were expected, and yet they seem surprised to see the other. Both sets of men are primed to meet not a friend but an enemy. The opening lines of both novel and play involve a night-time encounter in which the darkness and anxiety reflect the psychological pressure of war (imminent in *Hamlet*, actual in *Deathly Hallows*). The 'Who's there?' with which *Hamlet* opens serves to frame the questioning of existence and selfhood that the play explores. *Harry Potter* is also a work about identity. The hero's orphaned state and ignorance about his true nature function as metaphors for the universal human quest for self-knowledge and 'as the books conclude, the focus begins to narrow onto Harry, into his very own soul' (Wolosky, 2010, p.73). The subtle echo of *Hamlet* in the opening of *Deathly Hallows* – in which the hero's angst-ridden questioning of past certainties is mirrored in an opening encounter in which allies meet at night but do not recognise each other – reflects the way this final novel will be the climax of Harry's quest of self-discovery.

There is also a more humorous echo of Hamlet's troubled mind earlier in the series when, at the conclusion of commentating the Quidditch World Cup, Ludo Bagman points his wand to his throat and mutters 'Quietus' (*Goblet*, Chap 8, p.105). 'Quietus' is a rare word but it appears in what is perhaps the most famous passage in English literature: Hamlet's 'To be or not to be' soliloquy. In this speech Hamlet muses on suicide and wonders why anyone would put up with the sorrows and irritations of the world 'when he himself might his quietus make/ With a bare bodkin' (3.1.77–8) – or when, in other words, he could use a dagger to commit suicide. In their films of *Hamlet* actors such as Laurence Olivier and Kenneth Branagh have stressed this idea by pointing their dagger at their throats during this speech. This melodramatic gesture is echoed in a comically non-threatening way when Bagman makes his 'Quietus' by pointing his wand to his throat.

Shakespeare habitually mingles the tragic and the comic. He brings comedy into his tragedies and serious, painful reflections into his comedies. He also wrote a number of plays in the mixed genre of tragi-comedy; and the greatest of these, *The Winter's Tale*, is (as discussed in Chapter 2) the source for Hermione's name. Shakespeare's prestige is such that English writers have, perhaps, been particularly drawn to his method of mixing the dark and the light and one of the most quintessentially Shakespearean aspects of *Harry Potter* is the revelation of pathos in things that had previously made its audience laugh.

One of the funniest scenes in *Harry Potter* is the delivery of Ginny's valentine. This episode in *Chamber* contains a direct echo from *A Midsummer Night's Dream* and retains both the comedy and the pathos of Shakespeare's scene. To celebrate Valentine's Day Lockhart has dressed up some less-than-delighted dwarfs as gold-winged, harp-carrying cupids. The comic disjunction between the grumpiness of the dwarfs and their saccharine outfits is heightened by the disconnect between the love-messages they carry and the violence with which they insist on delivering them. A particularly grim-looking dwarf pursues Harry and tackles him to the floor when he tries to dodge hearing his valentine. The dwarf then sings the valentine – which compares Harry's eyes to fresh pickled toads and his raven locks to blackboards – while sitting on top of him (Chap 13, pp.177–8).

The valentine that Ginny has sent to Harry is a type of 'blazon', a tradition within love poetry in which specific features of the beloved (eyes, hair, lips etc.) are listed and compared with beautiful objects (usually flowers and jewels rather than toads and blackboards). Blazon traditionally breaks down a woman's beauty into its constituent parts and, in doing so, renders her rather a passive object of praise. It was a popular way of describing feminine beauty but it is in many ways an odd device for love poetry. It objectifies its subject and its imaginative and flamboyant dissection of the female body suggests that showing off his powers of poetic invention are rather more important to the poet than the woman he claims to be addressing. Traditionally the blazoning poet is always a 'he' and the poetic blazon is of a woman. Harry's powerlessness in the face of his valentine as he lies pinned to the floor echoes the emasculating nature of the poetic blazon and increases the comedy of the moment.

The comparison of Harry's green eyes to freshly pickled toad also recalls a specific Shakespearean comic blazon: Thisbe's lament over Pyramus at the end of *A Midsummer Night's Dream*. This blazon (which, like Ginny's, breaks with convention by being addressed by a woman to a man) is performed as part of the play-within-a-play that the artisans perform at Theseus and Hippolyta's wedding ceremony. This play is intended by Shakespeare to be a comic disaster and Thisbe mourns over her dead lover's beauty with a deeply improbable blazon:

> This cherry nose,
> These yellow cowslip cheeks,
>   Are gone, are gone:
>   Lovers, make moan:
> His eyes were green as leeks.
>
> (5.1.326–30)

Thisbe's similes are all strained, but the triumphantly worst one is left till last.

The performance of both of these blazons to their green-eyed lover have an audience within the fiction as well as outside it. Ginny's blazon causes the crowd of on-lookers to literally cry with laughter (and the strained pickled toad simile causes particular amusement [*Chamber*, Chap 13, pp.178–9]). The on-stage audience of 'Pyramus and Thisbe', likewise, mock the performance: Theseus comments of Pyramus' lament that 'this passion – and the death of a dear friend – would go near to make a man look sad' (5.1.283–4). While the constant interruptions of the play-within-a-play by its aristocratic audience are often amusing, however, they ignore the emotional truth behind the performance. In both *Dream* and *Chamber*, the somewhat brutal reaction of the fictive audience serves to make the real audience reflect on their own amusement. The line 'his eyes were green as leeks' always gets a laugh in the theatre but performers such as Sam Rockwell (in Michael Hoffman's 1999 film) manage to acknowledge the comic awkwardness of the simile, while still playing it for pathos. As with Ginny's comparison of Harry's eyes to the emerald green of a freshly pickled toad there is comedy in the poverty of poetic invention; but there is also something more. Ginny adores Harry and the discomfort of her public humiliation in this scene is underlined when Malfoy draws spiteful attention to it. Thisbe's mourning speech, likewise, begins as comedy. But the audience of *Dream*, like the reader of *Chamber*, may end the scene with an awakened sensibility towards those who have been the butt of the joke and a certain disquiet that they have fallen in with the mockery of the emotionally vulnerable by the powerful.

'THE MACBETH IDEA': PROPHECY IN *HARRY POTTER*

Rowling has called *Macbeth* 'possibly my favourite Shakespeare play' (2005c). She has referenced it in connection with her writing a number of times, including a jokey allusion to the theatrical superstition of calling *Macbeth* 'the Scottish Play' when she noted of her projected, but ill-fated, *Harry Potter Encyclopaedia* that 'we should call it something like "The Scottish Book"' (2007k). (The film of *Azkaban*, likewise, plays with the relevance of *Macbeth*'s witchy themes to *Harry Potter* by welcoming the students back to Hogwarts with a song with words drawn directly from Shakespeare's play.)

There is also a light-hearted allusion to *Macbeth* in the name of *Harry Potter*'s popular band, the Weird Sisters. The 'witches' in *Macbeth* are not, in fact, ever named as such in the play; they are referred to as 'the weird sisters' (1.3.30). In *Goblet* Harry wonders 'exactly who or what the Weird Sisters' might be and when Macbeth and Banquo meet the weird sisters on the heath, Macbeth, likewise, wonders not just who but *what* they are: 'what are you?' (Chap 22, p.341; 1.3.37, 45). Part of this confusion is due to the fact that *Macbeth*'s weird sisters have beards: 'you should be women,/ And yet your beards forbid me to interpret/ That you are so' (1.3.43–5). The hairiness of the Weird Sisters in *Harry Potter*, likewise, is frequently stressed; but although they are 'all extremely hairy' (*Goblet*, Chap 23, p.364) their gender is never specified. Just like Shakespeare's weird sisters, therefore, the Wizarding group could be male, female or some combination of the two. The hairiness of the Wizarding band draws directly on the gender-indeterminate nature of Shakespeare's bearded weird sisters (a subtlety that has been ironed out in the *Harry Potter* films and video games, in which the Weird Sisters are simply men). The appearance of the Weird Sisters in *Goblet* is a jokey reference to Shakespeare's most witchy play but it is also – given the importance of the *Macbeth*-style prophecy in the following novel – a hint of things to come.

The plot of *Phoenix* revolves around the prophecy that Trelawney makes just before Harry is born, stating that '*the one with the power to vanquish the Dark Lord approaches*' (Chap 37, p.741). In interview, Rowling has argued that this prophecy does not have power in and of itself, but only because Voldemort chooses to believe it – 'The *Macbeth* idea: the witches tell Macbeth what will happen and he then continues to make it happen.' She links Voldemort's belief in the prophecy with the superstitious paranoia of tyrants:

> Voldemort is of course a sort of Hitler. If you read books about megalo-mania types like Hitler and Stalin, it's interesting to find how superstitious these people are, with all their power. It's part of their paranoia, the desire to make themselves bigger than who they really are; they love talking about destiny and fate. I wanted Voldemort to also have those paranoid traits. But the fact that the prophecy from book five becomes true in the end is because Voldemort and Harry chose to let it come true. Not

because it is destined to. The *Macbeth* idea: the witches tell Macbeth what will happen and he then continues to make it happen.

(2007i)

Rowling has a sceptical attitude towards the prophecy in *Harry Potter* and she presents it as part of a literary tradition in which prophecies can often be understood in radically different ways.

The prophecy in *Phoenix* is uttered by Sybill Trelawney, a comic charlatan who turns out – rather unexpectedly – to possess the true seer's gift. While Trelawney 'is at least ninety per cent fraud' she has 'inherited more than she knows' (Rowling, 2015s) from her famous great-great-grandmother Cassandra, who (as her name suggests) was a genuine Seer. (Cassandra is the name of a prophetess in Greek myth. In one tradition Apollo promised her the gift of prophecy on condition that she would sleep with him, but when she refused he cursed her with speaking true prophecies that would always be ignored.) Sybill Trelawney's name brilliantly expresses her combination of fakery and insight: it is a synthesis of an ancient Cornish name ('suggestive of Sybill's over-reliance on her ancestry when seeking to impress') and a first name that, while it references 'the august clairvoyants of old', is also 'really no more than a variant of the unfashionable female name "Sybil"' (2015s). *Harry Potter*'s American editors tidied up Trelawney's name to 'Sibyl' (which clarifies her link with the inspired Greek Sibyls) but its original spelling balances this grand meaning with a comic allusion to the unfashionable name 'Sybil', which, for many English readers, is inextricably linked with the TV comedy series *Fawlty Towers*.

The Sibyls of Greek culture were inspired prophetesses, but their fame spawned a veritable industry in fake sibylline prophecies (Charlesworth, 1983, vol I, pp.324, 390). Sibylline oracles continued to command respect for many centuries – Michelangelo, for example, painted the Sibyls alongside Old Testament prophets on the ceiling of the Sistine Chapel – but over time the preponderance of these later, derivative sibylline oracles, meant that the wisdom of the Sibyls became discredited. Sybill Trelawney's name, therefore, asserts both her general chicanery and her ability to make occasional, genuine, prophecies, like the Sibyls of old.

Rowling has noted that 'prophecies . . . are usually open to many different interpretations. That is both their strength and their weakness' (2004–12a). Macbeth calls the weird sisters 'imperfect speakers' (1.3.70) and the interpretation he chooses to place on their words leads him astray. They speak the truth, but the most obvious interpretation of their words is not the correct one. The most famous example of this oracular ambiguity is the Delphic Sibyl. This Sibyl told Croesus (the proverbially wealthy ruler of Lydia) that if he attacked the Persians he would '*destroy a great empire.*' Croesus assumed that the great empire he would destroy would be the Persian Empire; as it turned out, however, it was his own (Parke, 1939, pp.151–3). Croesus also asked the Sibyl whether he would have a long reign. The answer (that his reign would last until '*a mule shall have become king of the Medes'*) made him believe that his kingdom would last forever; but it was shortly ended by Cyrus, king of the Medes (who could be considered a 'mule' – the offspring of a female horse and a male donkey – in that he had an aristocratic mother and poor father) (Parke, 1939, pp.152–3). Macbeth is likewise given confidence by the equivocal prophecy that 'no man that's born of woman/ Shall e'er have power upon thee' (5.3.6–7). Macbeth believes that this means he is safe, but his confidence turns out to be just as misplaced as that of Croesus, when he is killed by Macduff (who was born by Caesarean section). Both the Delphic Sibyl's and the weird sisters' prophecies appear to mean one thing, but turn out to mean the opposite.[1]

Somewhat surprisingly, even Trelawney's apparently fraudulent prophecies turn out to have a similarly equivocal relationship with the truth. In *Azkaban*, for example, Trelawney is ridiculed for her superstitious refusal to sit down for Christmas lunch on the grounds that if thirteen people share a meal, the first person to rise from the table will be the one who dies. (Trelawney's reasoning provokes McGonagall's sarcastic response: "'Tripe, Sybill?'" [Chap 11, pp.169–70]). In the following novel Trelawney remains laughably off the mark with her assertion that Harry was born in mid-winter. In both cases, however, there is something to these predictions, despite their apparently comic inaccuracy. In *Azkaban*, Ron's pet rat Scabbers is nestling in his pocket at the Christmas feast, so – unbeknownst to everyone – Peter Pettigrew is already at the table. Hence, thirteen people are already present and Trelawney is proved correct in her prediction as it is Dumbledore (who courteously rises to encourage her to take a seat) who will be the first to die (Harry Potter Wiki, 2016d). There is something, too, in Trelawney's guess that Harry was born in December for there is a piece of Voldemort's mid-winter soul secretly buried within Harry (and Voldemort was born on the 31st December, in a wintery echo of Harry's birth on the 31st July.)

These prophecies resonate not only because they turn out to be unexpectedly accurate, but also because of their subtly messianic overtones. Trelawney's predictions about thirteen diners and Harry's birthday both have a Christian aspect. The traditional superstition voiced by Trelawney – that when thirteen eat together the first to rise will be the first to die – is rooted in Christian tradition. Thirteen people were seated at the Last Supper and Judas – the first to leave the Last Supper as he set off to betray Jesus – was the first of the group to die. Likewise, Jesus is the quintessential baby born 'in the bleak midwinter' so Trelawney's belief that Harry was 'born in mid-winter' (*Goblet*, Chap 13, pp.177–8) carries a possible messianic significance.

Echoes of the Christian story are found likewise in Trelawney's first, and most important, prophecy. She tells of how a child will be born with '*the power to vanquish the Dark Lord.*' Jesus' birth, like Harry's, is heralded by prophecy (Matt 1.21–3). The news of the birth is unwittingly carried to Herod by the wise men, who tell him that a great ruler has been born: 'where is he that is borne King of the Iewes? For we haue seene his Starre in the East, and are come to worship him' (Matt 2.2). The star that heralds Jesus' birth suggests that he will have the power to vanquish the enemy of his people, for it recalls an earlier prophecy that 'there shall come a Star out of Jacob, and a Sceptre shall rise out of Israel, and shall smite the corners of Moab, and destroy all the children of Sheth' (Numbers 24.17). When Herod hears that a baby of great power is about to be born, he fears (like Voldemort) that his own strength is threatened by this portentous birth and unsuccessfully attempts to kill the infant who threatens him.

Rowling has drawn a connection between Trelawney's prophecy and 'the one the witches make to Macbeth' (2004–12b) but, perhaps even more clearly, it draws on the gospel narrative that also underlies *Macbeth*'s prophecy. In all three, a prophecy leads a powerful man to attempt the murder of a young boy because of the future that is prophesied for him. Trelawney's prophecy, however, is closer to the biblical story than *Macbeth*'s prophecy because it involves a baby and the sense that this baby is destined not simply to be a powerful leader but some more profound power for good when he vanquishes the Dark Lord.

It is *Macbeth*, however, with which Rowling has drawn parallels, due (in part) to the way she wants Trelawney's prophecy to be read. While biblical prophecy has an absolute truth-value, Rowling wants readers to take Trelawney's prophecy with a pinch of salt. Dumbledore repeatedly explains that the prophecy does not impinge on Harry's free will (*Half-Blood Prince*, Chap 23, pp.476–9) and Rowling, likewise, subscribes to a sceptical reading of this prophecy. She has argued that neither Harry nor Neville is 'pre-ordained' (2004–12b) to defeat Voldemort. Rowling compares her prophecy with *Macbeth* because she is confident that this sceptical reading is the one contained in Shakespeare's text, 'The *Macbeth* idea: the witches tell Macbeth what will happen and he then continues to make it happen.'

This, however, is not the only possible reading of Shakespeare's play. Orson Welles' 1948 film version of *Macbeth*, for example, begins with the witches fashioning a voodoo doll of Macbeth, suggesting that, far from being a free agent, he is simply their puppet. At the other end of the interpretative scale Laurence Olivier's acclaimed performance of Macbeth in the 1955 suggested that 'the witches did not implant the idea of Duncan's murder in him, but, with a distinct air of weariness, he recognised them as part of his mental landscape' (Williams, 2002, p.131). While Antony Sher's 1999 Macbeth seemed genuinely surprised by the prophecy, Henry Irving's Macbeth (performed over a century earlier) was – like Olivier's Macbeth – already thinking of murdering Duncan before he ever met them (Williams, 2002, pp.134, 129). Ian McKellen's 1976 Macbeth, like Voldemort, shared in the superstitions of a paranoid dictator and 'the visions the witches had shown him were only dolls, which he clung to like a cringing child until his death' (Williams, 2002, p.134). These performances of *Macbeth* show that texts, like prophecies, contain multiple interpretations. As Wolosky argues 'the prophecy is the most focal moment in the books, the moment in which interpretation is shown to be not a passive understanding of something that is given, but an active decision about what something means . . . . The prophecy thus changes from being an emblem of forced fate to being one of interpretative freedom and moral responsibility' (2010, p.92).

A MIDSUMMER NIGHT'S DREAM AND THE ABUSE OF POWER

In *Harry Potter* Rowling has created 'a fantastic world that has to live shoulder-by-shoulder with the real world' (2001e). In some fantasy writing, magical lands – such as Narnia or Middle Earth – remain resolutely separate from the 'real' world. Rowling, however, thinks that the way in which the Wizarding world runs parallel to our own is one of the main appeals of her creation: 'there's something delicious in this idea of hiding in plain sight, that there is a world within a world, that we could all access' (2016). *A Midsummer Night's Dream*, like *Harry Potter*, imagines a magical world within a world 'hiding in plain sight'.

In both *Harry Potter* and *Dream* invisibility cloaks prove useful aids to conceal-ment given this proximity. Harry, Ron and Hermione use the invisibility cloak when they venture into Muggle settlements to find food in *Deathly Hallows*, and Harry and Hermione use it to enter the jointly magical and Muggle settlement of Godric's Hollow. In *Dream*, likewise, magical folk make themselves invisible so that they will not be perceived by mortals: when the king of the fairies, Oberon, sees the lovers arriving in the forest he says, 'I am invisible' (2.1.186). Some of Shakespeare's other magical creations – such as Prospero and Ariel – are likewise regularly described as 'invisible'. This was probably achieved on stage with an 'invisibility cloak' – either, perhaps, a cloak with the word 'invisible' written on it, or a cloak designed to mimic some aspect of the scenery. One of Shakespeare's rival acting companies had 'a robe for to goo invisibell' (Rutter, 1999, p.133) and Prospero appears to hand Ariel a cloak of this kind when he tells him to 'be subject/ To no sight but thine and mine, invisible/ To every eyeball else' (*Tempest*, 1.2.304–306). Prospero's ability to make himself invisible could also be a property of the 'magic garment' (1.2.24) that he wears and Shakespeare's 'robe for to goo invisibell' may be one source for Harry's invisibility cloak.

Despite the attempts of the magical folk to stay out of the way, however, in both *Harry Potter* and *Dream* their actions have profound effects on the well-being of the mundane world. The fact that *Harry Potter*'s first Wizarding war concludes in 1945 marks the clear relationship between Wizarding and Muggle conflicts: 'it amuses me to make allusions to things that were happening in the Muggle world, so my feeling would be that while there's a global Muggle war going on, there's also a global Wizarding war going on' (Rowling, 2005c). In *Dream* the 'dissension' between Oberon and Titania – the warring fairy king and queen – has ruined the summer weather and replaced it with 'contagious fogs' (2.1.116, 90). These 'contagious fogs' caused by the magical conflict are similar to '"all this chilly mist in the middle of July"', which, as Fudge explains to the Muggle Prime Minister, is the consequence of the second Wizarding war (*Half-Blood Prince*, Chap 1, p.8). The fairy brawls in Shakespeare, like the Wizarding war in *Harry Potter*, result in meteorological problems for Muggles. (And, incidentally, given the way that *Dream*'s fog-generating magical wars seem to have influenced *Harry Potter*, it is noticeable that Shakespeare describes this unseasonal weather as a flowery tiara placed on the head of an old man: 'and on old Hiems' thin and icy crown/ An odorous chaplet of sweet summer buds/ Is, as in mock'ry, set' [2.1.109–111]. One might also think of a diadem placed incongruously on the 'chipped bust of an ugly old warlock' [*Half-Blood Prince*, Chap 24, p.493].)

Magical wars have unintended consequences for humankind, but both texts also present some magical folk as intentionally malicious towards oblivious mortals. Puck uses his supernatural abilities to play tricks on people. During the rehearsal of the 'Pyramus and Thisbe' play, for example, Puck uses his invisibility cloak to place ass's ears on Bottom's head (*Dream*, 3.1.71–111). This kind of comic abuse of power parallels the Muggle-baiting of *Harry Potter* and Puck is full of practical jokes that he delights in unleashing on unsuspecting humans. He boasts of his exploits, such as misleading 'night-wanderers, laughing at their harm' and pretending to be a stool and then disappearing so that 'the wisest aunt, telling the saddest tale' falls on her backside (2.1.39, 51). Puck's exploits, like Muggle-baiting, are an explanation for commonplace human problems. Puck is to blame in Shakespeare's world when travellers lose their way at night or milk fails to churn into butter; in *Harry Potter* Muggle-baiting is responsible for a number of more modern irritations such as not being able to find the door keys you thought you had put there only the minute before (*Chamber*, Chap 3, p.34).

Puck's practical jokes, like the weather disturbances caused by the fairy war, are part of a larger interference in mortal affairs by the fairies in *Dream*. The driving force behind the mistaken-identity plot that plagues the lovers is Oberon's attempt to sort out their love lives. This paternalistic, and slightly patronising, care is comparable to the attitude of Kingsley Shacklebolt, who guards the Muggle Prime Minister without his being aware of it and who encourages the listeners of *Potterwatch* to follow the example of those '"wizards and witches risking their own safety to protect Muggle friends and neighbours, often without the Muggles' knowledge"' (*Deathly Hallows*, Chap 22, p.357). The attitude of the magical world towards the mundane is that of the powerful towards the powerless: some exhibit paternalistic concern while others (such as Puck and Willy Widdershins) indulge in callous vindictiveness. The practical joke of shrinking keys in *Chamber* turns into something much more unpleasant in the vomiting toilets of *Phoenix*, and this latter offence is perpetrated by Willy Widdershins (a character whose name suggests his shady dealing: 'widdershins' means 'moving in an anticlockwise direction, contrary to the apparent course of the sun [considered as unlucky or sinister] . . . relating to the occult' [*Oxford English Dictionary*]). In *Phoenix* it is discovered that Willy Widdershins has not been prosecuted for this flagrant Muggle-baiting because he has been spying for the Ministry. This blatant corruption, as well as the increased nastiness of vomiting toilets over shrinking keys, might cause the reader to reflect more seriously on the moral implications of the effortless supremacy of the magical over the mundane world.

While Muggle-baiting is predominantly comic in *Harry Potter*, it opens up a dialogue about how people react to difference. Rowling has said that 'bigotry is probably the thing I detest most. All forms of intolerance, the whole idea of "that which is different from me is necessarily evil." I really like to explore the idea that difference is equal and good' (2000j). The comic motif of Muggle-baiting darkens with the unholy alliance of Umbridge and Widdershins, and becomes actively disturbing in the final revelation of Dumbledore's flirtation with Muggle domination.

Muggle domination involves wizards finally openly asserting their absolute power over Muggles and as such it is the ultimate end towards which the covert expression of this power (Muggle-baiting) points. *Harry Potter* expresses the moral repugnance of Muggle domination by linking it explicitly with Nazism. Grindelwald (the principle proponent of Muggle domination) is, like Hitler, defeated in 1945. Grindelwald also has both a symbol and a slogan that have clear parallels in Nazi ideology. Grindelwald's mark – like the Nazi swastika – co-opts a pre-existing sign that then becomes tainted by its later association. The swastika is an ancient religious symbol common to Hinduism, Jainism and Buddhism, but it remains difficult for people of faith to display this symbol in the West, due to its association with Nazism. Xenophilius Lovegood has a similar problem with the reception of the symbol of the Deathly Hallows (which Victor Krum can see only as Grindelwald's mark). Likewise Grindelwald's slogan 'For the Greater Good' is 'carved over the entrance to Nurmengard' (*Deathly Hallows*, Chap 18, p.294) in a reference to the infamous words written over the entrance to Auschwitz: 'Arbeit macht frei' ('Work makes you free').

The abuse of power practised on mortals in *Dream* – in Puck's practical jokes, in the bewitching of the lovers and in the use of Bottom as a mere prop for Oberon's revenge – remains comedic; but it nonetheless raises questions about other abuses of power in the play. There is evident injustice in almost all the ways in which power is wielded in *Dream*. Husbands exhibit tyranny over their wives, adults abuse their power over their children, and aristocrats lord their status over artisans during the play-within-a-play in which (as discussed above) the on-stage audience displays a deeply ungracious response to the performance into which so much loving, if inept, enthusiasm has been poured. This is all done with immense lightness of touch but by introducing one power relation (that of magical over mortal) in which every audience member would be on the losing side, *Dream* subtly encourages a new perspective on the abuse of power among those who might be used to wielding it unthinkingly. Rowling has spoken of *Harry Potter* as exploring 'the misuse of power' (1998b) and, like Shakespeare's play, it uses the mundane world's powerlessness in the face of magic to alert its audience to more pertinent inequalities.

Much Ado about Nothing

The humour in *Harry Potter* is often intended to make the reader think as well as laugh:

> 'Women,' [Ron] said wisely to Harry. 'They're easily upset.'
> 'And yet,' said Hermione, coming out of her reverie, 'I doubt you'd find a *woman* who sulked for half an hour because Madam Rosmerta didn't laugh at their joke about the hag, the healer and the *Mimulus mimbletonia*.'
> (*Half-Blood Prince*, Chap 21, p.438)

This is one of the many contentious exchanges between Ron and Hermione that are a leit-motif of the books from the moment she pours scorn on his failed spell when they meet on the Hogwarts Express. This exchange about Madam Rosmerta may make the reader smile as they enjoy Ron's wrong-footing, and in its recreation of a familiar, formulaic joke ('the hag, the healer and the *Mimulus mimbletonia*' is clearly a Wizarding version of the 'an Englishman, an Irishman and a Scotsman' formula). But it is also noticeable that Ron's comment rouses Hermione from her 'reverie': she notices what he is saying although it is not worthy of attention and she was deep in thought. While Ron and Hermione's barbed exchanges provide humour, they also provide a clue as to where their relationship is heading. Their bickering signals their underlying attraction for they follow in a long line of literary 'quarrelling couples' (such as Austen's Emma and Mr Knightley, and Elizabeth and Mr Darcy) where abrasive exchanges spring from repressed desire (Granger, 2009, p.239).

Hermione and Ron's caustic relationship also recalls that between Lily and James in Hogwarts' previous generation. The only time the reader gets to eavesdrop on Lily and James' conversation is when they hear him fail to ask her out on a date in the Pensieve. This moment casts James in the worst possible light – his bullying of Snape is grotesque and his conceit (boasting about his exam-performance and basking in Pettigrew's hero-worship) highly unappealing. Lily berates James for his behaviour: '"Messing up your hair because you think it looks cool to look like you've just got off your broomstick . . . walking down corridors and hexing anyone who annoys you just because you can"' (*Phoenix*, Chap 28, p.571). Harry cannot understand how someone who says such things could possibly fancy his father, and he is horrified by the thought that James might have somehow forced his mother into marrying him. Harry, however, is rather young in the ways of the world (as his ham-fisted interactions with Cho make abundantly clear). Lily castigates James for his behaviour – but she is also exceptionally clued-up about what that behaviour has been: she gives an exact run-down of what he has been up to and even considers the effect he has been intending to create: '"Messing up your hair . . . to look like you've just got off your broom-stick".' He has her attention.

This idea that attraction might be demonstrated more by attention than approval is basic to the quarrelling couples of both Austen and Shakespeare.

Elizabeth thinks, at the beginning of *Pride and Prejudice*, that she does not care about Mr Darcy, but she nonetheless has excellent recall of his conversation ("'I remember hearing you once say, Mr. Darcy, that you hardly ever forgave, that your resentment once created was unappeasable'", 1995 [1813], p.79). Shakespeare's most famously acerbic couple – Beatrice and Benedict – are, likewise, constantly attuned to what the other is doing. On the crowded stage at the beginning of *Much Ado about Nothing* they manage to have an almost private quarrel:

> *Beatrice.* I wonder that you will still be talking, Signior Benedick. Nobody marks you.
>
> *Benedick.* What, my dear Lady Disdain! Are you yet living?
>
> *Beatrice.* Is it possible disdain should die, while she hath such meet food to feed it as Signior Benedick? Courtesy itself must convert to disdain, if you come in her presence.
>
> (1.1.110–117)

They continue to trade insults for twenty-eight lines. This conversation is begun by Beatrice's disdainful remark – 'I wonder you are still talking Senior Benedick. Nobody marks you' – but it is a put-down that is self-evidently false. *She* is paying attention to him, or she would not have made it. As with James and Lily (and Hermione and Ron) the witty and comic antagonism between Beatrice and Benedick reveals a deeper intimacy.

> *Benedick.* I would my horse had the speed of your tongue, and so good a continuer. But keep your way, o' God's name. I have done.
>
> *Beatrice.* You always end with a jade's trick. I know you of old.
>
> (1.1.135–9)

Beatrice picks up on Benedick's horse metaphor; his 'continuer' is a horse with good stamina, her 'jade' is a spirited horse, liable to slip its collar. Such echoing of each other's imagery is further evidence that they listen carefully to what the other says. Beatrice's final comment – 'I know you of old' – suggests a previous entanglement and in spite of, or rather because of, their abusive repartee, it is clear that this flame continues to burn. However, the humour of the exchanges between Beatrice and Benedick, like those of Ron and Hermione, initially blinds the audience to their attraction. Readers of *Harry Potter* are likely to come to a growing rather than an immediate realisation that such verbal fireworks are a sign that these two characters belong together.

Harry Potter and Shakespeare both use comedy to divert their audiences from something more serious and Rowling often uses humour as misdirection in order to plant clues. Take for example the barman of the Hog's Head, who – unbeknownst to almost everyone – is Dumbledore's brother. Aberforth is a comic figure who generates laughter when he comes up in interviews

(2004b; 2007h), and the reader is led to believe that he is illiterate, uncivilised and has a dubious fondness for goats. The goaty odour pervading the Hog's Head is a subtle clue as to the barman's secret identity and this apparently unnamed minor character, distinguished for nothing more than running the dodgier pub in town, turns out to be crucial to the battle against Voldemort. The dismissal of Aberforth as a bit of a joke enables his anonymity, which turns out to be an essential aspect of his ability to spy for Albus and to save Harry's life.

Shakespeare's humorous characters, likewise, often turn out to be integral to his plotting. In *Much Ado*, against all the odds, the bumbling, comic Constable Dogberry and the Watch unwittingly discover and foil the plot of the evil Don Jon. Dogberry is famously someone who gets his words mixed up – telling a new recruit, for example, that 'you are thought here to be the most senseless and fit man for the constable of the watch' (3.3.22–3). Dogberry is, however, unintentionally accurate here for, as the Watch are all fools, a 'senseless' (stupid) man is in many ways the perfect man for the job. Shakespeare makes Dogberry's verbal mistakes – mistakes that glance unwittingly at the truth – parallel Dogberry's plot function in which his ineptitude inadvertently outwits the schemes of more intelligent men.

Shakespeare, however, is doing something more complex, and more political, than simply raising a laugh by having his fools outwit his villains. Behind the unwitting wisdom of Shakespeare's fools lies the idea that 'the wisdom of this world is foolishness with God' (1 Corinthians 3.19). This religious subtext is made particularly clear in *Dream* in which the clownish Bottom speaks Shakespeare's longest paraphrase of a biblical passage: 'I have had a most rare vision. I have had a dream past the wit of man to say what dream it was . . . . The eye of man hath not heard, the ear of man hath not seen, man's hand is not able to taste, his tongue to conceive, nor his heart to report what my dream was. I will get Peter Quince to write a ballad of this dream. It shall be called "Bottom's Dream", because it hath no bottom' (4.1.202–213). Like Dogberry, Bottom jumbles his words, but they are a scrambled version of the biblical affirmation of the unknowability of God's love: 'eye hath not seene, nor eare heard, neither haue entred into the heart of man, the things which God hath prepared for them that loue him' (1 Corinthians 2.9). The comedy of Bottom's mistakes, like the comedy of Dogberry's similarly confused language, has a kernel of wisdom. Shakespeare's drama performs the radical and biblical social agenda in which the ignorant and foolish are not outcasts but part of God's unexpected grace.

For Shakespeare, comedy is much more than simply a way of making an audience laugh. In *Harry Potter*, likewise, comedy performs another function than simple audience enjoyment. In *Harry Potter* humour often performs the function of misdirection, as it diverts the reader away from clues. Hannah Abbott raises a laugh when she goes around telling people that Black has got into the castle by transforming himself into 'a flowering shrub' (*Azkaban*, Chap 9, p.125) but this joke has both planted, and cleverly dismissed, the accurate idea that Black is entering Hogwarts in a different form. Similarly, the concept of magical effects strengthening over time is comic when it is introduced with the Love Potion of *Half-Blood Prince*: "'Was this potion within date?" asked Slughorn, now eyeing Ron with professional interest. "They can strengthen, you know, the longer they're kept"' (Chap 18, p.371). But this information, casually and humorously imparted to the reader, also means that the curse in Dumbledore's blackened hand 'strengthens over time' (*Deathly Hallows*, Chap 33, p.546) with fatal results. The strengthening of magical effects over time results in both Ron's ridiculous infatuation and Dumbledore's death-sentence, and the humour with which this information is first communicated makes it unlikely that the reader will spot its more serious application.

Hermione and Ron's habitually caustic exchanges, likewise, often hide the fact that a clue has been divulged. When Ron suggests that it would be safe for Hermione to ask her parents about Nicolas Flamel, she responds with a one-liner that ends the discussion: "'Very safe, as they're both dentists"' (*Philosopher's Stone*, Chap 12, p.146). The brusqueness of Hermione's rejoinder suggests that she is offended (the implication being that she thinks Ron has forgotten she is Muggle-born), but the abrupt humour also prevents the reader from spotting the hint encoded in Ron's suggestion. It *would* be worthwhile asking Hermione's parents about Flamel because he is a historical figure: in the Muggle world, too, rumours circulate that Flamel was an alchemist who discovered the philosopher's stone.

This technique is also discernible in the exchange quoted above about Ron and Madame Rosmerta. The reader's enjoyment of Hermione's put-down means they are not likely to note that it *is* surprising that Madam Rosmerta had failed to laugh along with Ron's 'the hag, the healer and the *Mimulus mimbletonia*' joke, however poor it may have been. Rosmerta shares her name with the Celtic goddess of abundance (the name means 'great provider': "'ro-" is an intensifying prefix, "smert-" means "looking after, providing"' [Viducus, 2014]). Rosmerta's name evokes her job as a provider of food and drink but also her warm, open nature. Earlier scenes in The Three Broomsticks have made it clear that she is a convivial soul: her voice is 'alive with curiosity' and 'breathless with interest' as she gossips with her customers (*Azkaban*, Chap 10, pp.151–2). The reader could, therefore, expect her to laugh along good-naturedly to even the feeblest of her customers' jokes. The humour of Ron's discomfiture, however, effectively blinds the reader from connecting Rosmerta's out-of-character behaviour with the fact that someone in Hogsmeade may have been Imperiused into giving Katie Bell the cursed necklace. This necklace was given to Katie at The Three Broomsticks and there is now an obvious, but likely to be overlooked, candidate.

These instances of comedy as misdirection point to the wider way in which *Harry Potter* uses comedy to undercut its moral seriousness. Rowling has spoken of how she sees the works as having a moral, although she does not 'set out to preach' (1998b). Humour is central to this balancing act.

Rowling frequently places writers of comic prose as among her favourite authors – she has chosen P. G. Wodehouse's collected works as a desert island book (2012e) and quoted from him from memory in interview (2012c). The next chapter explores the influence of the greatest English comic prose writer (and Rowling's favourite author) on *Harry Potter*. Rowling's description of what she admires in Austen shares some clear parallels with what fans love about *Harry Potter*: 'her characters are vividly alive, she had a wonderful facility for dialogue, a dry and sometimes scathing sense of humour and she crafted seamless plots with such lightness of touch it appears effortless' (2005h). Chapter 6 argues for the many influences of Austen on *Harry Potter* – from the explicit nod to *Mansfield Park* in the name of Filch's cat and the connections between characters such as Hermione and Emma (and Gilderoy Lockhart and Mrs Elton) to Hogwarts' echoes of the Gothic comedy of *Northanger Abbey* and the indebtedness of the novels' narrative voice to Austen's.

Note

1 This idea recurs in *Cursed Child* where Delphi and her Augurey tattoo recall both the Delphic Sibyl and the Roman religious practice of 'augury' (interpreting the future through observing the flight of birds). Delphi and her tattoo can be read one way, but turn out to mean something quite different.

6   Jane Austen

Rowling's favourite author

Austen is Rowling's 'favourite writer of all time' (2000c). As Lisa Hopkins has noted Austen's own tongue-in-cheek verdict on *Pride and Prejudice* (as 'rather too light & bright & sparkling' [1995, p.203]) seems to be remembered in the opening description of Dumbledore's eyes as 'light, bright and sparkling' (2011, p.55; *Philosopher's Stone*, Chap 1, p.12). Rowling's answer to which fictional character she would like to be was 'Elizabeth Bennet, naturally' and she has named Austen as one of the writers who 'represent untouchable ideals to me' (2012e; 2000b).[1]

Rowling re-reads Austen's novels in rotation: 'I've re-read all of Jane Austen so often I can actually visualize the type on the page' (2000c; 2013b). *Emma* is her favourite novel, and she considers it 'the most skilfully managed mystery I've ever read . . . . I must have read it at least twenty times' (2000c). Although Rowling is extremely cautious of acknowledging any specific literary influence ('it is impossible for me to say what my influences are; I don't analyse my own writing in that way' [2000b]) she does – at least implicitly – compare her work with Austen's. She says of the final plot twist in *Emma* that 'I have never set up a surprise ending in a Harry Potter book without knowing I can never, and will never, do it anywhere near as well as Austen did in *Emma*' (2000c). She has also noted that she and Austen share an authorial delight in 'pull[ing] the wool' (2005h) over their readers' eyes. *Emma*'s influence on *Harry Potter* is discernible not only in its hallmark surprise endings, but also in one of its central relationships. The passionate subtext in Emma's abrasive, argumentative, life-long friendship with Mr Knightley is one literary forbear of the slow-burning romantic relationship between Hermione and Ron.

Rowling herself hints that reading her novels with Austen in mind will be a fruitful exercise. In one interview she notes how: 'I read my favourite books over and over until they fall apart, literally. I've gone through three copies of *Emma* – they get dropped in the bath and I have to replace them. My ambition is to write books that the reader won't necessarily get completely at first. Nothing makes me happier than when a child brings me a copy of Harry that looks appalling – it proves they've read and read it' (2001c). Rowling draws an implicit parallel here between her own battered copies of *Emma* and her readers' tattered copies of *Harry Potter*. She reveals that she aims to emulate Austen in writing books whose intricacies encourage readers to return to them again and again. Rowling, the obsessive re-reader of Austen, has written books that repay re-reading in part because they draw on Austen's taut narrative style and careful plotting in which events and characters are seldom exactly what they first appear.

HOGWARTS AND HARTFIELD

Rowling often describes the *Harry Potter* novels as 'who-dunnits' (2012a) and *Emma*, likewise, has many of the characteristics of a classic detective story (James, 1999). Rowling's description of *Harry Potter* as something 'which is not really a detective novel, but it feels like one sometimes' (2005b) fits *Emma* as well as it does her own work. In both a central mystery is played out in a self-contained setting. Rowling loves crime fiction (and has, latterly, become an author of crime fiction herself): 'I've always loved it . . . . I think that the *Harry Potter* books are in many ways who-dunnits in disguise . . . . I enjoy the golden-age book . . . to take that finite number of suspects, the genuine who-dunnit style' (2014c). Classic 'golden-age' detective novels are set in a confined society so that the reader gets to know a distinct set of people, their characteristics and motivations (which function as clues to the solution of the mystery), and witnesses the emotional tensions that such enforced proximity brings.

Hogwarts is geographically close to, but effectively isolated from, the near-by village of Hogsmeade, in a way that parallels both the confined society of a classic mystery story and the setting of *Emma* (which centres on the heroine's home, Hartfield, and its neighbouring village of Highbury). In both *Emma* and *Harry Potter*, as in traditional detective novels, when strangers arrive they disturb the community's equilibrium and reveal something about the already-existing relationships. Viktor Krum's arrival, for example, like that of Frank Churchill in *Emma*, clarifies the relationship between the quarrelling couple – until then ostensibly just friends – as one of them begins to suffer the agitations of jealousy.

Structurally speaking the main 'stranger' in the *Harry Potter* series is the yearly changing Defence against the Dark Arts teacher. In *Chamber* the self-importance, vanity and unintentional humour of this teacher may well have been modelled on Mrs Elton, one of the outsiders who breaks in on Highbury society in *Emma*. Both Gilderoy Lockhart's and Mrs Elton's self-conceit forms the comic engine of their respective novels and Austen, like Rowling, mines this self-regard for comic gold: 'Mr. Knightley seemed to be trying not to smile; and succeeded without difficulty, upon Mrs. Elton's beginning to talk to him' (1966 [1816], p.312). Lockhart's vanity likewise provides comedy at an emotionally heightened moment when Harry enters Lockhart's office (to be questioned after Mrs Norris' Petrification) and sees 'several of the Lockharts in the pictures dodging out of sight, their hair in rollers' (Chap 9, p.107).

Mrs Elton and Lockhart have inflated views of themselves and both behave as though their fleeting and facile status – Mrs Elton's as a bride, Lockhart's as a man whose looks have captivated the readers of *Witch Weekly* – trumps the standing of the main character. Mrs Elton, like Lockhart, finds plenty of people willing to take it for granted that she is 'as clever and as agreeable as she professed herself' although in both novels the protagonist themselves are under no illusions:

> Emma was not required, by any subsequent discovery, to retract her ill opinion of Mrs Elton. Her observation had been pretty correct. Such as Mrs Elton appeared to her on this second interview, such she appeared whenever they met again, – self-important, presuming, familiar, ignorant, and ill-bred. She had a little beauty and a little accomplishment, but so little judgment that she thought herself coming with superior knowledge of the world, to enliven and improve a country neighbourhood.
>
> (p.283)

Lockhart, likewise, believes that he is the most exciting thing to have happened at Hogwarts for some time, and boasts at Flourish and Blotts of how wonderfully exciting it will be for Harry and his school friends to have him for a teacher.

The witty caricatures of Mrs Elton and Lockhart, however, have a serious point. Both characters expose the way that ministering to one's own ego often involves the maltreatment of others. Lockhart's oppressive patronage of Harry shares a number of similarities with Mrs Elton's ostentatious and unwanted championing of the orphan Jane Fairfax. Mrs Elton and Lockhart are both involved in the self-conscious display of their prestige through their condescension. Subconsciously, however, both are aware of the superiority of the person they patronise and they are actually attempting to bask in reflected glory by the connection they have forced on the other. And both orphans manage to subtly, but firmly, rebuff this 'kindness'. Harry's photographic-self ducks out of the photograph Lockhart forces on him and Jane Fairfax politely, but implacably, refuses to allow Mrs Elton to fetch her letters (one of Austen's many clues as to her novel's central mystery).

The intrusion of Mrs Elton into the settled world of Highbury society exposes truths about the relationships that exist there. Just as in a detective story, in both *Emma* and *Harry Potter* new-comers enter the self-contained setting and reveal things that have previously lain hidden.

NARRATIVE VOICE

One of the aspects that *Harry Potter* most clearly shares with Austen's novels is its narrative voice. Both employ a narrative voice (known as 'third person limited omniscient view') that is partial in its knowledge, yet appears omniscient to the reader caught up in the story. In both *Emma* and *Harry Potter* the third person is used ('he raised his wand' not 'I raised my wand') but the narration nonetheless largely shares the limited outlook of the protagonist who becomes '[the] narrative equivalent of speaker – that is, the consciousness whose point of view is reflected in the exposition' (Dry, 1977, p.99). It is a style of narration that effectively draws the reader into the protagonist's perspective while partially hiding from them (as a first person narrative voice would not) that they have accepted a limited view as objective truth. John Granger, in his invigorating discussion of this stylistic connection between Rowling and Austen, notes how useful it is for lulling 'the passive reader into traveling down the erring path' (2009, p.26).

Emma begins with an omniscient narrator but this 'objective' narrator becomes less and less present as the novel progresses: 'by the latter half of the book, Emma seems to have usurped the narrator's role and to be telling her own story' (Dry, 1977, p.88). *Philosopher's Stone*, likewise, begins with an omniscient narrative voice. There are three novels later in the series that open outside Harry's perspective, but it is only in *Philosopher's Stone* that scenes in which Harry is present have an omniscient narrative. This happens when he is a baby at the novel's opening, but also at the Quidditch match when the discussion of Harry's broom's odd behaviour and Hermione's solution to the problem, both occur without Harry's knowledge as he flies above (Chap 11, pp.139–41). The post-match celebrations, likewise, take place without Harry witnessing them: 'Harry heard none of this, though. He was being made a cup of strong tea back in Hagrid's hut' (p.141). Likewise, an omniscient narrator notes of Harry's dream about Quirrell's turban that, 'when he woke next day, he didn't remember the dream at all' (Chap 7, p.97). Events at Hogwarts are never again described from outside Harry's perspective. The omniscient narrative voice is confined to the start of the series (and the start of specific later novels) just as it was in *Emma*, as both authors progressively replace the omniscient narrative voice with one that draws the reader inexorably into the protagonist's world.

The third person limited omniscient voice is a brilliant device both for making a reader identify with the protagonist, and for springing surprises on them. It would, however, appear to suffer from the draw-back that it precludes the reader from knowing things that the protagonist does not. This is one reason that four novels – *Philosopher's Stone*, *Goblet*, *Half-Blood Prince* and *Deathly Hallows* – start in the third person omniscient voice. Clues, however, can be provided through a skilful deployment of the third person limited omniscient view, by providing evidence the protagonist ignores. In early books these can be quite explicit – such as Harry meeting Quirrell in Diagon Alley just before an attempt is made to steal the Philosopher's Stone – although later in the series, when the reader is primed to search for such clues, they grow in subtlety. When Harry wants to believe that his father might be the Half-Blood Prince, for example, he remembers that he has seen his father using one of the spells inscribed in the Prince's potions book (the *Levicorpus* spell) when he was inside Snape's memory in *Phoenix*. An attentive reader might note, however, that he has failed to notice that he had seen Snape use another of the book's handwritten spells (*Sectumsempra*) in the very same memory. It is the spell that Harry overlooks, not the one he notices, that provides the clue to the true identity of the Half-Blood Prince, but the reader could follow his reasoning and come to the correct conclusion.

Austen is arguably the most skilful practitioner there has ever been of the third person limited omniscient view, and never more so than in *Emma*. Emma, for example, is furious after meeting Mrs Elton, because of the latter's complacent remark that 'Knightley is quite the gentleman':[2]

> 'Insufferable woman!' was her immediate exclamation. 'Worse than I had supposed. Absolutely insufferable! Knightley! – I could not have believed it. Knightley! – never seen him in her life before, and call him Knightley! – and discover that he is a gentleman!'
>
> (p.280)

Emma then proceeds to muse on Frank Churchill and wonder what he would think about Mrs Elton, and laughs to herself – 'Always the first person to be thought of! How I catch myself out!' – but she has misremembered her own thoughts. Austen is giving the reader the clue that if the first person to be thought of is the cared for (as Emma suggests) then it is Mr Knightley, not Frank Churchill, she loves. Mr Knightley is so habitually first with Emma that she is not aware of his perpetual priority in her thoughts.

This moment forms a further clue as Mrs Elton's over-familiarity, likewise, hints at the secret love affair between Frank Churchill and Jane Fairfax:

> Mr. Elton had just joined them, and his wife was exclaiming,
>
> 'Oh! you have found us out at last, have you, in our seclusion?—I was this moment telling Jane, I thought you would begin to be impatient for tidings of us.'
>
> 'Jane!'—repeated Frank Churchill, with a look of surprise and displeasure.—'That is easy—but Miss Fairfax does not disapprove it, I suppose.'
>
> 'How do you like Mrs. Elton?' said Emma in a whisper.
>
> 'Not at all.'
>
> (p.322)

Frank, just like Emma, cannot stand Mrs Elton because of how she talks about the person he loves. The reader who is aware of Emma's love for Mr Knightley could use the similarity of these passages to discover that Frank Churchill is likewise in love with Jane. Mrs Elton's spurious assertion of intimacy through informal address ('Knightley', 'Jane') inadvertently reveals where true intimacy lies.

Emma and Frank's exchange above takes place at a ball, and the plot-importance of the Yule Ball in *Goblet* mirrors the centrality of balls in a number of Austen's novels. In particular the belief that Dumbledore has ordered stupendous quantities of mulled mead for the Yule Ball directly recall the rumours – which likewise prove false – about how many men Mr Bingley will bring to the ball in *Pride and Prejudice*. Frank's response at the dance in *Emma* to Mrs Elton's presumptuous reference to Jane Fairfax ('Jane!') is directly recalled by Ron's jealousy when he hears Hermione call Krum by his first name at the Yule Ball: '*Viktor?*' (*Goblet*, Chap 23, p.366).

RIDDLES, FIREBOLTS AND PIANOFORTES

The importance of riddles to *Harry Potter* is made explicit in the name of its villain. Tom Riddle's surname points to the way that his new identity is an anagram of his old name, but also the importance of such word games for the series as a whole. The logic puzzle that Hermione solves in *Philosopher's Stone*, likewise, is one of the many overt riddles in *Harry Potter* that operate as clues to the unexpected tricks the narrative will hold. As Wolosky has argued: 'literature is writing that always opens to further interpretations . . . and *Harry Potter* – with its riddles, puzzles, codes, and secrets – is also very much a story about interpretation. It tracks the characters' attempts to identify and penetrate the secrets and riddles, in an active pursuit that underscores the importance and vitality of interpretation itself' (Wolosky, 2010, p.1).

Harry meets a Sphinx in a maze during the final task in *Goblet*. The Sphinx of Greek legend guards the gate of Thebes and, like the riddling door of the Ravenclaw common room, it allows entrance only to those who answer it correctly. Its most famous riddle was correctly answered by Oedipus: 'What creature is four-footed in the morning, two-footed in the afternoon and three-footed in the evening?' The traditional riddle of the Sphinx, like that of the Ravenclaw common room door, is a conceptual riddle. The answer to Oedipus' riddle is 'man', because man crawls in the morning of his life, walks in adulthood and then uses a stick in old age. It is a solution that involves a change in perspective, in its re-imagining of a lifetime as the span of a day.[3] *Harry Potter*'s Sphinx, however, does not ask a traditional, conceptual riddle. The Sphinx in the maze asks instead a logical verse riddle in which the single syllable answers to each couplet are added together at the end to form the solution ('*spy*' '*d*' '*er*' = 'spider'). While this is not the form of the traditional Sphinx's riddle, it is exactly the form of the riddling 'charade' in *Emma*.

The conundrums in *Harry Potter* (like the riddles in *Emma*) are hints about the plot of the novel itself: clues that the books in which they occur will themselves have a twist in the tail. The first explicit riddle of *Harry Potter* – the logic puzzle in *Philosopher's Stone* – holds the key to the novel's main plot-twist.[4] Austen, likewise, highlights her first narrative conundrum (Mr Elton courts Emma not Harriet) by making it revolve around a word-game (or 'charade'). Emma challenges Mr Elton to write his own riddling charade for them and he responds with one that he claims was written by a friend:

To Miss -.
CHARADE
My first displays the wealth and pomp of kings,
    Lords of the earth! their luxury and ease.
Another view of man, my second brings,
    Behold him there, the monarch of the seas!

But ah! united, what reverse we have!
    Man's boasted power and freedom, all are flown;
Lord of the earth and sea, he bends a slave,
    And woman, lovely woman, reigns alone.

    Thy ready wit the word will soon supply,
    May its approval beam in that soft eye!

(p.97)

In *Harry Potter* and *Emma* these explicit riddles signal the twists and turns of the narrative, but this charade gives a more precise piece of evidence for the solution to the 'mystery' of the novel. Emma – like Hermione in *Philosopher's Stone* – is quick to decipher the riddle. However, while Emma solves the word-game easily ('courtship'), its deeper meaning – that Mr Elton means to the pay his addresses to *her* – is completely lost on her. The solution of the riddle is therefore also a clue: it primes the reader not to trust Emma's perspective. Emma's reading of the mystery of Jane Fairfax's secret lover will, likewise, be both acute and wildly off the mark.

The clandestine love-story between Frank and Jane, like the abortive romance of Mr Elton, is also announced with a conundrum, in this case the mysterious gift of a pianoforte. In *Azkaban*, too, an anonymously given gift holds the solution to the novel's central puzzle. In *Emma* Jane receives the anonymous, extravagant gift of a pianoforte, while in *Azkaban* Harry receives the anonymous, extravagant gift of the Firebolt. In both novels this enigmatic and valuable present enables the beneficiary to display their talent (which in both cases is considerable). Likewise, in both the recipient of the anonymous gift is an orphan and unused to receiving costly presents (someone is finally showing true appreciation of their worth). The gift is much discussed and pairs of friends in each novel (Emma and Mrs Weston/Harry and Ron) enjoy speculating as to who might have sent it. The mystery, however, is only fully resolved at the end of the novel when the true solution is revealed in an explanatory letter from the giver.

Hermione, like Emma, is particularly intent on finding out who the secretive benefactor might be (and, in both cases, this persistence rather against the wishes of the actual recipient of the gift). *Harry Potter*, however, teasingly inverts Austen's solution. Emma gets the secret benefactor's motivation correct (she assumes that the gift is from Jane's clandestine lover) but blunders as to the true identity of this person; Hermione gets the identity of the giver correct (the present *is* from Sirius Black) but blunders as to his motivation. For both the Firebolt and the pianoforte turn out to be gifts of love.

Rowling has quoted with approval Virginia Woolf's assessment of Austen's style: "'For a great writer, she was the most difficult to catch in the act of greatness,' which is a fantastic line. You're drawn into the story, and you come out the other end, and you know you've seen something great in action. But you can't see the pyrotechnics; there's nothing flashy' (2014b). One of the aspects of Austen's prose that is brilliant yet unshowy, is her economy. In *Azkaban* Ron wonders whether it might have been Lupin or Dumbledore who has sent the Firebolt, but these are simply guesses based on people who are fond of Harry – in Austen the guesses people make about the enigmatic benefactor reveal their own motivations. When it is suggested to Emma that Mr Knightley might have sent the pianoforte she is immediately sure that this cannot be the case. The real reason for her certainty is jealousy – she is in love with him herself so cannot bear the idea that he might be in love with Jane. The reason she gives, however, is that 'Mr. Knightley does nothing mysteriously' (p.234) and in this reasoning she expresses an essential truth about the man she loves. In articulating Mr Knightley's upright honourableness Emma unconsciously grows to love him more (to see, in effect, his superiority to the man who has actually made the mysterious gift – Frank Churchill).

Austen has likewise left numerous, subtle hints that Frank Churchill is in love with Jane. At the evening party (during which the present of the pianoforte is discussed) there is an unpremeditated little dance; but the evening ends after only two dances and Frank (who has been dancing with Emma) comments: "'Perhaps it is as well . . . . I must have asked Miss Fairfax, and her languid dancing would not have agreed with me, after your's'" (p.238). But the next day he asks Miss Fairfax to play a tune for him on the pianoforte:

> 'If you are very kind,' said he, 'it will be one of the waltzes we danced last night;—let me live them over again. You did not enjoy them as I did; you appeared tired the whole time. I believe you were glad we danced no longer; but I would have given worlds—all the worlds one ever has to give—for another half-hour.'
>
> (p.249)

If readers put these two comments together they will discover that Frank's whole heart is fixed on what he had claimed not to care about: a dance with Jane Fairfax.

Austen leaves another clue as to the true sender of the pianoforte: Frank has not only motive but also opportunity as he has previously journeyed to London (ostensibly to have his hair cut). As a cover story the haircut does not really wash: it is a ridiculous distance to travel for such a frippery and it seems unlikely he would have met his step-mother for the first time looking unkempt. Yet Austen embeds it so cleverly within her characterisation that the reader does not think to question it: for the jovial Mr Weston the haircut makes an amusing anecdote; for Mr Knightley it provides evidence to bolster his prejudice

against Frank ('"Hum! just the trifling, silly fellow I took him for"' [p.217]) and
it forces Emma into an over-rationalisation, because she is attempting to argue
herself into a love for Frank she does not actually feel – '"silly things do cease to
be silly if they are done by sensible people in an impudent way"' (p.222). The
clue is there in plain sight however: travelling to London to have one's hair cut
would be 'silly'; Frank is not an idiot and therefore he did not go to London to
have his hair cut (he went to order the pianoforte).

   Emma replays its plots: the whole Mr Elton sub-plot means that readers only
have themselves to blame when they share in the heroine's blindness about
Frank and Jane. *Harry Potter*, likewise, replays plot devices over the series as
a whole (such as in Harry's endless, and endlessly unfounded, suspicions of
Snape) and time after time the reader falls for Harry's version of events, only
to find that they have been tricked by his limited, although apparently omniscient, view (Granger, 2009, pp.30–33). Both *Emma* and *Harry Potter* 'pull the
wool' over their readers' eyes and, to add insult to brilliant injury, do so after
signposting these narrative twists with explicit riddles.

'I AM GOING TO TAKE A HEROINE WHOM NO ONE BUT MYSELF WILL MUCH LIKE'

The specific connection between the gifts of the pianoforte and the Firebolt
strengthen the parallels between Emma and Hermione. Rowling has noted
of her heroine that she is 'intense, clever, in some ways not terribly self-
aware . . . . She is part of me, although she is not wholly me' (2014a). Both
Emma and Hermione are intellectually brilliant but emotionally unaware – and
Rowling has compared both these heroines to herself.[5] Austen famously said of
Emma that 'I am going to take a heroine whom no one but myself will much
like' (Austen-Leigh, 2002 [1869/71], p.119). Rowling seems similarly invested
in her heroine – she has, for example, given Hermione her favourite animal as
her Patronus (an otter [2005i]) – yet cautious about how likeable her readers
will find her. This insecurity is suggested by her effusive response to the script-
writer of the *Harry Potter* movies: 'Firstly, Steve turned to me while food was
being ordered and said quietly, "You know who my favorite character is?" I
looked at him, red hair included, and I thought: *You're going to say Ron. Please,
please don't say Ron – Ron's so easy to love.* And he said: "Hermione." At which
point, under my standoffish, mistrusting exterior, I just melted, because if he
got Hermione, he got the books. He also, to a large extent, got me' (2011a).
Rowling's comment might not have the chutzpah of Austen's but both writers
combine great confidence in, and affection for, their heroine with an acknowledgement that their readers may find her uncongenial (though both are widely
loved by readers, in spite of – or because of – their faults).

   Hermione and Emma marry a striking intellect with gaps in their emotional
intelligence. Both heroines are authentically themselves and do not shrink
from doing things that will displease their friends. *Philosopher's Stone*, in particular, stresses aspects of Hermione's character that might lead readers, as well

as her classmates, to turn against her. On her first appearance she is insensitive to other peoples' feelings, oppressively confident in her own abilities, and her kindness in searching for Neville's toad has (like Emma's attitude towards Harriet Smith) a rather patronising air. Hermione largely grows out of her over-bearing behaviour, although even in *Azkaban* she persists in enumerating the logical flaws in Lavender's reasoning while the latter is still in floods of tears over the loss of her rabbit.

Hermione, like Emma, grows up and learns to understand her own heart while also recognising her faults, and her growth is one of the most interesting character changes of the series. Critics have perceptively pointed out, however, that there is a negative aspect in Hermione's new-found maturity as she grows out of a certain child-like wisdom in the early books. In *Chamber* she argues for the factual basis of legend when Professor Binns tries to quash the idea of the Chamber of Secrets but as she grows older she becomes more limited in her understanding of myth, refusing to believe that the Hallows could have a basis in reality. There is a clear connection between this narrowing of Hermione's vision and the character of Susan in the *Narnia* books, who grows out of her child-like wonder and hence is excluded from Narnia itself (Prinzi, 2009, pp.17–20). *Deathly Hallows*, however, presents Hermione's scepticism as an essential ingredient in Harry's mission. Far from meaning that Hermione (like Susan) is excluded from the happy ending, her scepticism keeps the trio on the trail of Horcruxes and (as Dumbledore explains [Chap 35, p.577]) creates space for Harry to come to the correct conclusion about his quest. It is important that Harry only knows the Hallows are real once he has grown in faith sufficiently to trust Dumbledore so that he can choose to seek Horcruxes not Hallows.

Rowling has, in fact, expressed her dislike of C.S. Lewis's treatment of Susan in the *Narnia* series: 'there comes a point where Susan, who was the older girl, is lost to Narnia because she becomes interested in lipstick. She's become irreligious basically because she found sex . . . . I have a big problem with that' (2005f). *Emma* forms an important – and far more positive – template for Hermione's development. *Emma* illustrates a contrary movement to Susan of a heroine who 'grows up' over the course of the novel and reaches (rather than is excluded from) enlightenment. *Harry Potter* shows Hermione maturing in positive ways that compensate for the lost innocence of childhood. Hermione's characterisation draws on Rowling's sense of her own development from a childish introversion (2007c; 1999d) as she grows into someone with emotional intelligence beyond her bookishness. In *Azkaban*, for example, Hermione is a genuine friend to Hagrid in her tireless work for Buckbeak's trial in a way that Harry and Ron are not. Her rather bossy kindness towards Neville on the Hogwart's Express in the first novel grows into a real empathy with his suffering in *Goblet* (when she recognises Neville's distress, and intervenes, when Moody psychologically tortures him by demonstrating the *Crucio* curse). Her new-found emotional intelligence allows her to explain Cho's conflicted emotions to Harry and Ron and to be a true friend to Ginny, as she helps her to become independent from, and simultaneously irresistible to,

Harry. By the end of *Emma*, likewise, Emma learns what true friendship with an equal might be like (when she finally seeks friendship with Jane Fairfax) as well as understanding whom it is she genuinely loves. Hermione, like Emma, not only learns sensitivity towards her friends, she learns to embrace the erotic underside to her fiery friendship with Ron, as Emma does with Mr Knightley.

MRS NORRIS

Rowling's frequent admiring references to Austen (and *Emma* in particular) in her early interviews are also in one sense a clue. They offer hints about the surprise ending of each *Harry Potter* book, and (more subtly) about where Ron and Hermione's friendship might be leading. They nudge the reader towards noticing echoes, such as the way in which Ron and Hermione fall out over her sudden infatuation for Crookshanks recalls Emma and Mr Knightley's disagreement over her friendship with Harriet Smith. Emma persists in her friendship with Harriet despite Mr Knightley's angry objections and Hermione, likewise, is resolutely committed to Crookshanks despite the fact that Ron cannot see the appeal.

The cats in *Harry Potter* are carefully named. Crookshanks recalls George Cruikshank, a nineteenth-century artist and satirist who illustrated both Dickens and the first English editions of Grimm's fairy tales. Crookshanks is an aggressive cat whose sharp teeth and claws are literal analogues to Cruikshank's biting satire. But more fundamentally they reflect the true nature of a satirist's job: not to be scathing but to reveal truth. Crookshanks' name points not only to his obvious and immediately displayed belligerence but also to his perspicacity (which the reader only discovers near the end of *Azkaban*). Crookshanks attacks Scabbers regularly throughout *Azkaban* not because Scabbers is what he seems (a rat whom a cat might be expected to attack) but because he is not. Crookshanks, in the best tradition of satirists, sees through Scabbers' disguise.

Filch's cat, likewise, has a name that reveals both her moral character and the importance of Austen to *Harry Potter*. Austen's Mrs Norris, one of the most unpleasant characters in fiction, is the self-appointed guardian of other people's behaviour and she is constantly vigilant about any rule-breaking (or joy) in which anyone else might be indulging. She is the heroine's aunt in *Mansfield Park*, and scolds her incessantly. The feline Mrs Norris' main characteristic, likewise, is her vindictive watchfulness and she is continually on the prowl for any student who might be out of bed to be spied on. She has a near-telepathic connection with her owner and, as Rowling has noted, 'the animal that acts most like a traditional familiar in the entire series is Mrs Norris' (2015f).

Mrs Norris is both the helpmeet for, and the feline alter-ego of, her owner Argus Filch, and Filch is likewise one of *Harry Potter*'s most suggestively named characters. The name Argus connotes vigilance: it is the name of the many-eyed guardian from Ovid's *Metamorphoses*. Juno employs Argus to watch Io, a beautiful woman Jove has slept with and then transformed into a heifer to allay his wife's suspicions that he may have been unfaithful yet again. The name

Argus is suitable for an ever-watchful caretaker for, according to Ovid, 'Argus' head was set about with a hundred eyes, which took their rest in sleep two at a time in turn, while the others watched and remained on guard' (Book 1, ll.625–8). Filch's Ovidian first name gives him a certain classical grandeur, but it is also suggestive of cruelty for Argus is a harsh guard to the innocent Io: 'he shut her up and tied an ignominious halter round her neck . . . and drove her, torn from her father's arms, to more distant pastures' (Book 1, ll.632, 665). The parallel with this watchman links Juno's propensity to punish the guiltless victims of her husband's attentions with Filch's similarly arbitrary enforcement of justice.

The two parts of Argus Filch's name, however, are in tension. While his first name brings to mind the epic anger of the famously resentful goddess Juno, his surname is rather less imposing. A 'filch' is a thief with small-time ambitions: the *Oxford English Dictionary* defines 'filch' as 'to steal, *esp.* things of small value; to pilfer.' Filch is therefore presented as the perpetrator of petty crimes rather than – as a caretaker should be – their preventer. Argus Filch is exactly the caricature of a bad caretaker that the contradictions within his name – both guardian and sneaking thief – suggest him to be. Argus Filch and Mrs Norris continually report on those who leave muddy footprints or drop litter but they are impotent when the castle's security is actually threatened. Trolls and (supposed) mass-murderers break into Hogwarts with impunity. Filch spends his time boarding up mouse-holes after Sirius Black has broken into Gryffindor common room: a perfect image of closing the stable door after the horse has bolted (and particularly so when the rat who actually threatens them is already living in the castle). Filch and Mrs Norris' apparent watchfulness is really a petty-minded obsession with small rules and a dereliction of a larger duty.

Austen's Mrs Norris, like her feline namesake, is sharp-eyed about little matters. She is quick to scold the heroine, for resting – '"you should learn to think of other people; and, take my word for it, it is a shocking trick for a young person to be always lolling upon a sofa"' (1966 [1814], p.101) – when she herself has made Fanny Price ill by over-working her. When the young people decide to perform a play, Mrs Norris is proud of her small part in reducing the expenses of the production: 'an enormous roll of green baize had arrived from Northampton, and been cut out by Mrs. Norris (with a saving by her good management of full three-quarters of a yard)' (p.155). The brackets mark the authorial voice's transmission of Mrs Norris' own words: she is proud of her fiscal prudence, which, as the reader well knows, is nothing more than miserliness. Austen has Mrs Norris unconsciously condemn herself out of her own mouth: when Fanny is unwell Mrs Norris says to her sister, '"Suppose you let her have your aromatic vinegar; I always forget to have mine filled"' (p.102). It is a moment of toe-curling brilliance – Mrs Norris is too mean to run the risk that someone else might inhale her vinegar. Her 'good management' of the green baize, however, has more important implications. She is proud of her meagre financial saving but in fact she is meant to be in charge of her nephews' and nieces' moral conduct: 'good management' of a far more important kind. Busy about the baize she ignores the fact that her nephews and nieces are performing a risqué play (Elizabeth Inchbold's *Lover's Vows*) that is 'totally improper', in Fanny's estimation, 'for home representation' (p.161). It is a play that ignites the jealous rivalry between the sisters and it involves the eldest daughter (Maria) acting out emotionally charged scenes with a man who is toying with her affections. When Sir Thomas returns after his long absence he realises that he was entirely mistaken to entrust his children to Mrs Norris' care.

The name of Mrs Norris in *Harry Potter* marks her out as vindictive and watchful but also signals that she and her owner are so caught up in policing petty rules that they will fail to protect the children in their care. Mrs Norris has been left in charge of Sir Thomas' children, just as Filch is in charge of guarding the pupils' physical safety, and while both characters stick obsessively to the rules (in Mrs Norris' case the rules of etiquette and economy) both entirely fail to fulfil their charge. Filch is a stickler for the rules that are intended to keep students safe, but he has become far more attached to official procedures than the safety they were meant to promote. Mrs Norris' keen-sightedness over little matters, likewise, is in reality blindness to what is important. She is blind to Maria's faults, Fanny's worth or the fact that her niece is falling in love with a man other than the one to whom she is engaged.

AUSTEN'S ALLUSIONS

Mrs Norris' name is a clue to the extent to which *Harry Potter* is enriched by putting it into dialogue with Austen. One of the things that is so appealing about these allusions to Austen is that they connect with Austen's own use of allusion. Rowling is following in the footsteps of her literary hero not only by echoing her novels but also in the habit of literary allusiveness itself. Austen, like Rowling, is drawn to allusion: a way of writing that (as discussed in the Introduction) brings the author's own reading into play and creates a working partnership between reader and author. Austen sported with allusion from her childhood when, as a stunningly precocious teenager, she wrote a comic *History of England* that knowingly inverted the truisms of the historical texts of her time.

Austen's most allusive novels are *Mansfield Park* and *Northanger Abbey*, both of which are involved in long-running conversations with other literary texts. Much of the plot of *Mansfield Park* revolves round an amateur performance of *Lover's Vows*. This play had been something of a smash-hit after it opened in Covent Garden in 1798 (and it was performed regularly in Bath while Austen was living there). Austen draws on her original audience's knowledge of *Lover's Vows* as she parallels her characters' motivations and morals with the parts that they take in the play. Many of these correspondences are straightforward: Mr Rushworth, for example, the soon-to-be jilted suitor in *Mansfield Park*, is cast as the soon-to-be jilted suitor in *Lover's Vows*. But they can also be subtle and complex. The linguistic similarities between Miss Crawford's dialogue and that of Amelia, for example, bring the reader to an acute awareness of the *difference* between the two women. Both speak with taboo-breaking honesty but Amelia's wide-eyed innocence throws the self-aware coquetry of Miss Crawford's utterances into sharper focus. Austen draws attention to the way that Miss Crawford is always aware of her audience: her kindness to Fanny, for example, is performed in part for Edmund's benefit. In effect, the role of Amelia is a literalisation of the artifice involved in Miss Crawford's presentation of herself as an artless young woman.

Austen's most thoroughgoing intertextual relationship (and the one most important to *Harry Potter*), however, is that between *Northanger Abbey* and the Gothic novel. Catherine Moreland, *Northanger Abbey*'s heroine, is a great novel reader. She adores the Gothic genre, to which she is introduced by her friend Isabella Thorpe, and spends her time in Bath absorbed in Mrs Radcliffe's *The Mysteries of Udolpho*. Austen draws explicit attention to the fact that her novel (unusually) has a heroine who is a great novel-reader, writing that, 'if the hero-ine of one novel be not patronized by the heroine of another, from whom can she expect protection and regard?' (1995 [1818], p.34). In this famous passage Austen celebrates novels as a form, calling them 'performances which have only genius, wit, and taste to recommend them.'

The Mysteries of Udolpho was the most influential Gothic novel of the period and as Catherine falls, rapt, under its spell she begins to interpret the real world around her in novelistic terms: she believes that she will find romantic secrets in locked cabinets and that the hero's handsome, brooding father must nurse a frightful secret. She has begun to see the world as the mirror of fiction and goes to Northanger Abbey with a mind 'craving to be frightened' (p.173). As Henry Tilney (the hero) teases her: '"And are you prepared to encounter all the horrors that a building such as 'what one reads about' may produce? – Have you a stout heart? – Nerves fit for sliding panels and tapestry?"' (p.138). Catherine arrives at the Abbey, in short, expecting to find what Harry actually does find when he arrives at Hogwarts, a Gothic edifice replete with moving staircases, rooms that come and go without warning, carriages that appear to drive themselves and tapestries covering hidden corridors and staircases. Indeed the first time such a concealed passageway is described in *Harry Potter* its 'slid-ing panels and hanging tapestries' (*Philosopher's Stone*, Chap 7, p.96) directly recall Henry Tilney's promise that Northanger Abbey will have passageways concealed behind 'sliding panels and tapestry'.

HOGWARTS AND THE GOTHIC

Gothic literature emerged immediately prior to Austen, towards the end of the eighteenth century. The Gothic is generally thought of as begin-ning with Horace Walpole's *The Castle of Otranto* (1764) and it proved astoundingly popular, accounting for a major proportion of the books pub-lished for the rest of the century. Gothic novels are full of mirrors and veils, castles and underground chambers, dark forests and supernatural events.

They form part of a movement intended to critique the rationalism that had held sway in intellectual circles during the Enlightenment and they champion the inner worlds of emotional experience and imagination over the ordered, external worlds of scientific explanation and symmetrical, neoclassical perfection. Radcliffe's *Mysteries of Udolpho* set the tone for the Gothic genre as a whole in 'its attention to surfaces, its reflections on literature and reading, its engagement with the horrors of subjective, familial and symbolic dissolution, the sublime threats of death, the doubles and ghosts haunting all its scenes with spectres of loss' (Botting and Townshend, 2004, vol 2, p.3). From its first appearance Gothic was recognised, as Sir Walter Scott put it, as 'appealing to those powerful and general sources of interest, latent sense and supernatural awe, and curiosity concerning whatever is hidden and mysterious' (quoted in Groom, 2012, p.83). 'Pure Gothic' was still all the rage when Austen was writing, but while it fell out of fashion shortly afterwards, its themes and devices have remained an undercurrent in the novelistic tradition ever since.

The Gothic uses a dramatic and uncanny setting to place in relief the familiar and universal experiences of fear, love and desire. The Gothic landscape of vast castles, stormy nights and wind-swept scenery is set against confined and secret spaces of locked doors and subterranean passages and the tension between the two gives physical expression to the interior life of the protagonist. (We might think of a boy who grows up locked in an under-stairs cupboard and escapes to a vast, unplottable castle.) Gothic novels share with fantasy fiction, their modern offspring, in the externalisation of psychological phenomena. This is something that is also germane to *Harry Potter* and objects such as the Mirror of Erised, Howlers, Boggarts and the Sorting Hat, render complex emotions in a readily comprehensible, physical form and as such, come straight from the Gothic genre (Klaus, 2012, pp.26–7).

The Gothic novel imagines the human subconscious in dramatic terms as a place in which the protagonist's emotional truth battles both society's strictures and the deep, dark recesses of their own soul. The typical topography of Gothic – its interplay between surface and depths – expresses psychological ideas through architectural forms: 'the fortress or castle, defiantly exposed to external elements, finds its power and darkness internalised in the ... labyrinthine spaces beneath its sovereign ramparts' (Botting and Townshend, 2004, vol 2, p.1). Hogwarts is a quintessentially Gothic edifice. It is an imposing, many-turreted ancient castle beneath whose grand battlements are concealed confined and secret spaces: dungeons, locked underground chambers, a room that disappears and a basement filled with an army of willing slaves. Rowling described Hogwarts as a 'big Gothic thing' in an early interview, and noted that it 'was the first thing I concentrated on. I was thinking of a place of great order but immense danger' (2002a). In the final battle, the stones of the citadel are blasted into pieces, Ron and Hermione disappear into its ancient underground chamber to seek basilisk fangs, and the hero must leave the protection of the castle and go out into the forest wilds to face death alone.

Harry Potter, with its prophecies and werewolves, magical mirrors and doubles, unbreakable vows and night-time adventures, is clearly indebted to the whole Gothic tradition (Gruss, 2013, pp.39–53; Granger, 2009, pp.65–104; Wolosky, 2010, pp.99–126). The Gothic genre, for example, is obsessed with surfaces, mirrors and doppelgängers. When this latter term is used for the many 'Harrys' created through Polyjuice Potion at the beginning of *Deathly Hallows*, it underscores the doubly-Gothic nature of the moment in which the hero's six 'doppelgangers' (Chap 4, p.49) recall Voldemort's own self-replicating Horcruxes. Such parallels between Voldemort and Harry, and the general mirroring of good and evil in *Harry Potter*, are a deeply Gothic aspect of the series (Granger, 2009, pp.80–84). The fundamentally Gothic nature of a hero who has a piece of the villain's soul buried within him reaches its apogee in Harry's dream-vision in which, standing alone in a darkened room, he looks into a 'a cracked, age-spotted mirror hung on the wall in the shadows' and sees not a reflection of his own face, but of the face that has haunted his nightmares (*Phoenix*, Chap 26, p.516). It is a Jekyll and Hyde moment when the hero discovers his enemy inside himself: 'I *was* You-Know-Who' (Chap 26, p.517). This mirroring of good and bad also occurs within Snape, *Harry Potter*'s compelling anti-hero, who embodies the brooding, Byronic aspects of the archetypal male Gothic lead (Millman, 2005, pp.39–52).

Harry Potter also contains more specific echoes of famous Gothic novels: the tank of brains in Department of Mysteries, for example, recalls the brain floating in its tank of amniotic fluid in Mary Shelley's *Frankenstein* (1818). Riddle's once handsome face, ruined by his evil deeds, recalls the picture of Dorian Gray in Oscar Wilde's 1890 novel in which, likewise, a face's slow disintegration from beauty to horror is the external manifestation of the corruption of a soul. The mysterious locket at the centre of Ann Radcliffe's *The Italian* (1797) may be recalled by the locket Horcrux of *Deathly Hallows*, particularly as the villain of *The Italian* – Schedoni, whose eyes 'were so piercing that they seemed to penetrate, at a single glance, into the hearts of men and to read their most secret thoughts' – has a number of links with the skilled Legilimens Snape (Millman, 2005, pp.39–52). Rowling also brings a vampire to the party in *Half-Blood Prince*. The excited anticipation Sanguini provokes among the students – and particularly the groups of girls who gather around him at Slughorn's party – is a humorous allusion to the well-known Gothic idea (typified by *Dracula* as well as the *Twilight* saga) that there is something erotically exciting about vampires.

In another Gothic link, Hogwarts' moving portraits recall the moving portrait of Walpole's *Castle of Otranto*, in which (in one of the novel's most famous and supernatural episodes) a painted figure leaves its canvas (2001 [1764], pp.24–5). *Harry Potter*'s moving portraits, however, are generally comic and never have the melodramatic grandeur of Walpole's. There is the portrait of a medieval Healer in St Mungo's, who (in order to carry on his argument with Ron) is not above thrusting the occupants of adjoining portraits out of his way, or the portrait of the Fat Lady, who likes chocolate, dislikes being roused from slumber and gets tipsy with her friends at Christmas. Her replacement

Sir Cadogan spends his time challenging students to duels and abusing them with medieval insults. Gothic novels tend to take themselves rather seriously but *Harry Potter* – like *Northanger Abbey* – infuses its Gothic with humour ("*Sanguini, stay here!*" [*Half-Blood Prince*, Chap 15, p.296]). The over-wrought seriousness of the moving portrait in *The Castle of Otranto* is replaced by a normalisation of the movement of characters out of their portraits, often with comic results.

Harry Potter is a synthesis of the ordinary and the uncanny – a dingy pub on the Charing Cross Road containing a magical portal to Diagon Alley, an Everyman-style hero with a splinter of the Dark Lord's soul embedded within him – and it was as just such a synthesis that Gothic first presented itself. The original Gothic novel, Walpole's *Castle of Otranto*, contained a preface explaining its author's vision for the genre he had created:

> It was an attempt to blend the two kinds of romance, the ancient and the modern. In the former, all was imagination and improbability: in the latter, nature is always intended to be, and sometimes has been, copied with success . . . . The author of the following pages thought it possible to reconcile the two kinds. Desirous of leaving the powers of fancy at liberty to expatiate through the boundless realms of invention, and thence of creating more interesting situations, he wished to conduct the mortal agents in his drama according to the rules of probability; in short, to make them think, speak, and act, as it might be supposed mere men and women would do in extraordinary positions.
>
> (Preface to the second edition, 2001 [1764], pp.9–10)

Gothic was invented as a mixed mode in which normal people find themselves in supernatural situations. *Northanger Abbey* and *Harry Potter* draw on this *ordinary* aspect of Gothic genre (an aspect that Walpole had insisted on, but which he rarely followed in practice). Walpole's idea of a genre that allows ordinary people to exist somewhere where the 'powers of fancy' run wild could be a description of the world reached in *Harry Potter* when the hero crashes through the wall between platforms 9 and 10 at King's Cross and finds himself in a new domain. *Harry Potter*'s blended world of an ordinary boarding-school in a magical universe stays true to its Gothic roots in its fusion of the conventional with the wildly imaginative. *Harry Potter*, as Walpole put it in his blue-print for the new Gothic genre, has characters who 'think, speak, and act, as it might be supposed mere men and women would do in extraordinary positions' while leaving 'the powers of fancy at liberty to expatiate through the boundless realms of invention.'

VANISHING CABINETS

Austen's *Northanger Abbey*, however, interrogates Walpole's idea that the uncanny can exist without complication in the ordinary world. Austen generates humour, not sublime fear, from the juxtaposition of a fevered imagination and real life. Catherine's 'powers of fancy' lead her to be gently mocked by Henry Tilney, who demystifies her world, when, during their journey to Northanger, he tells his own mock-Gothic tale at her expense. Henry imagines that, after arriving at Northanger, Catherine will hear rumours of a 'secret subterraneous communication between your apartment and the chapel of St. Anthony, scarcely two miles off' and upon searching her room during a violent storm, she will discover a door hidden by a tapestry and enter a small vaulted room behind it:

> 'you will proceed into this small vaulted room, and through this into several others, without perceiving anything very remarkable in either. In one perhaps there may be a dagger, in another a few drops of blood, and in a third the remains of some instrument of torture; but there being nothing in all this out of the common way, and your lamp being nearly exhausted, you will return towards your own apartment. In repassing through the small vaulted room, however, your eyes will be attracted towards a large, old-fashioned cabinet of ebony and gold, which, though narrowly examining the furniture before, you had passed unnoticed. Impelled by an irresistible presentiment, you will eagerly advance to it, unlock its folding doors, and search into every drawer; —but for some time without discovering anything of importance—perhaps nothing but a considerable hoard of diamonds. At last, however, by touching a secret spring, an inner compartment will open—a roll of paper appears: —you seize it—it contains many sheets of manuscript—you hasten with the precious treasure into your own chamber, but scarcely have you been able to decipher "Oh! Thou—whomsoever thou mayst be, into whose hands these memoirs of the wretched Matilda may fall"—when your lamp suddenly expires in the socket, and leaves you in total darkness.'
>
> (p.140)

Henry's parody makes the reader laugh but Austen is playing a double game here. *Northanger Abbey* is a satire of the Gothic genre, but it is not only a satire. Austen explicitly eschews well-worn Gothic images and yet her novel nevertheless enacts a classic Gothic romance. Her pure-hearted heroine falls in love with a stranger at a ball and, after secretly exploring his ancient home, she is turned out by his tyrant of a father to undertake a dangerous journey alone.

One of the most Gothic objects in *Northanger Abbey* is the black and gold cabinet that (in an echo of Henry Tilney's story) Catherine finds in her bedroom when she arrives at the Abbey. This cabinet is darkly exotic and – Catherine believes – must conceal some secret that only she will be able to fathom. It is an object linking *Harry Potter* with *Northanger Abbey*, for Hogwarts, like Northanger, has a black and gold cabinet that hides a secret. In *Chamber* Nearly Headless Nick – in a bid to distract Filch from punishing Harry – smashes this 'large black and gold cabinet' (Chap 8, p.99). Filch (believing that Peeves is the author of this destruction) gloatingly mutters that he will at last be able to punish Peeves because he has broken a valuable Vanishing Cabinet. This Vanishing Cabinet reappears, briefly, in *Phoenix* (when Montague is forced head-first into it by Fred and George) but in *Half-Blood Prince* it will finally become crucial to the plot.

In *Northanger Abbey* Henry spins Catherine a dream of Gothic romance in which she will discover 'a large, old-fashioned cabinet of ebony and gold', filled with secret papers, to which only she holds the key. The story is a complete fiction; Henry tells it to gently mock Catherine's romantic imaginings and Austen invents it as a wittily sardonic comment on the Gothic romance that has so captivated Catherine (and is likely to have captivated many of Austen's readers). Catherine realises that Henry is laughing at her, takes it in good part and – as with the smashed black and gold cabinet in *Chamber* – the moment is dismissed as simply humorous by the reader. But afterwards Catherine finds a real black and gold cabinet in her room and upon searching it (during a storm by the light of a guttering candle) she does find papers hidden within it. She is sure that she has uncovered a secret worthy of her Gothic fantasies. But when she discovers that these papers are nothing more than washing bills, she discards them, ashamed of her own over-heated imagination.

Harry Potter's 'large black and gold cabinet' is likewise slyly introduced as merely humorous, and apparently dismissed, while it will later turn out to be highly significant. It is a satisfying narrative technique that parallels the misdirection created by the third person limited omniscient narrative voice employed by both writers. Catherine dismisses the cabinet from her mind and the reader is encouraged to share in her disillusionment; but there is an anomaly here. The Abbey is replete with the servants, so the appearance of washing bills *is* slightly surprising. To whom do these bills belong? Likewise, from Harry's point of view, the damaged Vanishing Cabinet merits no further explanation (he is simply grateful for the reprieve it has earned him from Filch). But if the reader were not so absorbed in Harry's perspective they might pause to think: *Vanishing* Cabinet? Surely this cabinet has some unexplored potential? When Montague disappears into the cabinet in *Phoenix*, it is revealed that – like the underground passage Henry Tilney claims leads out of Catherine's room in the Abbey – the cabinet is a route out of the castle. It might, therefore, also be a means of entering it. The comedy of Filch's glee at the smashing of the cabinet, and of Fred and George's insouciance over Montague's disappearance ('"I dunno where we sent him," said Fred coolly' [Chap 28, p.552]), like the comic bathos when Catherine discovers the washing bills, mitigate the likelihood that the reader will think any further about what this cabinet might mean.

Northanger Abbey and *Harry Potter* both make comic capital out of some of the absurdities of Gothic, but both also place their naïve protagonists in highly Gothic settings. Hogwarts, in fact, could be argued as the realisation of Catherine's dreams (and Henry's promises) of Northanger. As mentioned above, the concealed passageways behind 'sliding panels and tapestry' with which Henry teases Catherine, become reality in Hogwarts, when on Harry's first journey into the castle he is led down corridors concealed by 'sliding panels and hanging tapestries.' The many secret underground passages that lead out of Hogwarts, enabling the hero to visit the Shrieking Shack and the cellar of Honeydukes, may likewise have been inspired by Henry's promise of a 'secret subterraneous communication between your apartment and the chapel of St. Anthony, scarcely two miles off.' Before Catherine visits Northanger 'she could not entirely subdue the hope of some traditional legends, some awful memorials of an injured and ill-fated nun' (p.125). The injured and ill-fated Grey Lady is her own 'awful memorial' as she wafts around the castle carrying the secrets of her past crimes and her bloody murder. Catherine had hoped for 'traditional legends' when she arrived at Northanger, and Hogwarts has these in heaping measure, such as the account that "'Slytherin, according to the legend, sealed the Chamber of Secrets so that none would be able to open it until his own true heir arrived at the school'" (*Chamber*, Chap 9, p.114). Catherine cherishes the idea that only she 'should be the first to possess the skill of unlocking [the] cabinet' (p.151) and Professor Binns' pupils are likewise excited by the idea of a secret chamber that only the true heir will be able to open. But while Binns is angrily dismissive of the whole idea, *Harry Potter* (as discussed in Chapter 2) rejects his rationalist approach and, by making the Chamber real, celebrates the Gothic championing of the imagination.

Harry Potter and *Northanger Abbey* both enjoy themselves at the expense of Gothic, but both also take something from it. The black and gold cabinet in *Northanger Abbey* encapsulates Austen's light-hearted humour at her Gothic-obsessed heroine's expense, but also her ultimate championing of Catherine (whose explorations in this cabinet have, unknown to herself, uncovered a secret). Hogwarts' own portentous black and gold cabinet is a direct echo of Austen's novel but also – in a more fundamental way – an engagement with Austen's own playful freedom with the Gothic genre.

Northanger Abbey is a work about innocence and understanding: the heroine is an ingénue who thinks that what people say is always an accurate guide to what they think and that everyone else is as pure and disinterested as herself. She believes that Gothic novels – in which heroines are rescued by handsome strangers from over-turned carriages and taken to castles in which unspeakable secrets lurk behind black veils – are useful guides to life. Much of the humour of *Northanger Abbey* lies in its parody of Gothic through the medium of a heroine who attempts to read life through its clichés. But *Northanger Abbey* is not simply a satire on a young woman who grows up and learns the error of her ways. Catherine, for all that her head appears to have been turned by reading too many Gothic novels, is quite correct in her judgements: Henry and Eleanor Tilney are essentially faultless, General Tilney is every bit as dark-hearted as she believes him to be and, as it turns out, the papers she finds in the cabinet do hide a romantic secret. At the very end of *Northanger Abbey* the papers hidden in the black and gold cabinet are finally explained:

The marriage of Eleanor Tilney, her removal from all the evils of such a home as Northanger had been made by Henry's banishment, to the home of her choice and the man of her choice, is an event which I expect to give general satisfaction among all her acquaintance. My own joy on the occasion is very sincere. I know no one more entitled, by unpretending merit, or better prepared by habitual suffering, to receive and enjoy felicity. Her partiality for this gentleman was not of recent origin; and he had been long withheld only by inferiority of situation from addressing her. His unexpected accession to title and fortune had removed all his difficulties; and never had the general loved his daughter so well in all her hours of companionship, utility, and patient endurance as when he first hailed her 'Your Ladyship!' Her husband was really deserving of her; independent of his peerage, his wealth, and his attachment, being to a precision the most charming young man in the world. Any further definition of his merits must be unnecessary; the most charming young man in the world is instantly before the imagination of us all. Concerning the one in question, therefore, I have only to add – (aware that the rules of composition forbid the introduction of a character not connected with my fable) – that this was the very gentleman whose negligent servant left behind him that collection of washing-bills, resulting from a long visit at Northanger, by which my heroine was involved in one of her most alarming adventures.

(pp.217–8)

Like Sirius's letter at the end of *Azkaban* (which clarifies that the sightings of the 'Grim' have been sightings of Harry's godfather) Austen's novel ends with a rationalisation of its Gothic 'terror'. Both Rowling's death omen and Austen's folded papers are found to have an entirely non-threatening explanation. But something more complex is going on with this late-in-the-day explanation than simply putting the Gothic machinery of uncanny alarm back into its box.

Austen's writing is the pinnacle of the prose-writer's art and the final sentence of the above extract – and its self-conscious, self-deprecating interpolation – is a work of genius. With the most delicate of touches Austen deepens the interrelation of her novel with the Gothic, and deftly implies that *Northanger Abbey* is not a simple satire but rather an 'anti-Gothic' novel: a work suffused with the romance of the genre that it ostensibly mocks. The word 'negligent' hints that 'the most charming man in the world' might have been paying Northanger Abbey a clandestine visit (or at least that the length of the visit may have gone beyond what General Tilney had sanctioned). He was certainly not meant to have left Northanger with the General's daughter's heart in his keeping. This nameless hero has long had Eleanor's love and has been 'withheld only by inferiority of situation from addressing her.' We have here a glimpse of a deeply romantic, Gothic tale. As in *Harry Potter*, where at the very end of the series the Grey Lady reveals the haunting story of unrequited love, bloody passion and eternal remorse that holds the key to the final clue; so in *Northanger Abbey*, likewise, a Gothic tale underlying the main narrative is finally revealed. A story of a mysterious lover with a chestnut mare, a yearning heroine suffering in silence and a secret romance hidden from the ogre of a father. Eleanor's love story is the Gothic romance hidden behind the common-sense façade of *Northanger Abbey*.

In both *Harry Potter* and *Northanger Abbey* the mysterious black and gold cabinet conceals important clues. The Vanishing Cabinet changes from comic to chilling, while the contents of Catherine's cabinet reveal a clandestine, Gothic romance. Although it is artfully concealed as a mere aside this fact overturns *Northanger*'s explicitly satiric stance. Austen, like Rowling, writes a moral satire that is nonetheless steeped in romantic possibilities. Catherine's imagination might be over-active but her instincts are true. Catherine is right about the romance of what she finds in the cabinet, just as she was right about the blackness of the General's heart and the perfection of his children. Austen brings realism to the centre of the Gothic genre but not merely in order to pour the cold light of day into Gothic's secret chambers. *Northanger Abbey*, like *Harry Potter*, puts the transformational power of love – the romantic passion that lies at the core of Gothic – at the heart of ordinary life.

AUSTEN, ROWLING AND THEIR READERS

Rowling has imagined her authorship in an Austenian mould: 'I imagined being a famous writer would be like being like Jane Austen. Being able to sit at home in the parsonage and your books would be very famous and occasionally you would correspond with the Prince of Wales's secretary' (2003b). One final puzzle in *Emma* connects Rowling's and Austen's mode of authorship in terms of their relationship with their readers. This is a word-game in which a set of children's letters from a box is used to create anagrams for anyone 'who would be puzzled' (p.343). As Mr Knightley realises, these seemingly innocent anagrams are being used for clandestine communication: 'it was a child's play, chosen to conceal a deeper game on Frank Churchill's part' (p.344) (and, as with the charade earlier in the novel, Emma proves adept at solving the anagrams without realising what they truly signify). After '*blunder*' and '*Dixon*', Frank creates a third anagram for Jane Fairfax, which is swept away before it can be deciphered. Within the novel the riddle of this word remains unsolved. Austen, however, responded to her fans' desires for an explanation of this anagram: 'she would, if asked, tell us many little particulars about the subsequent career of some of her people. In this traditionary way we learned that Miss Steele never succeeded in catching the Doctor; that Kitty Bennet was satisfactorily married to a clergyman near Pemberley . . . and that the letters placed by Frank Churchill before Jane Fairfax, which she swept away unread, contained the word "pardon"' (Austen-Leigh, 2002 [1869/71], p.119).

Rowling, like Austen, responds to her audience's desire to hear details about the 'subsequent career' of her characters, and thus gratify her readership, while also maintaining authorial control over such extra-textual details. One such example in *Harry Potter* is Hermione's response to the cauldron of

Amortentia, which Slughorn presents in the first Potions lesson of *Half-Blood Prince*. Suitably this Love Potion almost causes Hermione – from her habit of answering teachers' questions correctly – to reveal her feelings for Ron: '"it's supposed to smell differently to each of us, according to what attracts us, and I can smell freshly mown grass and new parchment and—". But she turned slightly pink and did not complete the sentence' (Chap 9, p.176). Just as Austen explained the unread third anagram to her readers (a clue to the love between Jane and Frank) so Rowling has explained this unspoken third smell (a clue to the love between Hermione and Ron). Rowling has said that it is the smell of Ron's hair: 'I think it was his hair. Every individual has very distinctive-smelling hair, don't you find?' (2007f).

In interview Rowling has noted that her readers, as well as herself, are fully aware of the importance of love in *Harry Potter*: 'there is one thing that Voldemort doesn't understand and that's the power that keeps Harry going. And we all know what that power is' (2003c). As this chapter has argued, *Harry Potter* plays many Austenian games in its presentation of erotic love – from the quarrelling couple of Hermione and Ron to the hidden Gothic love-story of the Bloody Baron and the Grey Lady. The next chapter looks more closely at the importance of love to the series and the many literary sources – from Petrarch and Shakespeare to Dickens and Hardy – that underlie its depiction in *Harry Potter*.

Notes

1 Elizabeth's emotion on receiving Darcy's (second) proposal are the words Rowling uses in trying to articulate the joy of discovering that her first book was being fought over by publishers (1999b).

2 To fail to use someone's title – in this case Mrs Elton has dropped the 'Mr' – was a sign of either intimacy or disrespect in Austen's England. Schools are one of the few places where this point of protocol remains in common usage and Dumbledore repeatedly 'corrects' Harry when he disrespectfully drops Professor Snape's title.

3 Rowling has said that *Harry Potter* responds to her belief that 'death is our destiny and we must face it' (2008a). This has an interesting relation to the riddle of the Sphinx for, in one reading of the riddle, it involves an acceptance of one's own mortality: 'the riddle of the Sphinx is the image of life itself through time – childhood, maturity, age, and death. When without fear you have faced and accepted the riddle of the Sphinx, death has no further hold on you, and the curse of the Sphinx disappears', Campbell and Moyers, 1988, p.151; quoted in McCauley, 2015, pp.156–7. For more on the importance on mortality in *Harry Potter* see Chapter 8.

4 Harry and Hermione have discussed how the two trials left must have been set by Snape and Quirrell: when they meet the potions riddle, they realise this must have been set by Snape, but both they (and almost certainly the reader) fail to spot what this means. If Snape sets the potions puzzle, then the previous trial – the troll – will have been set by Quirrell; and if Quirrell can control trolls then he is the most likely candidate for letting the troll into the castle earlier in the novel; and, as that troll provided distraction so that the stone could be stolen, so it is Quirrell, not Snape, who is trying to steal the stone.

5 Rowling has said of Emma that 'she annoys me because she is in some ways like me' (quoted in Smith, 2002, p.255) and has repeatedly said of Hermione, 'she's me' (2001e, 2000l).

7 Brewing the language of love
Victorian novels, sonnets, Shakespeare and Snape

In an interview for the publication of *Half-Blood Prince* Rowling spoke of how Voldemort had never loved anyone: 'if he had, he couldn't possibly be what he is. You will find out a lot more about that. It is a good question, because it leads us rather neatly to *Half-Blood Prince*' (2004b). *Half-Blood Prince* is the *Harry Potter* novel in which romantic love plays the most explicit role. It opens with the announcement of Fleur and Bill's engagement and ends with a reminder that their wedding will need to be attended before the Horcrux-hunting can begin. It is the novel in which the love between the adult characters is acknowledged to an unprecedented degree. At Dumbledore's funeral, the shocking pink of Tonks' hair informs the reader that Lupin has finally accepted their union; Molly reminisces about falling in love with Arthur; and Harry is taught by Dumbledore about Merope's tragic passion. This emphasis on erotic love among the adults forms a back-drop to the maturing of the trio. In *Half-Blood Prince* Ginny and Harry kiss for the first time and, while Ron and Hermione will not do so until the Battle of Hogwarts, the future of their relationship is made explicit as they embrace at Dumbledore's funeral.

The unusual stress of the *Half-Blood Prince* on romantic love is also a clue about the motivation of its titular hero. This novel is explicitly concerned with Love Potions and, tacitly, it concerns the Potions master's love. This is the novel in which we learn about Lily Evans' skill at Potions and this frequently repeated fact is the subtlest of hints that the two best Potions students of their year may have been friends. Perhaps Lily learnt some of her skills sharing a bench with Severus (as her son unwittingly does in *Half-Blood Prince*) or, perhaps, it was Snape's desire to impress Lily at her own best subject that led him to excel at Potions.

Potions turn up with unusual frequency in *Half-Blood Prince*: Amortentia, the Draught of Living Death, Hiccoughing Solution, Polyjuice Potion, an Elixir to Induce Euphoria, Shrinking Solution and Felix Felicis. Love Potions, in particular, form a recurring motif. When Harry and his friends enter Weasley's Wizard Wheezes Fred and George proudly show them their best-selling range of Love Potions. Christmas at the Burrow proceeds to the soundtrack of Celestina Warbeck's 'A Cauldron Full of Hot, Strong Love' and a cauldron of Amortentia (the most powerful Love Potion in the world) is bubbling away in corner during their first lesson with Slughorn. Harry, who is beginning to realise that he has fallen in love with Ginny, wants to keep his Felix Felicis to use as a kind of Love Potion. He does not partly because (like any hero) Harry has to put a public duty before personal fulfilment but also because true love in *Harry Potter* is not affected by potions (or, at least, not too much: Ginny and Dean do have a little misunderstanding when Harry bumps into her after taking Felix Felicis).

It is one of *Harry Potter*'s typical trajectories that magical objects and spells that are first introduced in a humorous context, grow into seriousness. When Love Potions first appear in the series, in *Chamber*, they produce a laugh as Lockhart suggests students might ask (a balefully glaring) Snape to whip up a Love Potion during the Valentine's Day celebrations. There is comedy again in Rita Skeeter's malicious suggestion in *Goblet* that Hermione's conquests may have been brought about by her skill in rustling up a Love Potion. They are also treated in a light-hearted vein as some of Fred and George's best-selling products when they first appear in *Half-Blood Prince*. But, reflecting the seriousness with which both Dumbledore and Slughorn insist love should be taken, by the end of the novel they have nearly caused Ron's death and have been revealed as the means by which Voldemort was conceived.

SEVERUS SNAPE AND SYDNEY CARTON

Snape, the erstwhile Potions master, is both the most romantic figure of the series and the titular hero of *Half-Blood Prince*. His dominance in this novel is illustrated by the opening chapter in which, for the first time, the reader encounters Snape without Harry's perspective intervening; and this chapter – 'Spinner's End' – also ensures that Snape's shadowy presence is felt behind the web Malfoy spins throughout the novel. It is no coincidence that it is this *Harry Potter* novel which is named after Snape. Rowling describes him as 'a very flawed hero. An anti-hero, perhaps. He is not a particularly likeable man in many ways. He remains rather cruel, a bully, riddled with bitterness and insecurity – and yet he loved, and showed loyalty to that love and, ultimately, laid down his life because of it' (2007f). But Snape's flaws serve to make him more completely the romantic hero. He loves Lily and, for that reason alone, he fights against the dark side.

Rowling is equivocal about Snape in interview (Millman, 2005) but she has nonetheless given him a fate mirroring that of one of the most romantic figures of nineteenth-century literature. In Paris, in a year abroad during her undergraduate studies, Rowling read Dickens' *A Tale of Two Cities* in one sitting and was profoundly moved by the fate of the novel's deeply romantic anti-hero: 'when I emerged in the evening I walked straight into Fernando who looked absolutely horrified. I had mascara down my face and he assumed I had just received news of a death which I had – Sydney Carton's' (quoted in Smith, 2002, p.96). Sydney Carton is a socially ostracised character who gives up his life for a woman whom he (unrequitedly) loves. He speaks the final words of the novel as he goes to the guillotine: "'It is a far, far better thing that I do, than I have ever done; it is a far, far better rest that I go to than I have ever known'" (1985 [1859], p.404). These are perhaps the most famous closing words of any novel, and Rowling considers them 'the most perfect last line of a book ever written' (quoted in Smith, 2002, p.96). In stressing her admiration for *Tale of Two Cities* as early as 2000 Rowling was leaving a clue about her own romantic anti-hero, who – in the final book of the series – will likewise be killed by a bloody neck-wound (Granger, 2009, pp.244–8).

The parallels with Sydney Carton – an outcast who dies to save not his beloved but, even more heroically, to save a man his beloved loves – form a powerful, literary analogue for the romantic aspect of Snape's characterisation. Carton, at his death, is given a prophetic vision of the future in which "'I see the lives for which I lay down my life, peaceful, useful, prosperous and happy.'" (And it is noticeable that Rowling's rather old-fashioned description of Snape's sacrifice above – he 'laid down his life' (2007f) – echoes Carton's description of his own sacrifice.) Carton looks into the future and sees Lucie's child naming his own son after the man who died to save them: "'I see him, foremost of just judges and honoured men, bringing a boy of my name, with a forehead that I know and golden hair, to this place . . . and I hear him tell the child my story, with a tender and a faltering voice'" (1985 [1859], p.404). In the epilogue to *Deathly Hallows* likewise, the reader discovers that nineteen years later Harry (the child of the woman Snape loves) will name Lily's grandson after Snape. And it will be Albus Severus alone of Harry's children who has inherited Lily's eyes, just as Lucie's grandson has inherited her golden hair. The most striking physical attribute of the woman Snape and Carton love is retained by the grandchild of hers who bears his name. Carton imagines this child being tenderly told his story and Albus Severus is told by Harry in this epilogue that the man he has been named after "'was probably the bravest man I ever knew".'

PETRARCHAN SONNETS AND THE LANGUAGE OF LOVE IN *ROMEO AND JULIET*

The first potion that is described in detail in *Harry Potter* is the Draught of Living Death, whose ingredients – asphodel (a type of lily) and bitterest wormwood – have been interpreted by fandom as symbolising Snape's deep regret for Lily's death: 'according to the Victorian Language of Flowers, asphodel is a type of lily meaning "my regrets follow you to the grave," and wormwood means "absence" and symbolizes bitter sorrow' (Lin, 2012). The Draught of Living Death also recalls the sleeping potion taken by Shakespeare's heroine in *Romeo and Juliet*, so powerful that it 'wrought on her/ The form of death' (5.3.254–5). This potion is made by Friar Laurence, whom the audience sees at the beginning of Act Two out gathering 'baleful weeds and precious-juicèd flowers' (2.2.8) in the very early morning, when their properties will be at their most potent. (This belief in the importance of the time potion ingredients are harvested is also found in *Harry Potter* where the Fluxweed for Polyjuice Potion must be picked at full moon and other ingredients are 'most efficacious if picked at twilight' [*Half-Blood Prince*, Chap 22, p.448].)

As in *Harry Potter*, and despite Friar Laurence's potion-making skills, love potions play no part in how Romeo and Juliet fall for each other. Shakespeare, instead, uses language to describe their love at first sight, which is as instantaneous as any produced by magical means. In *Romeo and Juliet*, prior to seeing Juliet, Romeo has been obsessed by Rosaline (a character the audience never see). This early infatuation is described with the formulaic hyperbole of sonneteering language. Romeo's speech at this point in the play is full of opposites and extremes – white swans and black crows, faith and heresy, fire and ice and eyes drowned in tears:

> When the devout religion of mine eye
>   Maintains such falsehood, then turn tears to fires;
> And these who, often drowned could never die,
>   Transparent heretics, be burnt for liars.
> One fairer than my love! – the all-seeing sun
> Ne'er saw her match since first the world begun.
>
>   (1.2.90–95)

This is pure Petrarchan cliché, mocking the way that the language of Petrarch's sonnets had become hackneyed in the hands of his many, less skilled, imitators. In an extraordinarily involved metaphor, Romeo's eyes (if guilty of thinking another woman more beautiful than Rosaline) will be 'transparent heretics' (punning on the clearness of their heresy and the translucence of the eye) who, as they have not drowned in their own tears of love for Rosaline, should be burnt as heretics instead.

Traditional sonneteering imagery reappears in Romeo's first exchange with Juliet, but the tone is quite different. The heroine of *Romeo and Juliet* stands on the cusp of her fourteenth birthday, and when he sees her, Romeo's language finds its true connection with the fourteen-line sonnet form. His language is no longer a parody of love, but the thing itself:

> *Romeo.* If I profane with my unworthiest hand
> This holy shrine, the gentler sin is this:
> My lips, two blushing pilgrims, ready stand
> To smooth that rough touch with a tender kiss.
> *Juliet.* Good pilgrim, you do wrong your hand too much,
> Which mannerly devotion shows in this.
> For saints have hands that pilgrims' hands do touch,
> And palm to palm is holy palmers' kiss.
> *Romeo.* Have not saints lips, and holy palmers, too?
> *Juliet.* Ay, pilgrim, lips that they must use in prayer.
> *Romeo.* O then, dear saint, let lips do what hands do;

They pray; grant thou, lest faith turn to despair.
Juliet. Saints do not move, though grant for prayers' sake.
Romeo. Then move not while my prayer's effect I take.

(1.5.92–105)

This shared sonnet contains poetic devices (such as the connection of love with religious devotion) that are familiar from Romeo's praise of Rosaline, but the entirely self-directed 'eyes as heretics' metaphor of his earlier infatuation has been transformed into a 'lips as pilgrims' metaphor that is used in pursuit of a connection with Juliet.

At first this appears to be a traditional sonnet in that the man strives for greater physical intimacy (Romeo is trying to get Juliet to agree to kiss him) while the woman keeps him at arm's length. But it is, in fact, a radical rewriting of the genre. While in traditional sonnets the lady remains aloofly chaste, in this sonnet desire wins the argument and – unlike any previous sonnet – it ends with a kiss. Juliet is, in fact, just as desiring of Romeo as he is of her and she will take the dominant role in the relationship (very unusually for the sixteenth century, it is Juliet who will propose marriage to Romeo).

While earlier sonnets tend to be written in a male persona this sonnet gives both a female and a male perspective for, uniquely, it is shared equally between male and female voices. Traditional sonneteering puts women on a pedestal but never allows them a voice. The shared sonnet of *Romeo and Juliet*, by contrast, witnesses to a genuinely equal relationship: the woman is not merely a desired object but a desiring partner. *Harry Potter*, likewise, attempts a degree of equality and reciprocity in the relationship between Harry and Ginny and, as in *Romeo and Juliet*, this is first hinted at through the inversion of the traditional poetic blazon (in which the woman is blazoned by the man). In *Chamber*, as discussed in Chapter 5, Ginny 'blazons' Harry in a love poem: comparing his hair to the blackness of a blackboard and his eyes to the green of a freshly pickled toad. In this first love-exchange of *Romeo and Juliet*, too, rather than the traditional division of the woman into her constituent parts, it is only Romeo's body that is poetically dissected, his red lips 'two blushing pilgrims'. The equality in desiring between Romeo and Juliet is found likewise in *Harry Potter* as Harry and Ginny's first kiss is initiated by Ginny (just as it is Hermione who initiates the kiss with Ron).

THE WHITE DOE: THE PETRARCHAN MISTRESS AND SNAPE'S PATRONUS

The Petrarchan sonnet tradition, by contrast, is famous for its depiction of unrequited love. Petrarch's fourteenth-century *Canzoniere* (or *Rime Sparse*) is a sonnet sequence that records his life-long passion for a young woman called Laura, who never returned his love. Laura's death does not end Petrarch's love for her, and while the first part of his sonnet sequence is dedicated to his love for Laura in life, the second part is devoted to Laura after her death.

The romantic melancholy of this undying, unrequited passion not only recalls Snape's fate, but the silver-white doe that embodies Snape's life-long love, is likewise the figure of Petrarch's unattainable beloved.

James and Lily's Patronuses are a stag and a doe; as the male and female versions of the same animal they form a perfect pair. This coupling is a visible sign of the happiness of their union: 'the Patronus often mutates to take the image of the love of one's life (because they so often become the "happy thought" that generates a Patronus)' (Rowling, 2007f). But while James and Lily form the erotically satisfying pair of a stag and doe, Snape's Patronus, formed from concentrating on the 'happy thought' that is Lily, is not a stag, but the doe itself. The strength of Snape's love is expressed in the form of his Patronus (as Rowling has commented, 'your Patronus only changes if it's eternal love, unchanging – part of you forever' [Twitter, 21 May 2015]). But the female form of Snape's Patronus also suggests a love that is truly self-abnegating: by taking on the gender as well as the form of his beloved, Snape's doe expresses both the intensity and the ultimate sterility of unrequited passion.

The importance of the doe Patronus is marked by the fact that she is given her own chapter title – 'The Silver Doe' (*Deathly Hallows*, Chap 19) – and this chapter contains one of the most haunting scenes in *Harry Potter*. As Harry sits alone in the dark forest, 'a bright silver light appeared right ahead of him, moving through the trees . . . . It was a silver-white doe . . . . He set off in pursuit . . . . She turned her beautiful head towards him once more, and he broke into a run, a question burning in him, but as he opened his lips to ask it, she vanished' (pp.298–9). This 'silver-white doe' exerts a resistless pull on the hero, leads him to a pool of water and then vanishes. In her other-worldly beauty, her mysterious, unattainable perfection, as well as her effect on the protagonist, she has stepped straight from Petrarch's *Rime* 190, one of his most famous sonnets:

> A doe of purest white upon the grass,
> With two golden horns appeared to me,
> Between two streams, beneath a laurel's shade,
> Upon the unripe rising of the sun.
> Her aspect was so sweetly disdainful
> That I must leave my work to follow her,
> Just like the miser whose search for treasure
> Delightfully honeys all his bitterness.
> 'Let no one touch me' was writ with topaz
> And diamonds around her lovely neck:
> 'It pleased my Caesar to create me free.'
> The sun by now had reached the midday heights,
> My eyes were sore, but had not gazed their fill,
> When I fell into water and she vanished.

This encounter with the white doe takes place at sunrise while Harry's takes place in a dark wood but in both the doe stands out in her dazzling purity against the wooded landscape. In both the doe, a symbol of the beloved, draws the hero inexorably to follow her. But in both her enigmatic charisma cannot be penetrated and she vanishes without being touched or questioned. The man who pursues her, meanwhile, falls (or, in Harry's case, jumps) into water.

The water in Petrarch's sonnet delivers a shock: its carries some of the reviving force of a slap as the reader of the poem as well as its speaker wake from the dream-vision into a cold reality. Harry's vision, likewise, recalls an actual dream (four years earlier he had dreamt of following a 'silvery white' animal through a dark wood [*Azkaban*, Chap 13, p.196]) and he is brought back to earth from the dream-like vision of the doe by a pool of icy water. What Harry wants from the doe is an answer – 'he broke into a run, a question burning in him' – although whether he has realised the reason for her 'inexplicable familiarity' (Chap 19, p.298) is left unanswered. The unspoken question burning within Harry echoes the implicit question of Petrarch's sonnet, which is silently repulsed before it is even articulated by the message of the diamond collar: 'It pleased my Caesar to create me free.' Petrarch's doe – and the woman she symbolises – will not be fettered by man or man's desires. The white doe in Petrarch, like Snape's Patronus, symbolises a woman who has rejected the man's love but remains adored. In both texts this woman, like the fleet-footed doe, remains out of reach but her unattainability only renders her more desirable.

The underlying imagery of Petrarch's sonnet – of a man setting off at sunrise to follow a deer – is drawn from hunting. The idea of the hunt, however, leaves only the faintest trace in this dream-like landscape suffused with symbolic meaning (the laurel tree from which the doe steps, for example, is not the shelter of an animal from its hunter, but a pun on 'Laura', the name of Petrarch's beloved). One of the reasons that this sonnet is well known in the English tradition is because it was paraphrased by Thomas Wyatt, England's first sonneteer. In Wyatt's version the mystic beauty of Petrarch is rewritten as a fully realised hunting scene, and the sexual implications of the hunt become apparent:

> Whoso list to hunt, I know where is an hind,
> But as for me, helas, I may no more.
> The vain travail hath wearied me so sore,
> I am of them that farthest cometh behind.
> Yet may I by no means my wearied mind
> Draw from the deer, but as she fleeth afore
> Fainting I follow. I leave off therefore
> Sithens in a net I seek to hold the wind.
> Who list her hunt, I put him out of doubt,
> As well as I may spend his time in vain.
> And graven with diamonds in letters plain
> There is written her fair neck round about:
> '*Noli me tangere* for Caesar's I am,
> And wild for to hold though I seem tame.'

(1978 [c.1526], p.77)

Wyatt's speaker, too, is inexorably drawn by the doe. Wyatt uses convoluted phrasing and a lack of punctuation at the end of the line – 'Yet may I by no means my wearied mind/ Draw from the deer, but as she fleeth afore/ Fainting I follow' – to express the breathless effort of the pursuit and the speaker's inescapable desire.

The 'fair' doe retains her appeal, but the mysticism of Petrarch's doe of 'purest white' has been replaced by the language of male conquest as Wyatt re-imagines the hunt in sexual terms. The aggressive stress that falls on the word 'her' (when the opening line 'Whoso list to hunt' is rephrased as 'Who list *her* hunt') encodes antagonism towards the woman symbolised by the doe. The aggression of the poem is poised between resentment at the woman's current sexual unavailability and the crude implication that she was not always so unavailable ('know' carried the meaning of sexual knowledge at this period – in the King James Bible men are always 'knowing' their wives).

Despite the speaker's sexual bitterness, however, Wyatt's poem retains something of Petrarch's mysticism. It alludes, like Petrarch, to a legend about deer who appeared three hundred years after the death of Caesar, bearing collars round their necks that read, 'Noli me tangere, Caesaris sum.' It also increases the significance of these words for, while Petrarch translated them into Italian, Wyatt retains the Latin phrase '*Noli me tangere.*' These are, famously, the words spoken by the risen Christ to Mary Magdalen and are often understood as a message to the believer to look beyond things of the flesh and towards those of the spirit. The phrase '*Noli me tangere*', therefore, keeps something of the enchanted tone of Petrarch's original and, in pointing beyond carnal understanding, it suggests that the poem, too, might contain a meaning beyond its literal one. It is in part this combination of the concrete and the mystical that makes this one of Wyatt's best – and most famous – poems. It hints at knowledge withheld and, while in Petrarch's sonnet it feels as if this knowledge lies beyond the reach of mortal man, there is a long tradition in Wyatt scholarship that reads the key to Wyatt's poem as an identification of 'Caesar' with Henry VIII, and the doe with Anne Boleyn. Rumours abound that Wyatt and Anne were once involved, but once the King became interested in Anne, Wyatt was forced to quit the field. In this reading Petrarch's sonnet is re-imagined by Wyatt as a Henrician hunt in which the King ('Caesar') has claimed the royal rights that the monarch always has over deer.

The Petrarchan moment of the white doe in the *Deathly Hallows*, likewise, holds a clue to the secrets of the heart that lie at the centre of the mystery. The submerged love-triangle of Wyatt's poem recalls the love-triangle between James, Lily and Snape while the haunting appearance of Snape's doe Patronus recalls the enchanted tone of the Petrarchan original and its unattainable beloved.

LOVE POTIONS, BLAZON AND PETRARCHAN CLICHÉ: LOVE-IN-VANE AND LOVE-IN-IDLENESS

While Petrarch's sonnets retain their freshness and power, the fashion for sonnet-writing that Petrarch initiated meant that the originality of his poems was replaced by the Petrarchan cliché of his imitators. *Romeo and Juliet*, as discussed above, uses this disjunction between the true Petrarchan language of love, and the platitudes of its imitators, in order to distinguish between Romeo's true love for Juliet and its pale imitation in his earlier infatuation for Rosaline. The convoluted language of Petrarchan cliché as Romeo languishes over Rosaline, is replaced by the innovative and intimate sonnet he shares with Juliet (Slater, 1988). *Harry Potter*, likewise, draws on both Petrarch and his hackneyed imitators to distinguish between true and false love. While *Harry Potter* draws on the haunting, genuinely Petrarchan image of the white doe for Snape's unrequited passion, it also enjoys mocking Petrarchan cliché in Ron's drugged, over-wrought infatuation for Romilda Vane.

The book *Fantastic Beasts and Where to Find Them* (published to raise money for Comic Relief in 2001) describes a creature called an Ashwinder, which, born of fire, has incredibly destructive potential: 'created when a magical fire is allowed to burn unchecked for too long. A thin, pale-grey serpent with glowing red eyes, it will rise from the embers of an unsupervised fire . . . . Ashwinder eggs are brilliant red and give off intense heat. They will ignite the dwelling within minutes if not found and frozen' (Scamander [Rowling], 2001, p.2). *Fantastic Beasts* contains a number of hints about things that will later become important in *Harry Potter*, such as Nifflers, Thestrals and Murtlap Essence. The Ashwinder is a foretaste of the Love Potions of *Half-Blood Prince* for its eggs, once frozen, are 'of great value for use in Love Potions.' These eggs (a union of fire and ice) are a subtle allusion to the Petrarchan sonnet tradition in which unrequited love is habitually described in these terms. Many Elizabethan sonneteers, drawing on Petrarch, described the misery of unrequited love as the painful disjunction between a burning passion and cold disdain. In Spenser's *Amoretti* (30), for example: 'my Love is like to ice, and I to fire' (1997 [1595], p.80). Petrarchan cliché of unrequited love as fire and ice – in which the lover is consumed while his mistress remains aloof – is literalised in the frozen, fiery Ashwinder eggs, an essential ingredient for the potion supposed to solve the problem of unrequited affection.[1]

Petrarchan lovers always love a distant, unattainable lady and Ron becomes a parody of a Petrarchan lover when he is accidentally drugged by Romilda Vane. Ron, after rhapsodising about Romilda, suddenly, without any consciousness of irony, admits that he has never met her: '"did you say Romilda? Harry – do you know her? Can you introduce me?"' (*Half-Blood Prince*, Chap 18, p.369). Love Potions, created through the Petrarchan formula of icy fire cause those who take them to spout Petrarchan cliché.

On the morning of Ron's birthday, when Harry sets off for breakfast as usual, he realises that Ron has not joined him but is leaning against his bed, staring vacantly out of the window. Very uncharacteristically he claims not to be hungry and when Harry asks why, Ron sighs out that he wouldn't understand. Ron's coy refusal to name his love echoes lovers through the ages who studiously pretend secrecy about what they are secretly bursting to share. Romeo, deep in his infatuation for Rosaline, is likewise coy when questioned by friend Benvolio: 'what sadness lengthens Romeo's hours?' 'Not having that which, having, makes them short' (1.1.160–161). Romeo, like Ron, appears to evade his friend's questions but his short, opaque answers invite requests for further confidences. Romeo, like the infatuated Ron, has this exchange early in the day: both texts poke fun at the longings and languishings of their would-be lovers making them pronounce their desire at the unromantic hour of breakfast time.

Romeo's earlier, hackneyed passion for Rosaline is mocked by his friend Mercutio in a parody of Petrarchan blazon:

> I conjure thee by Rosaline's bright eyes,
> By her high forehead and her scarlet lip,
> By her fine foot, straight leg, and quivering thigh
> And the demesnes that there adjacent lie.
>
> (2.1.17–20)

Ron likewise performs a blazon of his false beloved: "'Romilda Vane,' said Ron softly, and his whole face seemed to illuminate as he said it, as though hit by a ray of purest sunlight . . . . "I love her," repeated Ron breathlessly. "Have you seen her hair, it's all black and shiny and silky. . . and her eyes? Her big dark eyes? And her—'" (pp.367–8). Ron catalogues the beauty of each separate part of Romilda's face but this comic blazon, like Mercutio's, is not only humorous in its excess but could also be read as sharing in Mercutio's crudity. Mercutio conjures Romeo by 'her fine foot, straight leg, and quivering thigh/ And the demesnes that there adjacent lie.' Blazon's cataloguing of the female form usually skips the part that lies at the top of the thigh, but Mercutio's parody draws attention to the idea that there is something inherently pornographic in blazon's objectification of women. Blazon might shun sexual parts as indelicate, but it implicitly encourages the reader to think about them as it roves across a woman's body leaving only that part unnamed. Harry swiftly interrupts Ron's blazon: "'and her eyes? Her big dark eyes? And her—'". It may be that Harry simply cannot stand to hear any more of this, but he may put an abrupt end to Ron's rhapsodies because Ron (like Mercutio) is about to move on to other – less appropriate – parts of Romilda's body.

Shakespeare's most famous critique of blazon occurs in his sonnet 130: 'My mistress' eyes are nothing like the sun.' But it is a critique that also runs through his plays and in one case the man who utters one of these mock-blazons is – like Ron – under the influence of a love potion. In *A Midsummer Night's Dream* Lysander (who actually loves Hermia) blazons Helena because Puck has 'latched' his eyes with 'love juice' (3.2.36–7). Oberon instructs Puck to fetch a flower called 'love-in-idleness', the juice of which is a potent love potion and 'will make or man or woman madly dote/ Upon the next live creature that it sees' (2.1.168–72). Under the influence of this flower's juice Lysander declares:

> O Helen, goddess, nymph, perfect, divine!
> To what, my love, shall I compare thine eyne?

Crystal is muddy. O, how ripe in show
Thy lips, those kissing cherries, tempting grow!
That pure congealèd white – high Taurus' snow,
Fanned with the eastern wind – turns to a crow
When thou hold'st up thy hand: O, let me kiss
This princess of pure white, this seal of bliss!

(3.2.138–45)

Lysander's blazon is rendered comic through its rhetorical excess – he strains for rhymes, repeating the 'ow' rhyme four times (and rhyming it thrice internally with 'O') and using an old-fashioned plural for eyes ('eyne') to force a rhyme with 'divine'.

In the comic blazons of Lysander, Mercutio and Ron, however, it is not love that is mocked, but infatuation: blazon's objectification of women is held up as an example of what love is *not* like. The enslavement of love potions in *Dream* and *Half-Blood Prince* and the comic blazons of *Romeo and Juliet*, *Dream* and *Half-Blood Prince* are used by both authors to highlight the difference between love and its imitations. Infatuation – and its attendant quasi-Petrarchan posturing – is held up as a foil to what real love might be. When Demetrius and Lysander wake from their adventures in the woods they will be back in love with (respectively) Helena and Hermia. After the Love Potion has worn off, Ron lies recovering in the hospital wing and, after all his prolonged sighings after Romilda, utters the single word 'Er-my-nee' (Chap 19, p.376).

Ron's consumption of the Love Potion Romilda Vane had intended for Harry, and the ensuing comic chaos, echoes the plot of *Dream*. In Shakespeare's play a Love Potion is likewise accidentally given to the wrong young man leading to his declaration of undying love towards the wrong woman. Shakespeare's love potion involves a virtuoso piece of four-way confusion: Demetrius and Lysander have both been drugged into believing that they love Helena, Hermia believes that Helena must have bewitched Lysander and Helena believes that the other three are leagued together to mock her (as up till now both Lysander and Demetrius have been in love with Hermia). The situation is much simpler in *Harry Potter* but the basic humour of the confusion, and the conversation between a drugged lover and a rational interlocutor, remain. In both texts this confusion leads to the slapstick of a fight between friends. Lysander and Demetrius spend much of the middle of the play chasing each other round the stage and Ron punches Harry on the ear when the latter suggests that he must be joking about being in love with Romilda. Harry uses a spell to stop Ron from continuing the fight and Puck, likewise, magically separates Demetrius and Lysander so no real harm can ensue.

Half-Blood Prince also shares with *Dream* in its double use of the love-potion plot. In one part of the action the potion is accidentally given to the wrong person and produces mistaken-identity comedy (the lovers in the wood/ Ron and Romilda) but in another strand the potion is intentionally administered and the results are more serious. Titania is drugged by her husband Oberon, and Tom Riddle Snr by his wife-to-be Merope, and both the victims are horrified to discover whom they have slept with under the potion's influence: 'O, how mine eyes do loathe his visage now!' (4.1.78). Oberon's drugging of his wife is designed to humiliate her into submission, and Merope enslaves her husband through the potion. While (in both Shakespeare and *Harry Potter*) the passions that the Love Potions unleash in the purely comic part of the plot remain chaste, in the more serious plot it leads to a consummated union – suggestive of the way that sexual relationships cloud human judgement.

Three strands of *Dream*'s plot – Theseus and Hippolyta, Oberon and Titania, and the lovers in the wood – all question the interrelation between love and power. The playful aspects of the chaos created by the love potion among the lovers in the wood reflect more serious issues of the abuse of power in the other erotic relationships of the play. Shakespeare's use of a magical love potion to question power relations within sexual relationships is reflected in the Merope sub-plot of *Half-Blood Prince*. Oberon's abuse of power when he uses a love potion to humiliate Titania is echoed in Merope's similar use of a Love Potion to get what she wants at the cost of the freedom of another.

MEROPE AND FANNY ROBIN

Hermione explains to Harry about how the Love Potions (with which Romilda Vane and her friends are trying to entrap him) are being smuggled into the castle disguised as cough mixtures and perfumes. Harry wonders if Malfoy could have smuggled in the opal necklace by the same method and Hermione objects that the necklace was a dark object with a major curse on it that would have been picked up: '"and anyway, Love Potions aren't Dark or dangerous—" "Easy for you to say," muttered Harry, thinking of Romilda Vane' (Chap 15, p.288). Romilda Vane does indeed try to entrap Harry by slipping a Love Potion into his drink when she offers him a Gillywater as he returns to the common room. Harry, suspecting that Romilda has laced it with a Love Potion, does not accept the proffered refreshment, but this moment echoes the scenario of how Merope might have persuaded Tom Riddle Snr into drinking a Love Potion by offering him a seemingly innocuous drink of water (Chap 10, p.202). Merope's history colours Hermione's confident assertion that "Love Potions aren't Dark or dangerous", which – although it is only comically countered here by Harry – is overturned by Ron's near-death after he takes Romilda's Love Potion and the enslavement that results in Voldemort's birth.

Romilda attempts to make Harry fall for her by offering him a drink and this feels like a familiar literary idea (as old as Rebecca who becomes Isaac's wife because she is generous in providing drinking water in Genesis 24). Dumbledore imagines that it would have appealed to Merope as a romantic idea. Merope uses a Love Potion to enslave the affections of the heartless Tom Riddle Snr and Harry's guess that Merope might have used an Imperius Curse on him suggests that there is something worryingly close to an Unforgiveable Curse about the coercive power of a Love Potion. Rowling is harsh on Merope in interview, saying that Voldemort's conception under the influence of a Love Potions was 'a symbolic way of showing that he came from a loveless union . . . it shows coercion, and there can't be many more prejudicial ways to enter the world than as the result of such a union' (2007f). But *Half-Blood Prince* encourages the reader to sympathise with Merope's suffering (if not with her actions) through the literary parallels it draws. In addition to the Ovidian source of her name (discussed in Chapter 2) there are also links between Merope's story and that of Fanny Robin in Hardy's *Far from the Madding Crowd*.

Hardy's Fanny Robin and Merope Gaunt both endure a loveless child-hood and a life of servitude before they fall in love with a cold-hearted, flashy young man who does not return their affection. Fanny, like Merope, becomes pregnant, is deserted and dies giving birth to her child in an institution. Hardy stresses the pathos of Fanny's terrible end in order to combat the harsh judgement a Victorian audience would have felt towards an unmarried mother; and *Harry Potter* may be doing something similar. While Hardy's audience would have believed that sex outside marriage was a sin, a modern readership is likely to feel something similar about sexual coercion. Merope's abusive upbring-ing, desperate poverty and abandoned death work to create sympathy for her, despite her immoral action. There is nothing rational to be urged in Merope's favour – she *does* conceive her son by force – but empathy for her suffering is fostered through its echoes of Fanny Robin's fate.

Merope is an abused daughter whose horrific home life (and the ghastliness of the man she falls for) makes the reader inclined to sympathise with her rather than the man she enslaves. The fact that she feels true love, rather than simple lust, for Tom Riddle is shown by her decision to stop using the Love Potion. While in interview Rowling has denigrated Merope's feelings for Riddle as a 'silly infatuation', Dumbledore takes them more seriously. Dumbledore guesses that '"Merope, who was deeply in love with her husband, could not bear to continue enslaving him by magical means"' (Chap 10, p.203). While Merope hopes that Tom has genuinely fallen in love with her, her decision to stop drugging him – to do something to his advantage that is (potentially cataclysmically) against her own interests – is a sign that what she feels for him is something more than a 'silly infatuation'.

Merope and Fanny Robin share very similar death scenes: they both stag-ger through a bitterly cold night to die as abandoned woman giving birth to their children in an institution; but there are also further connections between the two characters and how their stories are told. Both leave a letter behind them to explain that they have run away from a life of service with a hand-some young man they hope to marry. Merope, like Fanny, is '"covered in rags and pretty far along"' when she meets a man who gives her money, in both cases an insufficient amount to save her from death in an institution (Chap 13, p.245; Hardy, Chap 39). Both Casterbridge Union (where Fanny dies) and the orphanage where Merope dies are staffed by unsentimental types, and both novels garner sympathy for the dying woman by showing how unresponsive to her need are those who witnessed her plight. In the chapter that Hardy devotes to Fanny's long journey through the darkness he describes how the lights of

Casterbridge 'lay before them like fallen Pleiads' (p.327). Rowling is a careful reader and, as she has noted, she is always particularly attentive to unusual names: 'I love names, as anyone who has read the book is going to see only too clearly. . . . I collect them. You know, if I hear a good name, I have got to write it down' (2000l). As mentioned in the introduction, another Hardy novel provided Dumbledore's name (and perhaps Hagrid's too) and it seems possible that Hardy's reference to the Pleiades here may have inspired the name of Merope (the 'lost Pleiad'; see Chapter 2) who shares Fanny Robin's fate.

Dumbledore counsels Harry against dismissing those who are engulfed by their suffering: '"do not judge her too harshly, Harry. She was greatly weakened by long suffering and she never had your mother's courage"' (Chap 13, p.246) and Merope's story does rouse compassion in Harry when he feels indignant on her behalf on hearing how little Caractacus Burke gave her for Slytherin's locket. Empathy is important in *Harry Potter*. While there is little explicit sympathy for Merope in *Half-Blood Prince* her literary analogues – both Ovid's Merope and Fanny Robin – encourages compassion for her fate. Empathy is something that *Harry Potter* constantly fosters, particularly through creating characters who appear as traditional bogey-figures – such as werewolves, giants and mass-murderers – and showing them to be the reverse of what the reader might have imagined. Nowhere is this empathy for the 'enemy' clearer, however, than in *Harry Potter*'s depiction of the hidden depths of its bullying Potions' master.

This chapter has looked at the Love Potions in *Harry Potter*, which form both a comic subtext (in the ill-fated romance of Romilda and Ron) and a serious back-story (with the story of Merope). In the first Potions lesson of *Half Blood Prince* Slughorn tells the smirking Slytherins (who, naturally, underestimate the power of love) that the Love Potion Amortentia is both more powerful and more perilous than any other potion in the room; and indeed the name 'Amortentia' derives both from the Latin for love (*amor*) and the Latin for death (*mors*). Love and death are entwined in *Harry Potter*. Dumbledore tells Harry that love is '"more wonderful and more terrible than death"' (*Phoenix*, Chap 37, p.743) and that it will be the power to defeat Voldemort, who is in some ways a symbol of death (Dunne, 2015). Rowling, too, habitually discusses love in relation to death: 'love wins . . . . It does win; we know it wins. When the person dies, love isn't turned off like a faucet. It is an amazingly resilient part of us' (2010b). The final chapter of this book argues for the essential importance of death to *Harry Potter*. This final chapter returns to the chiastic form of the novels (first discussed in Chapter 1) and argues that both this reflexive form and *Harry Potter*'s characteristic use of allusion respond to the importance of mourning and mortality to the series.

of first narrative

Note

1 A frozen Ashwinder egg – its fire glowing within a shell of solid ice – is shown in the 2016 film *Fantastic Beasts and Where to Find Them*.

8 In Memoriam

According to its creator *Harry Potter* is 'largely about death' (2006a). Rowling
has spoken of the way that 'the theme of death runs through every volume
of the Potter books' and stated that 'all of my characters are defined by their
attitude to death and the possibility of death' (2015j; 2007e; see also 2012a).
Rowling calls Harry 'the prism through which I view death' (2012g). Implicit
within many of these observations, however, is that it is grief, as much as mortality itself, that lies at the heart of *Harry Potter*: 'dealing with bereavement is a
strong part of the books. Dealing with loss' (2000i). Rowling effectively used
a joke about the so-called 'five stages' of grief (defined by Elisabeth Kübler-
Ross [2009 (1969)] as denial, anger, bargaining, depression and acceptance) to
parry an awkward question about Snape's true allegiance. She confirmed that
Dumbledore was dead and counselled: 'I think . . . all of you need to move
through the five stages of grief [crowd laughs], and I'm just helping you get
past denial. So, I can't remember what's next. It may be anger so I think we
should stop it here' (2006b). Through the series Harry has to learn to face up
to the deaths not only of his parents but also of many of those who have come
to replace them as parental figures. In *Deathly Hallows* Harry passes through
denial and anger in his grief for Dumbledore and it is only once he has reached
a degree of acceptance for that loss that he is able to face his own mortality.

The grieving process is given a physical expression within *Harry Potter* in
the Thestrals. Thestrals can only be seen 'when you really understand death in
a broader sense, when you really know what it means . . . . Anyone who has
suffered a bereavement knows that there is the immediate shock but that it
takes a little while to appreciate fully that you will never see that person again.
Until that had happened, I did not think that Harry could see the Thestrals'
(Rowling, 2004b). Rowling has written that Luna, unlike Harry, can see
the Thestrals very soon after her mother dies: 'because she is intuitive, spiritual and unafraid of the afterlife' (2015s). Thestrals are characteristic of *Harry
Potter* in their externalisation of a psychological phenomenon. As argued in
Chapter 6, the series regularly invents objects and creatures – such as Boggarts
and Dementors – that render complex emotions in a readily comprehensible,
physical form. Thestrals embody the grieving process and the ability to see

them equates with emotional insight. Once Harry has become accustomed to the Thestrals he can even find beauty in them (*Phoenix*, Chap 33, p.672).

This chapter argues for the relation between *Harry Potter*'s exploration of grief and the chiastic structure of the series (discussed in the opening chapter of this book). This structure, in which the closing of the series echoes its opening, reflects the structure of grief in which the mourner, even as they move forward, instinctively looks back to the past. Mourning, like chiasmus, is reflective and compares the present with the past, the past with the present. Rowling has spoken of how completing *Harry Potter* took her back to its conception:

> I was incredibly low. I think what – what – what is probably hard for people to imagine is how wrapped up the seventeen years' work is with what was going on in my life at the time . . . .. I was mourning the loss of this world that I had written for so long and loved so much. I was also mourning the retreat it had been from – from ordinary life, which it has been. And it forced me to look back at seventeen years of my life and remember things. And it was very linked to my mother dying, which happened – because, you know, a huge – this big long passage from my life is now rounded off. So inevitably you think about what was happening at the beginning of that passage.
>
> (2007e)

The deaths of characters the reader has got to know in *Harry Potter* begins with the death of Cedric Diggory in *Goblet* and continues in each of the novels in the second half of series. The 'pivotal' nature of *Goblet* has been noted by Rowling – 'it's literally a central book, it's almost the heart of the series, and it's pivotal' (2000f) – and this is one way that its pivotal nature is marked: 'this is the book in which the deaths start. I always planned it this way. It's become a bit of an *idée fixe* with me' (2000d).

After the publication of *Deathly Hallows* Rowling regularly reiterated that *Harry Potter* had taken her seventeen years to write, and – coincidentally – Tennyson also took seventeen years to write *In Memoriam*, perhaps the greatest poem of mourning in English. This poem – which Tennyson began in 1833 when he first heard of the death of his friend Arthur Hallam, and which he continued to write and revise right up to its publication in 1850 – embodies its author's deep grief. And, like *Harry Potter*, it responds to the backwards-looking nature of grief with a chiastic form. Tennyson writes *In Memoriam* in a chiastic rhyme-scheme – '*abba*' – in which the first line of the quatrain rhymes with the last, arching over the rhymed couplet in the centre of the verse:

> But, for the unquiet heart and brain,
>   A use in measured language lies;
>   The sad mechanic exercise,
> Like dull narcotics, numbing pain.
>
> (Section V)

Both Tennyson and Rowling turned to a highly structured form of writing in their grief, and both found it therapeutic. Tennyson writes that his poetry 'brings myself relief' (LXXV) and Rowling has likewise spoken of her writing as a 'retreat' and an 'escape' from her grief (2007e; 1997b; 2008a).

The title of Tennyson's poem – *In Memoriam* – means 'to the memory of', and the phrase is used as a chapter title within *Harry Potter*. It is the title of the second chapter of *Deathly Hallows* (the first chapter in which the grief-struck Harry appears in the novel). Due to Tennyson's poem, 'in memoriam' (originally a Latin phrase at the beginning of an epitaph) has come to describe a memorial poem or piece of writing. Elphias Doge's rose-tinted obituary of Dumbledore is just such a piece of writing, and its presence in this 'In Memoriam' chapter is the beginning of the novel's exploration of grief and memory; and the way that Rita Skeeter's very different response to Dumbledore's death makes Harry begin to doubt him.

T. S. Eliot's famous assessment of *In Memoriam* is that 'it is not religious because of the quality of its faith, but because of the quality of its doubt. Its faith is a poor thing, but its doubt is a very intense experience' (2004 [1936], p.138). Rowling has, similarly, described the impact of her own doubts on *Harry Potter*: 'my faith is sometimes that my faith will return . . . it's something that I wrestle with a lot. It preoccupies me a lot, and I think that's very obvious within the books' (2007g). In both *In Memoriam* and *Harry Potter* doubt revolves around the relationship of the living with those they have loved and lost.

In Memoriam's response to mortality and mourning connects in a number of ways with *Harry Potter*. Tennyson suggests, for example, that excessive grief can lead to a form of petrification or narcissism:

> I will not shut me from my kind,
>   And, lest I stiffen into stone,
>   I will not eat my heart alone,
> Nor feed with sighs a passing wind . . .
>
> What find I in the highest place,
>   But mine own phantom chanting hymns?
>   And on the depths of death there swims
> The reflex of a human face.
>
> (CVIII)

Tennyson paraphrased these verses as 'grief shall not make me a hermit, and I will not indulge in vacant yearnings and barren aspirations . . ... I find nothing but reflections of myself' (2004 [1850], pp.81–2). The Narcissus myth echoes through this passage, as it does with the Mirror of Erised episode. The fear of a self-consuming grief that echoes in the sighs of the wind, leads naturally to the fear that the Narcissus myth will be fully realised if the 'reflex of a human face' Tennyson's speaker sees is nothing but a reflection of himself. Both *Philosopher's*

Stone and *In Memoriam* daringly use Ovid's tale of self-absorption to suggest the dangers and false attraction of an all-consuming grief: '"it does not do to dwell on dreams and forget to live."'

In Memoriam embodies the grief of its author within its chiastic form and *Harry Potter* likewise grew out of Rowling's own bereavement. Rowling has spoken of the way that her mother's death 'depth-charged me. It changed my life' (2006a). Rowling's mother is enshrined within the books in Lily's emblematically perfect motherhood, in the warm, protective presence of Molly Weasley and in Hagrid's surprisingly maternal aspects (discussed in Chapter 4). Rowling believes in the profound influence of her mother's death on her writing: 'the books are what they are because she died . . . because I loved her and she died' (2010b). Rowling's mother died six months after Rowling had begun her series 'and I really think from that moment on, death became a central, if not the central theme of the seven books' (2007e). *Harry Potter* memorialises Rowling's mother in its chiastic championing of maternal love: it is maternal love that saves Harry in both his first and his final encounters with Voldemort.[1]

One of the essential differences between Harry and Voldemort lies in their attitude to death: 'Harry Potter overcomes his fear of death while Lord Voldemort is running away from death.'[2] Voldemort's fear of death is connected to the pain of Rowling's own bereavement, and she has left a subtle hint of this within his name. Rowling is a fluent French-speaker (she studied French as an undergraduate and was once a French teacher) and Voldemort's name – which she pronounces as a French word (without the 't' [Twitter, 9 Sept 2015]) – is rich in meaning. 'Vol de mort' means both 'flight of death' and 'flight from death'. This double meaning encapsulates *Harry Potter*'s moral in which an overwhelming fear of death – a sense that nothing is worthwhile except one's own life – is a form of capitulation to death: Voldemort's 'flight from death' transforms him into little more than a simulacrum of death (a 'flight of death'). 'Vol' also means 'theft' as well as 'flight' so Voldemort's name also means 'theft of death'. Voldemort's attempt to circumvent death is a theft as well as a flight: a morally dubious attempt to overturn the natural order and a subtle inversion of the 'gifts of death' crucial to the *Deathly Hallows* (and its title in a number of translations).[3]

There is, however, another – more startling – source for Voldemort's name. Rowling's interest in French stems in part from her mother's French roots, and when she took part in the TV series *Who Do You Think You Are?* in 2011, Rowling explained that her mother, Anne Volant, had always wanted to know more about her French history: 'a huge motivation in looking into my family history is my mother . . . .. It's very bound up in that loss' (2011c). Rowling has said that she took the inspiration for Voldemort's name from her mother's maiden name because Volant ('flying') was the first French word she knew.[4]

Rowling's explicit link of Voldemort's name with her mother's maiden name indicates the extent to which her mother's death (mort de Volant) is central to the exploration of mortality in *Harry Potter*: 'her death infuses the whole Harry Potter series' (2012g); it 'bled into Harry at every level:

an awareness of mortality, what death means, what it means for the people who are left behind' (2012b). Rowling's use of 'Volant' as an inspiration for 'Voldemort' makes it explicit that it was her mother's death, the pain of that death, which makes Rowling both understand Voldemort's desire to fly from death and her need to confront that desire head on: 'I so understand why Voldemort wants to conquer death' (2006a). Rowling believes that both she and her hero had to learn that 'it's mortality that gives life meaning' (2008a).

HARRY POTTER'S CHIASTIC STRUCTURE: 'CLOSING THE CIRCLE'

For years Rowling believed that *Harry Potter* would end with the word 'scar' to signal the way that Harry was still marked by his parents' death after so many years: 'we all repeat the lie again and again, that time heals everything. And it's not true. There are things that do not heal, like when someone you love dies' (2008a). Rowling was 'writing *Harry Potter* the night my mother died' and when she finished, its ending took her back to its beginning: 'this big long passage from my life is now rounded off. So inevitably you think about what was happening at the beginning of that passage' (2012c). Rowling has noted both that finishing the first and last books felt 'strangely similar' and that completing the series 'felt like a bereavement' (2007h), bringing her back as it did to the time when she had just lost her mother.

This cyclical aspect of grief is mirrored in the chiastic structure of *Harry Potter*. As discussed in the first chapter, the final novel of the series recalls the first. Rowling has called this 'closing a circle' (2012h) and within the text itself it is hinted at when Harry receives the Resurrection Stone with the words '*I open at the close*' (*Deathly Hallows*, Chap 34, p.559). The first and the last novels revolve around a stone that has power over death and Dumbledore and Flamel's decision to destroy the Philosopher's Stone in the first novel prefigures Harry's more momentous decision to relinquish the Resurrection Stone in the *Deathly Hallows*. One of the most important echoes of the first novel in the last is the way that the temptation of the Resurrection Stone recapitulates Harry's response to the Mirror of Erised. Harry's heroic decision to leave the Resurrection Stone in the forest is the final realisation of his acceptance of Dumbledore's advice not to seek the Mirror of Erised, and his ability to see within it not his past for which he mourns but the future that he must create. The Mirror of Erised shows Harry the Philosopher's Stone because he has overcome its temptations of immortality and endless wealth but also because he has overcome another (harder) temptation: the Mirror's temptation to live in the lost land of memory. Dumbledore's destruction of the Philosopher's Stone in the first novel was intended 'to show that Dumbledore accepts his mortality' and when Harry discards the Resurrection Stone it symbolises that 'just like Dumbledore Harry has made his peace with death' (Rowling, 2008a). Dumbledore accepts his own mortality but he dies (cursed when he tries to wear the Resurrection Stone) because of his inability to accept the mortality of those he loves. Harry, uniquely, masters the lure of both the Philosopher's Stone and the Resurrection Stone, learning both that 'death is our destiny and we must face it' (2008a) and that mortality of those we love is 'tougher on the living, and you've just got to get past it' (2001e).

The chiastic form of *Harry Potter* connects the two magical objects that tempt Harry 'to live with dead people' (*Deathly Hallows*, Chap 22, p.346). It also links the internal structure of the series with Rowling's own renewed grief when she completed the series. *Harry Potter* is littered with Rowling's 'personal passwords': 'when I need a date or number, I use something that relates to my personal life. I do not know why I do that, it's a tic. Harry's birthday is mine, for example. The numbers and dates that appear in the books relate to me' (2008a).[5] These personal passwords often involve her family (the driver and conductor of the Knight Bus, for example, are named after her grandfathers Ernest and Stanley [2015l]) and in particular her parents (2015k). The most important of these personal passwords is the way that the linked temptation that Harry faces in the first and last novels echoes Rowling's own desires. As Rowling has said of the Mirror of Erised, 'I would definitely see what Harry sees. I would have seen my mother' (2007e), although it was only when she re-read Chapter 12 of *Philosopher's Stone* that she fully realised, 'I had given Harry almost entirely my own feelings about my mother's death' (1999f). In post-*Deathly Hallows* interviews, however, Rowling notes not only the parallel between her own and her hero's desire but also the importance of moving through this stage: 'my temptation would be Harry's, i.e. the Stone. But I believe, as does Harry ultimately, that the greatest wisdom is in accepting that we must all die, and moving on' (2007f). One interviewer noted that Rowling had said in the past that she would, like Harry, have chosen the Resurrection Stone, and she replied: 'and I would've been wrong . . .. Resurrection is a huge temptation but it's dangerous' (2008b).

CHIASMUS WITHIN *IN MEMORIAM*

In Memoriam's chiastic verse form is echoed in its larger structural parallels. It contains, for example, many repeated passages and phrases, such as the recurring Christmas and spring sections of the poem, and the repeated, paired sections on the yew tree and the darkened house. These include the repetition of the famous early line – ''Tis better to have loved and lost/ Than never to have loved at all' (XXVII) – near the end of the poem:

> This truth came borne with bier and pall,
> I felt it, when I sorrow'd most,
> 'Tis better to have loved and lost,
> Than never to have loved at all—
>
> (LXXXV)

These repeated lines and passages of *In Memoriam* chart the diminution, or resurgence, of grief over time. Tennyson reflects on the way that grief affects the relationship between the present and the past, and he does this within a rhyme-scheme that likewise relates its end to its beginning:

> And is it that the haze of grief
>> Makes former gladness loom so great?
>> The lowness of the present state,
> That sets the past in this relief?
>
> Or that the past will always win
>> A glory from its being far;
>> And orb into the perfect star
> We saw not, when we moved therein?

(XXIV)

Tennyson's *abba* rhyme-scheme is relatively unusual in English poetry. The much commoner *abab* quatrain communicates a clear sense of progression, but with an *abba* rhyme-scheme the end of the verse seems not to escape its beginnings. John Lennard has written of the way that Tennyson's verse-form works to embody an inescapable grief:

> the mirror symmetry of the rhyme would split the quatrain in the middle, *ab–ba*, but the central – *bb* – couplet is fastened across the breaking point, giving to the lines the tension of an arch and the sense of coming back to the ground (or even coming home, like a return to the tonic key in music) at the end of each stanza . . . .. Grief, the rhyme-scheme suggests, is not really changed by the passage of time: Tennyson wrote *In Memoriam* over 17 years and in its form – the self-contained stanzas and repeated iambic tetrameter – his unremitting grief lived out through the repetitious form. In many lines the symmetry of rhyme is reflected in a central caesura splitting the line symmetrically 2–2. Both are prosodic expressions of the rocking movement of grief, back and forth; and one could say that the continuity of form expresses the persistence of Tennyson's grief; but it might be the other way around. Tennyson's grief was remarkably prolonged, and he wrote the earliest of the 'In Memoriam' poems within a few days of hearing that Hallam was dead. In them the form, and the grieving rock of the lines and quatrains, is from the first fully achieved: so the question becomes whether Tennyson instinctively divined the form that he would need for the extended grief he was just entering, or whether the form he seized upon in his first grief came to trap him within that grief, and to prolong its grip on him.

(1996, pp.32, 161)

Harry's grief, too, does not simply fade with time, it resurfaces at different periods of his life and *Harry Potter*, like *In Memoriam*, explores the cyclic nature of grief.

Tennyson's chiastic form chimes with the experience of mourning: 'the *abba* form enacts in the outer rhymes the mourner's desire to "travel" rather than to "arrive," to continue missing Hallam rather than to cease loving him. The fourth line circles back to the first line via the rhyme; the stanza returns to its beginning; and thus like the thoughts of the mourner "recedes from its affirmations"' (Gates, 2004 [1999], p.231). The chiastic structure of Tennyson's verse, and the pairing of lines and sections over the poem as a whole, enact the stasis of grief, but the speaker does – painfully – move forward to a truth 'borne with bier and pall'. In the poem's 'sport of random sun and shade' (Epilogue) the speaker comes finally to an ecstatic vision of the person they have loved and lost as eternally present:

> Thy voice is on the rolling air;
>> I hear thee where the waters run;
>> Thou standest in the rising sun,
> And in the setting thou art fair.
>
> What art thou then? I cannot guess;
>> But tho' I seem in star and flower
>> To feel thee some diffusive power,
> I do not therefore love thee less:
>
> My love involves the love before;
>> My love is vaster passion now;
>> Tho' mix'd with God and Nature thou,
> I seem to love thee more and more.
>
> Far off thou art, but ever nigh;
>> I have thee still, and I rejoice;
>> I prosper, circled with thy voice;
> I shall not lose thee tho' I die.

(CXXX)

The speaker's finding of his beloved friend as present in the eternal is very close to the comfort offered by the quotation from William Penn with which *Deathly Hallows* opens: 'Death is but crossing the world, as friends do the seas; they live in one another still. For they must needs be present, that love and live in that which is omnipresent. In this divine glass they see face to face; and their converse is free, as well as pure. This is the comfort of friends, that though they may be said to die, yet their friendship and society are, in the best sense, ever present, because immortal.' *Deathly Hallows*, like *In Memoriam*, holds out the hope that love once given, will never be lost. In the epigraph to *Deathly Hallows*, as in Tennyson's ecstatic vision, faith in 'that which is omnipresent' helps the bereaved to believe that death will not obliterate love: 'Love wins . . .. It does win; we know it wins. When the person dies, love isn't turned off like a faucet. It is an amazingly resilient part of us' (Rowling, 2010b).

Tennyson's speaker expresses a mystical understanding of his love as present in, and entwined with, nature: 'I hear thee where the waters run;/ Thou standest in the rising sun'. These lines may lie behind the turning point in *Deathly Hallows* when Harry watches the dawn over the sea and – in a passage that is both unusually mystical and unusually responsive to natural beauty – finally comes to peace and understanding: 'he looked out over the ocean and felt closer, this dawn, than ever before, closer to the heart of it all . . .. Harry stood quite still, eyes glazed, watching the place where a bright gold rim of dazzling sun was rising over the horizon' (Chap 24, p.391). The spiritual intensity of this passage is strengthened by the way that, as Harry communes with the Dumbledore 'in his head', the headmaster's characteristic gesture of putting his fingertips together is, for the first time, compared with hands joined in prayer.

In Memoriam, like *Harry Potter*, ends on a note of hope with an epilogue that celebrates the marriage of Tennyson's sister. The movement of Tennyson's elegy is typical of the form: 'the grief of the opening has passed at the close into triumph: at first the singer thinks only of loss and death, and at last his eyes are fixed upon the vision of a new and greater life' (Bradley, 2004 [1901], p.123). This vision is described in words that recall *Harry Potter*'s closing words:

> And hear at times a sentinel
> > Who moves about from place to place,
> > And whispers to the worlds of space,
> In the deep night, that all is well.
>
> And all is well, tho' faith and form
> > Be sunder'd in the night of fear;
> > Well roars the storm to those that hear
> A deeper voice across the storm,
>
> > . . .While thou, dear spirit, happy star,
> > O'erlook'st the tumult from afar,
> And smilest, knowing all is well.
>
> (CXXVI, CXXVII)

The phrase thrice repeated as *In Memoriam* concludes – 'all is well' – is virtually identical to the three words that close *Harry Potter*: 'all was well' (Epilogue, p.607). Both texts echo Julian of Norwich's famous affirmation of faithful hope that 'all shall be well, and all shall be well, and all manner of thing shall be well' (Garrett, 2010, p.100). In Julian's thirteenth 'showing' she receives this answer to the problem of sin:

> In my folly, before this time, I often wondered why, by the great foresee-ing wisdom of God, sin was not prevented, for then, I thought, all should have been well . . .. But Jesus in this vision informed me of all that I needed . . .. He answered in these words and said, 'Sin is necessary . . . but all shall be well and all manner of thing shall be well.'
>
> (1978 [1373], p.60)

As noted above, Rowling had said (prior to the publication of *Deathly Hallows*) that the final word of the series would be 'scar', a symbol of the wounds that time cannot heal (2008a; 2007e). It is perhaps a sign of how the passage of time had, in the end, softened grief that her text, like Tennyson's, ends instead with an affirmation, a calm echo of Julian's transcendent vision: 'all was well.'

WRITING TO REACH YOU: LITERARY ALLUSION AND MEMORY

Allusion – such as *Harry Potter*'s connections with *In Memoriam* – is one specific example of the general truth that texts create a relationship between those who write and those who read them. Rowling has spoken of the way in which 'the experience of reading requires that the imaginations of the author and the reader work together to create the story' (2011b): 'When you do that, the reader and the author are having sort of a conversation. . . . the reader is very aware of what's in the author's mind' (1999g). Stephen Greenblatt considers all literary study an attempt to form a relationship with the past: he opens his *Shakespearean Negotiations* (1988) with the words 'I began with the desire to speak with the dead' (p.1). This perception of reading as a form of conversation is one that Rowling shares. In her Harvard Commencement Address she spoke of Seneca (whose work she encountered as an undergraduate) as someone she 'met' (2008d) when she studied his texts. She also replied to the question whether one job of a writer is to provide companionship, with an enthusiastic affirmation: 'yes, yes, it is, and certainly, I discovered I wasn't alone through books, I think, arguably more than I did through friendships in my early days, 'cause I was quite an introverted child, and it was through reading that I realised I wasn't alone on all sorts of levels' (2005g).

There is one text in *Harry Potter* that Harry reads particularly carefully. When he finds his mother's letter in *Deathly Hallows* he concentrates first on the handwriting itself – the way that the 'g's are like his own ('each felt like a friendly little wave glimpsed from behind a veil') – and then imagines how 'her warm hand had once moved across this parchment, tracing ink into these letters' (Chap 10, p.150). The phrase 'warm hand' stresses both the immediacy of this experience – the way the text connects with the living person at the moment of composition – and its distance: that hand is now cold. This paradox of how a manuscript simultaneously conveys a sense of closeness to and separation from its author also forms its own connection with another text; for it echoes the arresting opening of John Keats' *Fall of Hyperion*. Keats writes about the power that writing has to communicate ideas and dreams; to form imaginative connections between people across time:

> Fanatics have their dreams, wherewith they weave
> A paradise for a sect, the savage too
> From forth the loftiest fashion of his sleep
> Guesses at Heaven; pity these have not

Traced upon vellum or wild Indian leaf
The shadows of melodious utterance.
But bare of laurel they live, dream, and die;
For Poesy alone can tell her dreams,
With the fine spell of words alone can save
Imagination from the sable charm
And dumb enchantment. Who alive can say,
'Thou art no Poet; may'st not tell thy dreams'?
Since every man whose soul is not a clod
Hath visions, and would speak, if he had loved
And been well nurtured in his mother tongue.
Whether the dream now purposed to rehearse
Be poet's or fanatic's will be known
When this warm scribe my hand is in the grave.

(1995 [1819], ll.1–18)

Keats writes of 'this warm scribe my hand' inscribing words that are 'traced upon vellum' as *Deathly Hallows* describes Lily's 'warm hand' 'tracing ink' upon parchment. In both cases the written word has a quasi-magical ability to connect the living with the dead. Keats uses strikingly magical imagery for writing in this passage – of the ability of the 'fine spell of words' to rescue imagination 'from the sable charm/ And dumb enchantment.'

Keats also imagines, as Rowling does, that everyone must feel the pull of authorship as strongly as he: 'every man whose soul is not a clod/ Hath visions, and would speak.' Rowling has spoken likewise of writing as a vocation she assumes all share: 'as soon as I knew that people *wrote* books – they didn't just arrive – I don't know. . . out of nowhere – like plants – I knew that's what I wanted to do. I can't ever remember not wanting to be a writer. It's a bit mysterious to me as well, but . . . .. And yet, it *isn't* mysterious to me. You see, I can't honestly understand why *you* don't want to be a writer. I can't understand why the whole world doesn't want to be a writer. What's better than it?' (2001e). The ability of Lily's writing to reach through and touch the lives of Harry and Snape after her death intimates the power that all writing has to connect writers and readers.

Reading Lily's letter is 'like listening to a half-remembered voice' (Chap 10, p.150) and all reading is a form of communication with those who have gone before: 'a friendly little wave glimpsed from behind a veil.' Allusion deepens this communication for it forms an interpretative network – the writer alludes to their own reading, and the reader (in the moment of spotting the connection) shares with the writer in their own experience of reading the earlier work. Allusion is the reaching of hands between authors and readers across time and space: 'this seems one of the most profound experiences available in reading, the realization of Alberto Manguel's fanciful notion that in a library, "One book calls to another unexpectedly, creating alliances across different cultures and centuries." Charming as it is to think of books conversing with each other, it is only people, readers and writers, who can do this'

(Hamlin, 2013, p.81). Hogwarts' books, however, can converse with their readers in a peculiarly literal way: the books in the Restricted Section of Hogwarts' library scream when opened illicitly, Harry and Ron's homework planners order them around ('*do it today or later you'll pay!*' [*Phoenix*, Chap 23, p.443]), Riddle's diary writes back to those who write in it, and when Hermione snaps shut *Magick Moste Evile* in frustration 'it let out a ghostly wail' (*Half-Blood Prince*, Chap 18, p.357). It is perhaps a sign of the importance of allusion to *Harry Potter* that it creates a world in which books *can* 'call to another unexpectedly' and when Harry enters Hogwarts' library at night he hears the books whispering to each other.

VOICES BEHIND THE VEIL

Harry sees his mother's writing as 'a friendly little wave glimpsed from behind a veil' and death is often described as a veil in *Harry Potter*. The dead beloved of Cadmus Peverell, who is raised to a half-life by the Resurrection Stone, remains cold and sad and 'separated from him as by a veil' (*Deathly Hallows*, Chap 21, p.332). In a chapter entitled 'Beyond the Veil' Sirius falls, fatefully, 'behind the veil' (*Phoenix*, Chap 35, p.711). This euphemism for death is present likewise in *In Memoriam*:

> O life as futile, then, as frail!
>   O for thy voice to soothe and bless!
>   What hope of answer, or redress?
> Behind the veil, behind the veil.

(LVI)[6]

This section of *In Memoriam* despairs at death as the universal doom and cries out for 'thy voice' to speak comfort and reassurance to him that death is not the end. The voice does not materialise but the implication is that the answer, if answer there is, will only be known 'behind the veil.' Tennyson's sense of an afterlife as voices that lie 'behind the veil' is shared by the end of *Phoenix*. Harry enters a room in the Department of Mysteries with a veiled archway on a dais, and he is transfixed by the veil and the voices he thinks he can hear speaking from behind it.

  The only person who can bring any kind of solace to Harry's grief at Sirius' loss when he falls 'behind the veil' is Luna. Luna – a light in the darkness – not only embodies that fact that bereavement is a shared, not a unique, fate; but also communicates some kind of hope in the afterlife. She, too, has heard what Harry remembers as 'voices behind the veil': "'you heard them, just behind the veil, didn't you?'" (Chap 38, p.761). Luna starts this episode expressing her confidence that her belongings will be returned to her, a comic parallel for her hopeful faith that the dead, too, are not lost to the living (Spencer, 2015, p.98). Out of the mists of Harry's grief he realises that he is not alone: Luna has lost loved ones too. Harry's empathy for Luna is one reason that he feels suddenly more able to bear his suffocating grief; but it is also that the companionship she brings enables his hope in another kind of companionship – of voices that speak 'behind the veil.'

Ricks argues that the allusions in *In Memoriam* create a form of textual companionship to compensate for that which Tennyson has lost through Hallam's death (2002, pp.179–216). Literary allusions for Rowling, likewise, not only link her to other writers but also memorialise her love for the most literary person in her life: her mother. Ricks has written of all allusion as 'the generous spending of an inheritance' (2002, p.9) and this is true in a peculiarly personal way for Rowling, for she owes her love of literature to her mother (2001e): 'she was the one who read to us when we were little, filled the house with books, loved discussing her favourite novels and never sat down without something to read, so I would have to say [that I owe her] a love of literature' (2005h). Rowling's literary allusions form more than one act of memory.

Asked whether her own writing is a form of 'Resurrection Stone' Rowling replied 'yes, of course' (2008b).

Note

1 As might be expected, given the pivotal nature of the fourth novel in the chiastic structure of the series, *Goblet* also has a self-sacrificing mother (Mrs Crouch).
2 This is not a direct quotation but an assessment by an audience member of Rowling's main argument in her 'Morality and Mortality in Harry Potter' talk, 10 Feb 2014 (Fraser, 2014).
3 *Harry Potter and the Gifts of Death* is the title of the final *Harry Potter* novel in Russian, Italian, Bulgarian, Afrikaans and Albanian (Harry Potter Wiki, 2016b).
4 As reported by an audience member at Rowling's 'Morality and Mortality in Harry Potter' talk, 10 Feb 2014 (Thakrar, 2014).
5 A very specific example of this is that the date Lavender Brown is dreading is '"Friday the sixteenth of October"' (*Azkaban*, Chap 6, p.80). This is not only the date of Rowling's wedding to her ex-husband but also the correct *day* of the week, for Rowling was married in 1992 (when the 16th October fell on a Friday) although in the 'world' of *Harry Potter Azkaban* takes place in 1993 (when it fell on a Saturday).
6 With thanks to Beth Sutton-Ramspeck for this connection.

Afterword

If it's true that Harry got people reading – anyone who wouldn't otherwise have enjoyed books or started to enjoy books, then that's the best thing anyone could say to me.

(Rowling, 2007e)

Rowling has advised aspiring authors to 'read as much as you can, I'd say, read anything' (2001e). Hogwarts boasts a magnificent library – 'tens of thousands of books; thousands of shelves' (*Philosopher's Stone*, Chap 12, p.145) – and, as this book has argued, *Harry Potter* is inspired by Rowling's own reading. As a child Rowling was nourished by books – 'basically, I lived for books, and was sustained by literary characters with whom I could identify' (2013b) – and books also sustain her own literary creations. *Harry Potter*'s literary inheritance is hinted at by the power and importance of books in its plots (Hopkins, 2003). When Harry mocks the idea that Riddle's diary might be dangerous, Ron tells him of books impounded by the Ministry that burned out their readers' eyes, compelled them to spout limericks or were literally un-put-down-able (*Chamber*, Chap 13, p.172). The plots of *Chamber* and *Half-Blood Prince* both revolve around a book – a book that is transformed by its reader, and which in turn transforms the reader.

Rowling has written, 'I lived in books. That's where all writers begin' (Twitter, 24 Nov 2015). She is 'someone for whom reading is the stuff of life' (2012c) and she remains strongly attached to works she has read. Rowling has said that what she would most like readers to take from *Harry Potter* is 'what I take away from my favourite books, which is the knowledge that there is always somewhere you can go that you love' (2012f). Rowling brings her own loved literary places, her own reading, and the allusive and symbolic techniques of the literary tradition that she loves, to her own literary creation.

Rowling has said that she sees magic as a metaphor – 'a beautiful metaphor for other things in life' (2001b) – and she has drawn attention to literary aspects of *Harry Potter*. She has spoken, for example, of how the novels echo Harry's own development in their structure. The newly international focus of

Goblet is 'symbolic. Harry's horizons are literally and metaphorically widening as he grows older' (2000j). When taken to task by a young fan for Hedwig's death, Rowling explained that 'the loss of Hedwig represented a loss of innocence and security . . . killing her marked the end of childhood' (2007f). (And rather suitably, the Sisters of St Hedwig – the saint after whom Harry's owl is named – were established to educate orphan children.) Likewise Rowling explains the reason for the existence of Slytherin in Hogwarts:

> the deeper answer, the non-flippant answer, would be that you have to embrace all of a person, you have to take them with their flaws, and everyone's got them . . . . [In addition] I wanted them to correspond roughly to the four elements. So Gryffindor is fire, Ravenclaw is air, Hufflepuff is earth, and Slytherin is water, hence the fact that their common room is under the lake. So again, it was this idea of harmony and balance, that you had four necessary components and by integrating them you would make a very strong place.
>
> (2005c)

ROWLING AND DICKENS

Allusion is a crucial part of *Harry Potter*'s literariness. When Rowling finished writing *Deathly Hallows* she turned to one, final, allusion and quoted the preface of *David Copperfield* to explain how it felt to have completed all seven novels and be 'mourning the loss of this world that I had written for so long and loved so much' (2007e):

> Charles Dickens put it better than I ever could: 'It would concern the reader little, perhaps, to know how sorrowfully the pen is laid down at the close of a two-years' imaginative task; or how an Author feels as if he were dismissing some portion of himself into the shadowy world, when a crowd of the creatures of his brain are going from him for ever.'
>
> (2007b)

Rowling turns here to the companionableness of allusion to express the experience of authorship, and it is significant that she chooses Dickens to do this, for he is one of the writers whose experience of authorship relates most closely to her own. The death of Little Nell was a national event in 1841, as the possible and actual deaths of *Deathly Hallows* were in 2007.

Dickens is one of Rowling's favourite authors (2012a, 2012e) and he is the most famous English author to have published his novels in serial form. *Harry Potter* echoes Dickens in its orphan hero (Granger, 2009, pp.17–9), its exuberant naming and in the story of Snape's unrequited love (see Chapter 7). It also echoes Dickens in its serial publication. It was originally planned for the novels to be published yearly (as the first three were) and Rowling has spoken of these 'instalments' as a serial publication of a single novel: 'one huge novel that has been divided up for the reader's convenience into seven' (2002b); 'I call it one big book' (2005c).

Serial publication affects the way a story is experienced by its audience. As Dickens critics have noted, it also affects the dynamic between the author and reader, fostering 'a public more delicately responsive, who made their views known during the progress of a novel both by writing to him and by reducing or increasing their purchases. Through serial publication an author could recover something of the intimate relationship between story-teller and audience which existed in the ages of the sagas and Chaucer' (Butt and Tillotson, 1957, p.16; see also: Jump, 1972). In the case of both Dickens' novels and Rowling's, the staggered revelations of an on-going story helped to foster their readership's investment in the narrative. Both Dickens and Rowling created a fan base whose enthusiasm was intensified by the delay between each instalment, which enabled them to discuss and predict the outcome of the story among themselves.

Regular publication encourages communal consumption of the texts as anticipated 'events' – and Dickens' novels (like Rowling's) were often read aloud: one charwoman's landlord read Dickens' latest instalment to her on the first Monday of every month (Patten, 2011, p.530).[1] Robert Patten writes that Dickens '*belonged*' to his readers and that this 'belonging was enhanced by the gap between instalments and the long time it took for the novel to run its course; the characters and events were talked about, predictions were made, old parts were reread for clues, and in countless other ways the events in the novel became part of people's lives' (2011, p.530). It is a description that could have been written to describe the experience of Rowling's readership. *Harry Potter* has, for many, formed the basis of social, storytelling gatherings in the way that Dickens' novels did in nineteenth-century England, and folk tales and bardic song did in pre-literate societies (Falconer, 2009, pp.60–61).

The publication of *Harry Potter* over a ten-year period meant that Rowling, like Dickens or an oral storyteller, could be both responsive to, and sustained by, her audience. This influence is visible in the novels themselves. *Potter*-mania first became visible after the publication of *Azkaban* in 1999: this was the period when on-line fan sites began to proliferate (MuggleNet, for example, started in 1999) and publishers confidently printed the novels in far larger numbers. In Germany, for example, the first edition print run of *Azkaban* was around 30,000, while for *Goblet* it was over thirty times that (Fenske, 2006, p.451). This massive surge in popularity is inscribed within the form of the books themselves. While the novels up to and including *Azkaban* average 264 pages in length, the final four novels average 654 pages each (an increase of almost 250 per cent). After the publication of *Azkaban* Rowling is newly confident that there is an appetite for as many pages of *Potter* as possible, and as surely as an oral storyteller viewing rapt faces, she knew that the story she was telling was going to find an attentive audience.

DRAGON'S BLOOD

This book has aimed to open up the width and depth of *Harry Potter*'s allusiveness and in so doing open up new perspectives on the text. The transformative pleasure of discovering literary depth is something C. S. Lewis describes in a way that resonates both within his own writing and, perhaps, within *Harry Potter*:

> I did not in the least feel that I was getting in more quantity or better quality a pleasure I had already known. It was more as if a cupboard which one had hitherto valued as a place for hanging coats proved one day, when you opened the door, to lead to the garden of the Hesperides; as if a food one had enjoyed for the taste proved one day to enable you (like dragon's blood) to understand the speech of birds.
>
> (1982, p.121)

Rowling has, as discussed in the Introduction, compared one of C. S. Lewis's imagined portals between worlds – the Wood between the Worlds in *The Magician's Nephew* – with a library. This passage suggests that Lewis also saw his fictional portals as metaphors for the transportative pleasure of reading, for when – four years later – Lewis published his first Narnia book his readers were able to join with him in that transformational moment when 'a place for hanging coats proved one day, when you opened the door, to lead to the garden of the Hesperides'.

Harry Potter may also draw on Lewis's description of reading in an unspoken undercurrent to one of its magical objects: 'as if a food one had enjoyed for the taste proved one day to enable you (like dragon's blood) to understand the speech of birds.' Harry reads about Dumbledore's achievements on his first chocolate frog card: alchemical innovations with Nicholas Flamel, defeating Grindelwald in 1945 and his '*discovery of the twelve uses of dragon's blood*' (*Philosopher's Stone*, Chap 6, p.77). The information about Nicholas Flamel will prove crucial to the plot of *Philosopher's Stone*, but this also provides the reader with a further clue about the importance of the rest of the card's information. This chocolate frog card carries clues about the series as whole. The parallel between the date of the allies' defeat of Nazi Germany and the date for the defeat of Grindelwald, for example, suggests some of *Harry Potter*'s larger ambitions for resonance between the magical and Muggle worlds (Rowling, 2005c).

The oft-mentioned, but never explained, twelve uses of dragon's blood are also a clue: a clue about the allusive way in which *Harry Potter* is written. The magical properties of dragon's blood were not invented by Rowling, but remind the reader of the way in which her imagined world is entwined with the history of traditional folklore. Rowling sees her own narrative method – of reworking existing material, and patching together the invented with the traditional – as in keeping with British folklore's own genesis: 'I've taken *horrible* liberties with folklore and mythology, but I'm quite unashamed about that, because British folklore and British mythology is a totally bastard mythology. You know, we've been invaded by people, we've appropriated their gods, we've taken their mythical creatures, and we've soldered them all together to make, what I would say, is one of the richest folklores in the world, because it's so varied' (2005g). The traditional ability of dragon's blood mentioned above by Lewis, that it enables the taker to understand the speech of birds, is never mentioned in *Harry Potter*. But in a subtle folkloric echo Dumbledore does indeed appear to have the magical skill traditionally conferred by dragon's blood, when he converses with Fawkes: '"We will need," Dumbledore said very quietly to the bird, "a warning." There was a flash of fire and the phoenix had gone' (*Phoenix*, Chap 22, p.415).

The wardrobe into Narnia is Lewis' explicit connection of his enchanted world with the way that literature opens up new horizons in the imagination: 'a place for hanging coats proved one day, when you opened the door, to lead to the garden of the Hesperides'. Rowling, too, has left a clue to the link between the joy of reading and the entrance to her magical world. The wall of the Leaky Cauldron – the first portal that Harry takes between the mundane and the Wizarding world – is on London's Charing Cross Road, a road 'famous for its bookshops, both modern and antiquarian. This is why I wanted it to be the place where those in the know go to enter a different world' (2015m).

Note

1 For evidence of *Harry Potter* being read aloud, see Sunderland et al., 2016, Chapter 6.

Bibliography

This book's quotation of Rowling's interviews has been assisted by the dedication of those who have ensured that they remain available on the web. My particular gratitude is due to Deborah Skinner and Lisa Bunker, who founded the invaluable website 'Accio Quote!'

All internet sources in this bibliography were accessed on 15 September 2016.

Acocella, J. (2000) 'Under the Spell', *New Yorker*, 31 July. Available at: http://www.newyorker.com/archive/2000/07/31/2000_07_31_074_TNY_LIBRY_000021373

Alton, A. H. (2003) 'Generic Fusion and the Mosaic of *Harry Potter*', in Heilman, E. E. (ed.) *Harry Potter's World: Multidisciplinary Critical Perspectives*. New York: Routledge Falmer, pp.141–62.

Andrade, G. (2008) 'Hermione Granger as Girl Sleuth', in Cornelius, M. G. and Gregg, M. E. (eds) *Nancy Drew and Her Sister Sleuths: Essays on the Fiction of Girl Detectives*. London: McFarland, pp.164–78.

Andrewes, L. (1592) *The Wonderfull Combate (for Gods glorie and Mans saluation) betweene Christ and Satan*. London: Richard Smith.

Arden, H. and Lorenz, K. (2003) 'The Harry Potter Stories and French Arthurian Romance', *Arthuriana*, 13.2, pp.54–68.

Ariosto, L. (2009 [1532]) *Orlando Furioso: A New Verse Translation*. Slavitt, D. R. (trans.) Cambridge, MA: Belknap Press.

Asher-Perrin, E. (2013) 'Neville Longbottom Is the Most Important Person in Harry Potter – And Here's Why', Tor.com, 19 Nov. Available at: http://www.tor.com/blogs/2013/11/neville-longbottom-is-the-most-important-person-in-harry-potter

Auerbach, E. (2003 [1946]) *Mimesis: The Representation of Reality in Western Literature*. Princeton, NJ: Princeton University Press.

Augustine (1955 [c.397–8, 421]) *Augustine: Confessions and Enchiridion*. Outler, A. C. (ed. and trans.) London: SCM Press.

Aulen, G. (1931) *Christus Victor: An Historical Study of the Three Main Types of the Idea of the Atonement*. Herbert, A. G. (trans.) London: Society for Promoting Christian Knowledge.

Austen, J. (1966 [1816]) *Emma*. Blythe, R. (ed.) Harmondsworth: Penguin.

Austen, J. (1966 [1814]) *Mansfield Park*. Tanner, T. (ed.) Harmondsworth: Penguin.

Austen, J. (1995) *Jane Austen's Letters*. Le Faye, D. (ed.) 3rd edn. Oxford: Oxford University Press.

Austen, J. (1995 [1818]) *Northanger Abbey*. Butler, M. (ed.) Harmondsworth: Penguin.

Austen, J. (1995 [1813]) *Pride and Prejudice*. Jones, V. (ed.) Harmondsworth: Penguin.

Austen-Leigh, J. E. (2002 [1869/71]) *Memoir of Jane Austen and Other Family Recollections*. Sutherland, K. (ed.) Oxford: Oxford University Press.

Bale, J. (1986) *The Complete Plays of John Bale*. Happé, P (ed.) 2 vols. Bury St Edmunds: D.S. Brewer.

Bartel, T. (2015) 'The Canonization of Neville Longbottom: The Development of Identity in Rowling's Supporting Cast', in Pazdziora, J. P. and Snell, M. (eds) *Ravenclaw Reader: Seeking the Artistry and Meaning of J.K. Rowling's Hogwarts Saga – Essays from the St Andrews University Harry Potter Conference*. Oklahoma City: Unlocking Press, pp.145–57.

Beadle, R. (ed.) (1982 [c.1470]) *The York Plays*. London: Edward Arnold.

Bilson, T. (1599) *The effect of certaine Sermons touching The Full redemption of mankind by the death and bloud of Christ Jesus*. London.

Boll, J. (2013) 'Harry Potter's Archetypal Journey', in Steveker, L., Berndt, K. and Nelson, C. (eds) *Heroism in the Harry Potter Series*, Ashgate Studies in Childhood, 1700 to the Present. Farnham: Ashgate, pp.85–104.

Botting, F. and Townshend, D. (eds) (2004) *Gothic: Critical Concepts in Literary and Cultural Studies*. 4 vols. London: Routledge.

Bradley, A. C. (2004 [1901]) 'The Structure and Effect of *In Memoriam*', in Gray, E. (ed.) *In Memoriam*. 2nd edn. New York: W. W. Norton & Company, pp.122–34.

Brown, S. A. (2012) *A Familiar Compound Ghost: Allusion and the Uncanny*. Manchester: Manchester University Press.

Bullein, W. (1888) *A Dialogue against the Fever Pestilence*. Bullen, M. W. and Bullen, A. H. (eds) EETS extra series 52. London: Early English Texts Society.

Burrow, C. (1993) *Epic Romance: Homer to Milton*. Oxford: Oxford University Press.

Butt, J. and Tillotson, K. (1957) *Dickens at Work*. London: Methuen.

Campbell, J. and Moyers, B. D. (1988) *The Power of Myth*. New York: Doubleday.

Carey, B. (2003) 'Hermione and the House-Elves: The Literary and Historical Contexts of J.K. Rowling's Antislavery Campaign', in Anatol, G. L. (ed.) *Reading Harry Potter: Critical Essays*. Westport: Praeger, pp.103–15.

Carroll, L. (1963 [1871]) *Alice in Wonderland and Through the Looking Glass*. New York: Grosset & Dunlap.

Caselli, D. (2004) 'Reading Intertextuality. The Natural and the Legitimate: Intertextuality in "Harry Potter"', in Lesnik-Oberstein, K. (ed.) *Children's Literature: New Approaches*. Basingstoke: Palgrave Macmillan, pp.168–88.

Charlesworth, J. H. (ed.) (1983) *The Old Testament Pseudepigrapha*. 2 vols. London: Darton, Longman & Todd.

Chaucer, G. (1987) *The Riverside Chaucer*. Benson, L. D., Robinson, F. N. et al. (eds) Oxford: Oxford University Press.

Colbert, D. (2007) *The Magical Worlds of Harry Potter: A Treasury of Myths, Legends and Fascinating Facts*. London: Michael O'Mara Books.

Coleridge, S. T. (1863) *The Poems of Samuel Taylor Coleridge*. Coleridge, D. and S. (eds) London: Edward Moxon & Co.

Cooper, H. (2004) *The English Romance in Time: Transforming Motifs from Geoffrey of Monmouth to the Death of Shakespeare*. Oxford: Oxford University Press.

Dickens, C. (1985 [1859]) *A Tale of Two Cities*. Woodcock, G. (ed.) Harmondsworth: Penguin.

Dry, H. (1977) 'Syntax and Point of View in Jane Austen's "Emma"', *Studies in Romanticism*, 16.1, pp.87–99.

Dunne, J. A. (2015) 'The Death of Death in the Death of the Boy Who Lived: The Morality of Mortality in Harry Potter', in Pazdziora, J. P. and Snell, M. (eds) *Ravenclaw Reader: Seeking the Artistry and Meaning of J.K. Rowling's Hogwarts Saga – Essays from the St Andrews University Harry Potter Conference*. Oklahoma City: Unlocking Press, pp.31–46.

Dupree, M. G. (2011) 'Severus Snape and the Standard Book of Spells: Ancient Tongues in the Wizarding World', in Reagin, N. R. (ed.) *Harry Potter and History*. Hoboken, NJ: Wiley, pp.39–53.

Edinburgh-flats (2016) 'Edinburgh Landmarks and Attractions'. Available at: http://www.edinburgh-flats.com/landmarks-and-attractions/

Eliot, T. S. (2004 [1936]) '*In Memoriam*', in Gray, E. (ed.) *In Memoriam*. 2nd edn. New York: W. W. Norton & Company, pp.135–9.

Falconer, R. (2009) *The Crossover Novel: Contemporary Children's Fiction and Its Adult Readership*. New York: Routledge.

Fenske, C. (2006) *Muggles, Monsters and Magicians: A Literary Analysis of the Harry Potter Series*. Frankfurt: Peter Lang.

Fichter, A. (1982) *Poets Historical: Dynastic Epic in the Renaissance*. New Haven, CT: Yale University Press.

Fidelia (2008) 'Chaucer, J.K. Rowling, and All of Us', *The Leaky Cauldron*. Available at: http://www.the-leaky-cauldron.org/features/essays/issue24/Chaucer

Fish, S. (1997 [1967]) *Surprised by Sin: The Reader in Paradise Lost*. 2nd edn. London: Macmillan.

Fraser, H. (2014) 'JK Rowling at Exeter College, Oxford', Storynory, 10 Feb. Available at: http://www.storynory.com/2014/02/10/jk-rowling-at-exeter-college-oxford/

Fraser, L. (2001) *Conversations with JK Rowling*. New York: Scholastic.

Friedman, A. B. and Osberg, R. H. (1977) 'Gawain's Girdle as Traditional Symbol', *The Journal of American Folklore*, 90.357, pp.301–15.

Furnivall, F. J., Brock, E. and Clouston, W. A. (eds) (1872) *Originals and Analogues of some of Chaucer's Canterbury Tales*. London: Chaucer Society.

Garber, M. (2003) *Quotation Marks*. London: Routledge.

Garrett, G. (2010) *One Fine Potion: The Literary Magic of Harry Potter*. Waco, TX: Baylor University Press.

Gates, S. (2004 [1999]) 'The Stanza Form of *In Memoriam*', in Gray, E. (ed.) *In Memoriam*. 2nd edn. New York: W. W. Norton & Company, pp.229–42.

Granger, J. (2008a) *Deathly Hallows Lectures: The Hogwarts Professor Explains Harry's Final Adventure*. Allentown, PA: Zossima Press.

Granger, J. (2008b) The Aeschylus Epigraph in 'Deathly Hallows', Hogwarts Professor, 20 Oct. Available at: http://www.hogwartsprofessor.com/the-aeschylus-epigraph-in-deathly-hallows/

Granger, J. (2009) *Harry Potter's Bookshelf: The Great Books Behind the Hogwarts Adventures*. New York: Berkley Publishing Group.

Granger, J. (2011) 'On Turtleback Tales and Asterisks: Picturing the Harry Potter Novels and Their Many Interrelationships', in Prinzi, T. (ed.) *Harry Potter for Nerds: Essays for Fans, Academics, and Lit Geeks*. Oklahoma City: Unlocking Press, pp.37–81.

Granger, J. (2015) 'The World Turned Inside-Out and Right-Side Up: What *Harry Potter* Teaches Us about Reading, Writing, and Literary Criticism', in Pazdziora, J. P. and Snell, M. (eds) *Ravenclaw Reader: Seeking the Artistry and Meaning of J.K. Rowling's Hogwarts Saga – Essays from the St Andrews University Harry Potter Conference*. Oklahoma City: Unlocking Press, pp.203–24.

Gray, D. (ed.) (1992) *English Medieval Religious Lyrics*. Exeter: Exeter University Press.

Greenblatt, S. (1988) *Shakespearean Negotiations: The Circulation of Social Energy*. Oxford: Clarendon Press.

Gresseth, G. K. (1970) 'The Homeric Sirens', *Transactions and Proceedings of the American Philological Association*, 101, pp.203–18.

Grimes, M. K. (2002) 'Harry Potter: Fairy Tale Prince, Real Boy, and Archetypal Hero', in Whited, L. A. (ed.) *The Ivory Tower and Harry Potter: Perspectives on a Literary Phenomenon*. Columbia, MO: University of Missouri Press, pp.89–122.

Groom, N. (2012) *The Gothic: A Very Short Introduction*. Oxford: Oxford University Press.

Groves, P. (2012) *Grace: The Cruciform Love of God*. Norwich: Canterbury Press.

Gruss, S. (2013) 'The Diffusion of Gothic Conventions in *Harry Potter and the Order of the Phoenix* (2003/2007)', in Steveker, L., Berndt, K. and Nelson, C. (eds) *Heroism in the Harry Potter Series*, Ashgate Studies in Childhood, 1700 to the Present. Farnham: Ashgate, pp. 39–54.

Hamlin, H. (2013) *The Bible in Shakespeare*. Oxford: Oxford University Press.

Hardy, E. B. (2011) 'Horcruxes in Faerie Land: Edmund Spenser's Influence on Voldemort's Efforts to Elude Death', in Prinzi, T. (ed.) *Harry Potter for Nerds: Essays for Fans, Academics, and Lit Geeks*. Oklahoma City: Unlocking Press, pp.225–40.

Hardy, T. (1985 [1874]) *Far from the Madding Crowd*. Blythe, R. (ed.) Harmondsworth: Penguin.

Hardy, T. (1985 [1886]) *The Mayor of Casterbridge*. Seymour-Smith, M. (ed.) Harmondsworth: Penguin.

Harry Potter Wiki (2016a) *Black Quill*. Available at: http://harrypotter.wikia.com/wiki/Black_Quill

Harry Potter Wiki (2016b) *List of titles of Harry Potter Books in other languages*. Available at: http://harrypotter.wikia.com/wiki/List_of_titles_of_Harry_Potter_books_in_other_languages

Harry Potter Wiki (2016c) *The Ballad of Nearly Headless Nick*. Available at: http://harrypotter.wikia.com/wiki/The_Ballad_of_Nearly_Headless_Nick

Harry Potter Wiki (2016d) *Thirteen*. Available at: http://harrypotter.wikia.com/wiki/Thirteen

Harry Potter Wiki (2016e) *Tom Riddle*. Available at: http://harrypotter.wikia.com/wiki/Tom_Riddle#Translations_of_the_name

Hatt, C. A. (2015) *God and the Gawain-Poet: Theology and Genre in Pearl, Cleanness, Patience and Sir Gawain and the Green Knight*. Cambridge: D.S. Brewer.

Herbert, J. A. (ed.) (1905) *Titus & Vespasian or The Destruction of Jerusalem in Rhymed Couplets*. London: Roxburghe Clube.

Hopkins, G. M. (1959) *Journals and Papers of Gerard Manley Hopkins*. House, Humphry and Storey, Graham (eds). London: Oxford University Press.

Hopkins, L. (2003) 'Harry Potter and the Acquisition of Knowledge', in Anatol, G. L. (ed.) *Reading Harry Potter: Critical Essays*. Westport, CT: Praeger, pp.25–34.

Hopkins, L. (2011) 'Harry and His Peers: Rowling's Web of Allusions', in Berndt, K. and Steveker, L. (eds.) *Heroism in the Harry Potter Series*. Farnham: Ashgate, pp.55–66.

Hunter, J. (2015) 'Folktale Structure, Aesthetic Satisfaction, and the Success of *Harry Potter*', in Pazdziora, J. P. and Snell, M. (eds) *Ravenclaw Reader: Seeking the Artistry and Meaning of J.K. Rowling's Hogwarts Saga – Essays from the St Andrews University Harry Potter Conference*. Oklahoma City: Unlocking Press, pp.95–114.

James, F. (2008) *Charles Lamb, Coleridge and Wordsworth: Reading Friendship in the 1790s*. Basingstoke: Palgrave Macmillan.

James, M. R. (ed. and trans.) (1924 [c.350]) 'The Gospel of Nicodemus', in *The Apocryphal New Testament*. Oxford: Clarendon Press. Available at: http://www. masterandmargarita.eu/estore/pdf/esen002_nicodemus.pdf

James, P. D. (1999) 'Emma Considered as a Detective Story', in *Time to Be in Earnest: A Fragment of Autobiography*. London: Faber and Faber, pp.250–66.

Joseph, A. (2014) '"What I did at the weekend" by Anjali, Age 22½', *Latimer*, 18 Feb. Available at: http://latimergroup.org/what-i-did-at-the-weekend-by-anjali-age-22-%C2%BD/

Julian of Norwich (1978 [1373]) *Julian of Norwich's Revelations of Divine Love: The Shorter Version ed. from B.L. Add. MS 3770*. Beer, F. (ed.) Heidelberg: Carl Winter.

Jump, J. D. (1972) *Dickens and His Readers*. Manchester: The John Rylands Library.

Keats, J. (1995 [1819]) *The Poems of John Keats*. Allott, M. (ed.) London: Longman.

Kelly, A. (2011) 'The Audience Expects: Penelope and Odysseus', in Minchin, E. (ed.) *Orality, Literacy and Performance in the Ancient World*. Leiden: Brill, pp.1–24.

Klaus, A. (2012) 'A Fairy-tale Crew? J. K. Rowling's Characters under Scrutiny', Hallett, C. J. and Huey, P. J. (eds.) *J. K. Rowling: Harry Potter, New Casebooks*. Basingstoke: Palgrave Macmillan, pp.22–35.

Kübler-Ross, E. (2009 [1969]) *On Death and Dying: What the Dying Have to Teach Doctors, Nurses, Clergy and Their Own Families*. 40th anniversary edn. London: Routledge.

Langland, W. (1995 [c.1370–90]) *The Vision of Piers Plowman: A Critical Edition of the B-Text based Trinity College Cambridge MS B.15.17*. Schmidt, A. V. C. (ed.) 2nd edn. London: Everyman.

Lee, J. S. (2011) 'There and Back Again: The Chiastic Structure of J. K. Rowling's Harry Potter Series', in Prinzi, T. (ed.) *Harry Potter for Nerds: Essays for Fans, Academics and Lit Geeks*. Oklahoma City: Unlocking Press, pp.17–35.

Lennard, J. (1996) *The Poetry Handbook: A Guide to Reading Poetry for Pleasure and Practical Criticism*. Oxford: Oxford University Press.

Lewis, C. S. (1982) *On Stories: and Other Essays on Literature*. Hooper, W. (ed.) New York: Harcourt Brace Jovanovich.

Lin, Y. (2012) 'What Are Some Amazing Hidden Plot Details Later Linked Together in the Harry Potter Series?', *Huffington Post*, 28 Sept. Available at: http://www. huffingtonpost.com/quora/what-are-some-amazing-hid_b_1921331.html

Lord, A. B. (2001) *The Singer of Tales*, Mitchell, S. and Nagy, G (eds.) 2nd edn. Cambridge, MA: Harvard University Press.

Lurie, A. (1999) 'Not for Muggles', *New York Review of Books*, 16 Dec, pp.6–8.

Luther, M. (2001 [1533]) *Sources and Contexts of The Book of Concord*. Kolb, R. and Nestingen, J. A. (eds) Minneapolis, MN: Fortress Press.

Machacek, G. (2007) 'Allusion', *PMLA*, 122.2, pp.522–36.

McCauley, P. (2015) *Into the Pensieve: The Philosophy and Mythology of Harry Potter*. Atglen, PA: Schiffer Publishing.

MacKenzie, G. (2015) 'The Roots and Rhetoric of the Forbidden Forest', in Pazdziora, J. P. and Snell, M. (eds) *Ravenclaw Reader: Seeking the Artistry and Meaning of J.K. Rowling's Hogwarts Saga – Essays from the St Andrews University Harry Potter Conference*. Oklahoma City: Unlocking Press, pp.75–88.

Matikkala, A. (2008) *The Orders of Knighthood and the Formation of the British Honours System, 1660–1760*. Woodbridge: The Boydell Press.

Millman, J. (2005) 'To Sir, With Love', in Lakey, M. (ed.) *Mapping the World of Harry Potter*. Dallas, TX: Benbella Books, pp.39–52.

Milton, J. (1997 [1671]) *Milton: The Complete Shorter Poems.* Carey, J. (ed.) Longman: London.

Milton, J. (2007 [1667]) *Paradise Lost.* Fowler, A. (ed.) 2nd ed. rev. Harlow: Pearson Longman.

Neal, C. (2008) *The Gospel According to Harry Potter: The Spiritual Journey of the World's Greatest Seeker.* Westminster: John Knox Press.

Nel, P. (2001) *J. K. Rowling's Harry Potter Novels: A Reader's Guide.* New York: Continuum.

Niditch, S. (2010) 'Hebrew Bible and Oral Literature: Misconceptions and New Directions', in Coote, R. B. and Weissenrieder, A. (eds) *The Interface of Orality and Writing: Speaking, Seeing, Writing in the Shaping of New Genres.* Tübingen: Mohr Siebeck.

Ostry, E. (2003) 'Accepting Mudbloods: The Ambivalent Social Vision of J. K. Rowling's Fairy Tales', in Anatol, G. L. (ed.) *Reading Harry Potter: Critical Essays.* Westport: Praeger, pp.89–101.

Parke, H. W. (1939) *A History of the Delphic Oracle.* Oxford: Basil Blackwell.

Patten, R. (2011) 'Serial Literature', in Schlicke, P. and Callow, S. (eds) *The Oxford Companion to Charles Dickens,* anniversary edn. Oxford: Oxford University Press, pp.527–31.

Penn, W. (1718) *More Fruits of Solitude: Being the Second Part of Reflections and Maxims, Relating to the Conduct of Human Life.* London: J. Sowle.

Prinzi, T. (2009) *Harry Potter & Imagination: The Way Between Two Worlds.* Allentown, PA: Zossima Press.

Reschan, S. C. (2015) 'A Bridge To Dystopia: Reading the Harry Potter Series as a Collapsing Utopia', in Pazdziora, J. P. and Snell, M. (eds) *Ravenclaw Reader: Seeking the Artistry and Meaning of J.K. Rowling's Hogwarts Saga – Essays from the St Andrews University Harry Potter Conference.* Oklahoma City: Unlocking Press, pp.121–37.

Richards, J. C. (2015) 'Towards a Pattern of Paternal Atonement: The Role of Snape in *Harry Potter*' in Pazdziora, J. P. and Snell, M. (eds) *Ravenclaw Reader: Seeking the Artistry and Meaning of J.K. Rowling's Hogwarts Saga – Essays from the St Andrews University Harry Potter Conference.* Oklahoma City: Unlocking Press, pp.163–73.

Ricks, C. (2002) *Allusion to the Poets.* Oxford: Oxford University Press.

Rowling, J. K. (1997a) *Harry Potter and the Philosopher's Stone.* London: Bloomsbury.

Rowling, J. K. (1997b) Interview with Judith Woods, *The Scotsman,* 20 Nov. Available at: http://www.accio-quote.org/articles/1997/1197-scotsman-woods.html

Rowling, J. K. (1998a) *Harry Potter and the Chamber of Secrets.* London: Bloomsbury.

Rowling, J. K. (1998b) Interview with Anne Simpson, *The Herald,* 7 Dec. Available at: http://www.accio-quote.org/articles/1998/1298-herald-simpson.html

Rowling, J. K. (1998c) STVEntsandComedy (2010) *Harry Potter author JK Rowling in early interview.* Available at: https://www.youtube.com/watch?v=kn7nlfoMcwQ

Rowling, J. K. (1998d) 'What was the Name of that Nymph Again? Or Greek and Roman Studies Recalled', *Pegasus* 41, pp.25–7.

Rowling, J. K. (1999a) *Harry Potter and the Prisoner of Azkaban.* London: Bloomsbury.

Rowling, J. K. (1999b) Interview with Joanna Carey, *Guardian Unlimited,* 16 Feb. Available at: http://www.accio-quote.org/articles/1999/0299-guardian-carey.htm

Rowling, J. K. (1999c) Interview with Judy O'Malley, *Book Links,* July. Available at: http://www.accio-quote.org/articles/1999/0799-booklinks-omalley.html

Rowling, J. K. (1999d) Interview with James Naughtie, *BBC Radio 4 Bookclub,* 1 Aug. Available at: http://www.bbc.co.uk/programmes/p00fpv7t

Rowling, J. K. (1999e) Interview with Christopher Lydon, *The Connection* (WBUR Radio), 12 Oct. Available at: http://www.accio-quote.org/articles/1999/1099-connectiontransc2.htm#p18

Rowling, J. K. (1999f) Interview with Diane Rehm, *The Diane Rehm Show*, 20 Oct. Available at: http://thedianerehmshow.org/shows/1999-12-24/jk-rowling-author-harry-potter-series-scholastic-originally-aired-1020

Rowling, J. K. (1999g) Interview with Stephanie Loer, *The Boston Globe*, 18 Oct. Available at: http://www.accio-quote.org/articles/1999/1099-bostonglobe-loer.html#eyes

Rowling, J. K. (2000a) *Harry Potter and the Goblet of Fire*. London: Bloomsbury.

Rowling, J. K. (2000b) Interview with Brad Crawford, *Writer's Digest*, 11 March. Available at: http://www.writersdigest.com/writing-articles/by-writing-genre/young-adult-childrens/jk_rowling_on_setting_priorities

Rowling, J. K. (2000c) 'From Mr Darcy to Harry Potter by way of Lolita', *The Sunday Herald*, 21 May. Available at: http://www.accio-quote.org/articles/2000/autobiography.html

Rowling, J. K. (2000d) Interview with Ann Treneman, *The Times*, 30 June. Available at: http://www.accio-quote.org/articles/2000/0600-times-treneman.html

Rowling, J. K. (2000e) Answering readers' questions on *South West News Service*, 8 July. Available at: http://www.accio-quote.org/articles/2000/0700-swns-alfie.htm

Rowling, J. K. (2000f) Interview with Lizo Mzimba, *cBBC Newsround*, 8 July. Available at: http://www.accio-quote.org/articles/2000/0700-cbbc-mzimba.htm.

Rowling, J. K. (2000g) Interview with Anne Johnstone, *The Herald* (Glasgow), 8 July. Available at: http://www.accio-quote.org/articles/2000/0708-herald-johnstone.html

Rowling, J. K. (2000h) Interview with Alan Cowell, *New York Times*, 10 July. Available at: http://www.accio-quote.org/articles/2000/0700-nyt-cowell.htm

Rowling, J. K. (2000i) Interview with Evan Solomon, *CBCNewsWorld: Hot Type*, 13 July. Available at: http://www.accio-quote.org/articles/2000/0700-hottype-solomon.htm

Rowling, J. K. (2000j) Interview with Jeff Jensen, *Entertainment Weekly*, 7 Sept. Available at: http://www.accio-quote.org/articles/2000/0900-ew-jensen.htm

Rowling, J. K. (2000k) Answering readers' questions, *Scholastic.com*, 16 Oct. Available at: http://www.accio-quote.org/articles/2000/1000-scholastic-chat.htm#cats

Rowling, J. K. (2000l) Interview with Larry King, *Larry King Live*, 20 Oct. Available at: http://transcripts.cnn.com/TRANSCRIPTS/0010/20/lkl.00.html

Rowling, J. K. (2000m) Interview with Max Wyman, *The Vancouver Sun*, 26 Oct. Available at: http://www.accio-quote.org/articles/2000/1000-vancouversun-wyman.htm

Rowling, J. K. (2000n) Interview with Sue Lawley, *Desert Island Discs*, 10 Nov. Available at: http://www.bbc.co.uk/programmes/p00949j1

Rowling, J. K. (2000o) abyhjp666 (2008) *Stephen Fry Interview with J.K. Rowling 2000 Part 3*. Available at: https://www.youtube.com/watch?v=z_XczgqkMic

Rowling, J. K. (2001a) Red Nose Day Chat, *BBC Online*, 12 March. Available at: http://www.accio-quote.org/articles/2001/0301-bbc-rednose.htm#potters

Rowling, J. K. (2001b) Interviewer unknown, *Detroit News*, 19 March. Available at: http://www.accio-quote.org/articles/2001/0301-detroitnews.htm

Rowling, J. K. (2001c) Interview with Jennie Renton, *Candis Magazine*, Nov. Available at: http://www.accio-quote.org/articles/2001/1101-candis-renton.html

Rowling, J. K. (2001d) Answering readers' questions in *Toronto Star*, 3 Nov. Available at: http://www.accio-quote.org/articles/2001/1101-torontostar.htm

Rowling, J. K. (2001e) 'Harry Potter and Me', *BBC*, 28 Dec. Available at: http://www.accio-quote.org/articles/2001/1201-bbc-hpandme.htm

Rowling, J. K. (2002a) Interview with Lindsay Fraser, *The Scotsman*, Nov. Available at: http://www.accio-quote.org/articles/2002/1102-fraser-scotsman.html

Rowling, J. K. (2002b) Persephone Diggen (2016) *J.K. Rowling and Harry Potter 60 Minutes – CBS News*. Available at: https://www.youtube.com/watch?v=5oOukI4EjY8

Rowling, J. K. (2003a) *Harry Potter and the Order of the Phoenix*. London: Bloomsbury.

Rowling, J. K. (2003b) Interview with Jeremy Paxman, *BBC Newsnight*, 19 June. Available at: http://www.accio-quote.org/articles/2003/0619-bbcnews-paxman.htm

Rowling, J. K. (2003c) Interview with Stephen Fry at the Royal Albert Hall, 26 June. Available at: http://www.accio-quote.org/articles/2003/0626-alberthall-fry.htm

Rowling, J. K. (2004a) Answering readers' questions at World Book Day Chat, 4 March. Available at: http://www.accio-quote.org/articles/2004/0304-wbd.htm

Rowling, J. K. (2004b) Answering readers' questions at Edinburgh Book Festival, 15 Aug. Available at: http://www.accio-quote.org/articles/2004/0804-ebf.htm

Rowling, J. K. (2004–12a) Archived content of JK Rowling's old website. Available at: http://www.accio-quote.org/jkrwebsite.html

Rowling, J. K. (2004–12b) Additional archived content of JK Rowling's old website. Available at: http://www.harrypotterspage.com/the-magic-makers/j-k-rowling/jk-rowling-website-updates/

Rowling, J. K. (2005a) *Harry Potter and the Half-Blood Prince*. London: Bloomsbury.

Rowling, J. K. (2005b) Interview with Melissa Anelli and Emerson Spartz, 16 July (part 2). Available at: http://www.the-leaky-cauldron.org/features/interviews/jkr2

Rowling, J. K. (2005c) Interview with Melissa Anelli and Emerson Spartz, 16 July (part 3). Available at: http://www.accio-quote.org/articles/2005/0705-tlc_mugglenet-anelli-3.htm

Rowling, J. K. (2005d) Edinburgh cub reporter press conference, *ITV*, 16 July. Available at: http://www.accio-quote.org/articles/2005/0705-edinburgh-ITV cubreporters.htm

Rowling, J. K. (2005e) Interview with Emma Coad, *ITV*, 17 July. Available at: http://www.accio-quote.org/articles/2005/0705-itv-coad.htm

Rowling, J. K. (2005f) Interview with Lev Grossman, *Time Magazine*, 17 July. Available at: http://www.accio-quote.org/articles/2005/0705-time-grossman.htm

Rowling, J. K. (2005g) Interview with Stephen Fry, *BBC Radio 4*, 10 Dec. Available at: http://www.accio-quote.org/articles/2005/1205-bbc-fry.html

Rowling, J. K. (2005h) Interview with Carrie Blake, *Girl Guiding Scotland*, undated (c.2005). Available at: http://www.accio-quote.org/articles/2005/0805-girlguiding-blake.html

Rowling, J. K. (2005i) EJohnson1988 (2009) *JK Rowling Interview 2005*. Available at: https://www.youtube.com/watch?v=pig7DhMqfG4

Rowling, J. K. (2006a) Interview with Geordie Greig, *Tatler*, Feb. Available at: http://mobile.jkrowling.com/uploads/documents/en_GB-press-specialjk-1373472608.pdf

Rowling, J. K. (2006b) Answering readers' questions, Radio City Music Hall, New York, 2 Aug. Available at: http://www.accio-quote.org/articles/2006/0802-radiocityreading2.html#petunia

Rowling, J. K. (2006c) gazconvery (2006) *jk rowling discussing Hagrid*. Available at: https://www.youtube.com/watch?v=a6Fdzl87RoY

Rowling, J. K. (2007a) *Harry Potter and the Deathly Hallows*. London: Bloomsbury.

Rowling, J. K. (2007b) Rowling's on-line diary, 6 Feb. Available at: http://www.hp-lexicon.org/about/sources/jkr.com/jkr-com-diary.html

Rowling, J. K. (2007c) Interview with Jonathan Ross, on *Friday Night with Jonathan Ross*, 6 July. Available at: http://www.accio-quote.org/articles/2007/0706-bbc-ross.html

Rowling, J. K. (2007d) *Blue Peter (CBBC)*, 20 July. Available at: http://www.accio-quote.org/articles/2007/0720-bluepeter.html

Rowling, J. K. (2007e) Interview with Meredith Vieira, *Today Show (NBC)*, 26 July. Available at: http://www.accio-quote.org/articles/2007/0726-today-vieira2.html

Rowling, J. K. (2007f) Bloomsbury Live Chat, 30 July. Available at: http://www.accio-quote.org/articles/2007/0730-bloomsbury-chat.html

Rowling, J. K. (2007g) Interview with Shawn Adler, *MTV News*, 17 October. Available at: http://www.mtv.com/news/1572107/harry-potter-author-jk-rowling-opens-up-about-books-christian-imagery/

Rowling, J. K. (2007h) Answering readers' questions at Carnegie Hall, 20 Oct. Available at: http://www.the-leaky-cauldron.org/2007/10/20/j-k-rowling-at-carnegie-hall-reveals-dumbledore-is-gay-neville-marries-hannah-abbott-and-scores-more/

Rowling, J. K. (2007i) Interview with Wilma de Rek, *Volkskrant*, 11 Nov. Available at:http://www.the-leaky-cauldron.org/2007/11/19/new-interview-with-j-k-rowling-for-release-of-dutch-edition-of-deathly-hallows.

Rowling, J. K. (2007j) Writing in the auction catalogue for *The Tales of Beedle the Bard* (auctioned 13 Dec). Available at: http://www.accio-quote.org/

Rowling, J. K. (2007k) Interview with Pottercast, 23 Dec. Available at: http://www.the-leaky-cauldron.org/2007/12/23/transcript-of-part-1-of-pottercast-s-jk-rowling-interview/

Rowling, J. K. (2007l) szarka86 (2011) *J.K. Rowling – A Year in the Life (TV, 2007)*. Available at: https://www.youtube.com/watch?v=p6-6zaa4NI4

Rowling, J. K. (2007m) Answering readers' questions, *Beyond Hogwarts*. Available at: http://www.beyondhogwarts.com/harry-potter/articles/jk-rowling-goes-beyond-the-epilogue.html

Rowling, J. K. (2008a) Interview with Juan Cruz, *El Pais*, 8 Feb. Available at: http://elpais.com/diario/2008/02/08/cultura/1202425201_850215.html.

Rowling, J. K. (2008b) Interview with Juan Cruz, *El Pais*, 8 Feb (translated longer version). Available at: http://www.the-leaky-cauldron.org/2008/02/09/jkr-discusses-dursley-family-religion-us-presidential-election-and-more-in-new-interview/

Rowling, J. K. (2008c) Interview with Adeel Amini, *The Student*, 4 March. Available at: http://gallery.the-leaky-cauldron.org/default/fullpic/207264

Rowling, J. K. (2008d) Harvard Commencement Address, 'The Fringe Benefits of Failure, and the Importance of Imagination', 5 June. Available at: http://harvardmagazine.com/2008/06/the-fringe-benefits-failure-the-importance-imagination.

Rowling, J. K. (2008e) Bloomsbury Publishing (2008) *J.K. Rowling at The Tales of Beedle the Bard launch*. Available at: https://www.youtube.com/watch?v=123piPzHq2Y

Rowling, J. K. (2010a) Answers readers' questions at the White House Easter Egg Roll, 5 Apr. Available at: http://www.accio-quote.org/articles/2010/0405-white-house-eggroll.html

Rowling, J. K. (2010b) Interview with Oprah, *The Oprah Winfrey Show*, 1 Oct. Available at: http://www.oprah.com/oprahshow/The-Brilliant-Mind-Behind-Harry-Potter

Rowling, J. K. (2010c) Hans Christian Andersen award acceptance speech, 19 Oct. Available at: http://www.alwaysjkrowling.com/j-k-rowling/speeches/hans-christian-andersen/

Rowling, J. K. (2011a) 'When Steve Met Jo: *Harry Potter's* Creator Remembers Her Collaboration with Steve Kloves', *Written By* (April/May). Available at: http://bluetoad.com/publication/?i=67460&p=36

Rowling, J. K. (2011b) The Telegraph (2011) 'JK Rowling unveils Pottermore website'. Available at: https://www.youtube.com/watch?v=M3ZYNOlgy1s

Rowling, J. K. (2011c) Interview with Claire Vaughan, *Who Do You Think You Are?* Oct. Available at: http://mobile.jkrowling.com/uploads/documents/en_GB-press-wdytya-1373364821.pdf

Rowling, J. K. (2012a) Interview with Mark Lawson, *Frontrow*, 27 Sept. Available at: http://www.bbc.co.uk/programmes/b01mx27g

Rowling, J. K. (2012b) Interview with Jennifer Byrne, posted by SnitchSeeker.com, 27 Sept. Available at: https://www.youtube.com/watch?v=VEy3uVfphP4&feature=player_embedded

Rowling, J. K. (2012c) Interview with Jennifer Byrne, *The Age*, 29 Sept. Available at: http://www.theage.com.au/lifestyle/life-after-harry-20120928-26fr5.html

Rowling, J. K. (2012d) Interview with Ian Parker, *The New Yorker*, 1 Oct. Available at: http://www.newyorker.com/magazine/2012/10/01/mugglemarch?currentPage=all.

Rowling, J. K. (2012e) 'J. K. Rowling: By the Book', *New York Times*, 11 Oct. Available at: http://www.nytimes.com/2012/10/14/books/review/j-k-rowling-by-the-book.html?_r=0

Rowling, J. K. (2012f) Scholastic webchat, 11 Oct. Available at: http://www.snitchseeker.com/harry-potter-news/live-video-jk-rowlings-new-webchat-and-interview-from-harry-potter-reading-club-91343/

Rowling, J. K. (2012g) Dan Radcliffe (2012) *jkr* [Interview with Charlie Rose, 19 Oct]. Available at: https://www.youtube.com/watch?v=ZvmcT9vRmK0

Rowling, J. K. (2012h) Jessi Morganster (2012) *The Women of Harry Potter – Special from the Deathly Hallows II*. Available at: https://www.youtube.com/watch?v=etNcsShL3F0

Rowling, J. K. (2012i) the1harrypotterfan (2012) *#1 Harry Potter Fan reads Personal Letter from JK Rowling*. Available at: https://www.youtube.com/watch?v=6ryDS3VdVR8

Rowling, J. K. (2012j) Interview to advertise *The Casual Vacancy* (undated, unnamed interviewer). Available at: https://www.littlebrown.co.uk/Articles/jk-rowling-interview.page

Rowling, J. K. (2012–14). Writing on 'Platform Nine and Three-Quarters' in 'The Hogwarts Express' moment in *Philosopher's Stone* on the old *Pottermore* website. Available at: http://pottermore.wikia.com/wiki/

Rowling, J. K. (2013a) Emily Temple (2013) Photograph for the grid of *Order of Phoenix* from Rowling's old website. Available at: http://flavorwire.com/391173/famous-authors-handwritten-outlines-for-great-works-of-literature/2

Rowling, J. K. (2013b) Interview with J. J. Marsh, *Words with Jam*, 25 May. Available at: http://www.wordswithjam.co.uk/2013/05/tea-cake-with-jk-rowling-need-we-say.html.

Rowling, J. K. (2013c) 'The Power of Charm Bracelets', *Harpers Bazaar*, Dec. Available at: http://www.harpersbazaar.co.uk/fashion/jewellery-watches/j-k-rowling-on-charm-bracelets

Rowling, J. K. (2013d) HarryPotterAdmirer (2013) *A Conversation between JK Rowling and Daniel Radcliffe.* Available at: https://www.youtube.com/watch?v=7BdVHWz1DPU

Rowling, J. K. (2013e) Farah Mohamud (2013) *Plotting Potter.* Available at: https://www.youtube.com/watch?v=V_m0V1OLaKo

Rowling, J. K. (2014a) Interview with Emma Watson, *Wonderland,* 7 Feb. Available at: http://www.hypable.com/jk-rowling-ron-hermione-interview/

Rowling, J. K. (2014b) 'What's on J.K. Rowling's Bookshelf?', *OMagazine,* 19 June. Available at: http://www.oprah.com/omagazine/JK-Rowlings-Bookshelf

Rowling, J. K. (2014c) abyhjp666 (2014) *Val McDermid interviews JK Rowling (Robert Galbraith) at Harrogate International Festival 2014.* Available at: https://www.youtube.com/watch?v=TbvJbbgFhrQ

Rowling, J. K. (2014d) Potty (2014) *Harry Potter Bonus DVD 2: Interview auters (J.K. Rowling et Steve Kloves.* Available at: https://www.youtube.com/watch?v=LPX_q3JVFSw

Rowling, J. K. (2015a) 'Azkaban', *Pottermore.* Available at: https://www.pottermore.com/writing-by-jk-rowling/azkaban

Rowling, J. K. (2015b) 'Beauxbatons Academy of Magic', *Pottermore.* Available at: https://www.pottermore.com/writing-by-jk-rowling/beauxbatons-academy-of-magic

Rowling, J. K. (2015c) 'Cauldrons', *Pottermore.* Available at: https://www.pottermore.com/writing-by-jk-rowling/cauldrons-

Rowling, J. K. (2015d) 'Dolores Jane Umbridge', *Pottermore.* Available at: https://www.pottermore.com/writing-by-jk-rowling/dolores-umbridge

Rowling, J. K. (2015e) 'Draco Malfoy', *Pottermore.* Available at: https://www.pottermore.com/writing-by-jk-rowling/draco-malfoy

Rowling, J. K. (2015f) 'Familiars', *Pottermore.* Available at: https://www.pottermore.com/writing-by-jk-rowling/familiars

Rowling, J. K. (2015g) 'Gilderoy Lockhart', *Pottermore.* Available at: https://www.pottermore.com/writing-by-jk-rowling/gilderoy-lockhart

Rowling, J. K. (2015h) 'Hogwarts Ghosts', *Pottermore.* Available at: https://www.pottermore.com/writing-by-jk-rowling/hogwarts-ghosts

Rowling, J. K. (2015i) 'Hogwarts's School Subjects', *Pottermore.* Available at: https://www.pottermore.com/writing-by-jk-rowling/hogwarts-school-subjects

Rowling, J. K. (2015j) 'Illness and Disability', *Pottermore.* Available at: https://www.pottermore.com/writing-by-jk-rowling/illness-and-disability

Rowling, J. K. (2015k) 'King's Cross Station', *Pottermore.* Available at: https://www.pottermore.com/writing-by-jk-rowling/kings-cross-station

Rowling, J. K. (2015l) 'The Knight Bus', *Pottermore.* Available at: https://www.pottermore.com/writing-by-jk-rowling/the-knight-bus

Rowling, J. K. (2015m) 'The Leaky Cauldron', *Pottermore.* Available at: https://www.pottermore.com/writing-by-jk-rowling/the-leaky-cauldron

Rowling, J. K. (2015n) 'Naming Seers', *Pottermore.* Available at: https://www.pottermore.com/writing-by-jk-rowling/naming-seers

Rowling, J. K. (2015o) 'Order of Merlin', *Pottermore.* Available at: https://www.pottermore.com/writing-by-jk-rowling/order-of-merlin

Rowling, J. K. (2015p) 'Polyjuice Potion', *Pottermore.* Available at: https://www.pottermore.com/writing-by-jk-rowling/polyjuice-potion

Rowling, J. K. (2015q) 'Remus Lupin', *Pottermore.* Available at: https://www.pottermore.com/writing-by-jk-rowling/remus-lupin

Rowling, J. K. (2015r) 'The Sword of Gryffindor', *Pottermore*. Available at: https://www.pottermore.com/writing-by-jk-rowling/the-sword-of-gryffindor

Rowling, J. K. (2015s) 'Sybill Trelawney', *Pottermore*. Available at: https://www.pottermore.com/writing-by-jk-rowling/sybill-trelawney

Rowling, J. K. (2015t) 'Thestrals', *Pottermore*. Available at: https://www.pottermore.com/writing-by-jk-rowling/thestrals

Rowling, J. K. (2015u) 'Wand Woods', *Pottermore*. Available at: https://www.pottermore.com/writing-by-jk-rowling/wand-woods

Rowling, J. K. (2016) The Rowling Library (2016) *J.K. Rowling at the Fantastic Beasts European Premiere in London (November 15, 2016)*. Available at: https://www.youtube.com/watch?v=rkd1WA5XBww

Rutter, C. C. (ed.) (1999) *Documents of the Rose Playhouse*. Manchester: Manchester University Press.

Sax, B. (2013) *Imaginary Animals: The Monstrous, the Wondrous and the Human*. London: Reaktion Books.

Saxena, V. (2012) *The Subversive Harry Potter: Adolescent Rebellion and Containment in the J.K. Rowling Novels*. Jefferson, NC: McFarland.

Scamander, N. [J.K. Rowling] (2001) *Fantastic Beasts and Where to Find Them*. London: Bloomsbury and Obscurus Books.

Seymour, M. C. (ed.) (2002) *The Defective Version of Mandeville's Travels*, EETS 319. Oxford: Early English Text Society.

Shakespeare, W. (1986) *The Complete Works*. Wells, S. and Taylor G. (eds) Oxford: Oxford University Press.

Skyinsane (2013) *REDDIT Today I learned*. Available at: http://www.reddit.com/r/todayilearned/comments/1acfy6/til_that_vol_de_mort_means_flight_from_death_in/

Slater, A. P. (1988) 'Petrarchism Come True in *Romeo and Juliet*', in D. J. Palmer et al. (eds) *Images of Shakespeare: Proceedings of the Third Congress of the International Shakespeare Association*. Newark, DE: University of Delaware Press, pp.129–50.

Smith, K. M. (2003) 'Harry Potter's Schooldays: J.K. Rowling and the British Boarding Novel', in Anatol, G. L. (ed.) *Reading Harry Potter: Critical Essays*. Westport, CT: Praeger, pp.69–87.

Smith, S. (2002) *J.K. Rowling: A Biography*. London: Arrow Books.

Snyder, S. (1979) *The Comic Matrix of Shakespeare's Tragedies: Romeo and Juliet, Hamlet, Othello and King Lear*. Princeton, NJ: Princeton University Press.

Spector, S. (ed.) (1991 [c.1425–75]) *The N-Town Play: Cotton MS Vespasian D.8*. 2 vols. Oxford: The Early English Text Society.

Spencer, R. A. (2015) *Harry Potter and the Classical World: Greek and Roman Allusions in J.K. Rowling's Modern Epic*. Jefferson, NC: McFarland.

Spenser, E. (1997 [1595]) *Edmund Spenser's Amoretti and Epithalamion: A Critical Edition*. Larsen, K. J. (ed.) Tempe, AZ: Medieval and Renaissance Texts and Studies.

Spenser, E. (2001 [1590/96]) *The Faerie Queene*. Hamilton, A. C., Yamashita, H. and Suzuki, T. (eds) London: Longman.

Steege, D. K. (2002) 'Harry Potter, Tom Brown, and the British School Story: Lost in Transit?', in Whited, L. A. (ed.) *The Ivory Tower and Harry Potter: Perspectives on a Literary Phenomenon*. Columbia, MO: University of Missouri Press, pp.140–56.

Steveker, L. (2015) 'Alternative Worlds: Popular Fiction (Not Only) for Children', in Berberich, C. (ed.) *The Bloomsbury Introduction to Popular Fiction*. London: Bloomsbury, pp.147–62.

Stevens, M. and Cawley, A. C. (ed.) (1994 [c.1450]) *The Towneley Plays*. 2 vols. Oxford: Early English Texts Society.

Stouffer, T. (2007) *The Complete Idiot's Guide to The World of Harry Potter*. New York: Penguin.

Sunderland, J., Dempster, S. R. and Thistlethwaite, J. (2016) *Children's Literacy Practices and Preferences: Harry Potter and Beyond*. Abingdon: Routledge.

Tennyson, A. (2004 [1850]) *In Memoriam*, Gray, E. (ed.) 2nd edn. New York: W. W. Norton & Company.

Thakrar, N. (2014) *J.K. Rowling*. Available at: http://www.findingfabulous.co.uk/blog/jk-rowling

Tolkien, J. R. R. (1997) *The Monsters and the Critics and Other Essays*. Tolkien, C. (ed.) London: HarperCollins.

Tolkien, J. R. R., Gordon, E. V. and Davis, N. (eds) (1966 [c.1390?]) *Sir Gawain and the Green Knight*, 2nd edn. Oxford: Oxford University Press.

Viducus (2014) *Deae Rosmertae: to the Goddess Rosmerta*. Available at: http://www.deomercurio.be/en/rosmertae.html

Villaluz, N. S. (2008) *Does Harry Potter Tickle Sleeping Dragons?* Seattle, WA: Ramance Press.

Wallis Budge, E. A. (1896) *An Egyptian Reading Book For Beginners*. London.

Walpole, H. (2001 [1764]) *The Castle of Otranto*, Gamer, M. (ed.) London: Penguin.

Wannamaker, A. (2008) *Boys in Children's Literature and Popular Culture: Masculinity, Abjection, and the Fictional Child*. New York: Routledge.

Williams, S. (2002) 'The Tragic Actor and Shakespeare', in Wells, S. and Stanton, S. (eds) *The Cambridge Companion to Shakespeare on Stage*. Cambridge: Cambridge University Press, pp.118–36.

Wolosky, S. (2010) *The Riddles of Harry Potter: Secret Passages and Interpretative Quests*. New York: Palgrave Macmillan.

Wyatt, T. (1978 [c.1526]) *Sir Thomas Wyatt: The Complete Poems*. Rebholz, R. A. (ed.) London: Penguin.

Index

Taylor & Francis eBooks

Helping you to choose the right eBooks for your Library

Add Routledge titles to your library's digital collection today. Taylor and Francis ebooks contains over 50,000 titles in the Humanities, Social Sciences, Behavioural Sciences, Built Environment and Law.

Choose from a range of subject packages or create your own!

Benefits for you

» Free MARC records
» COUNTER-compliant usage statistics
» Flexible purchase and pricing options
» All titles DRM-free.

Benefits for your user

» Off-site, anytime access via Athens or referring URL
» Print or copy pages or chapters
» Full content search
» Bookmark, highlight and annotate text
» Access to thousands of pages of quality research at the click of a button.

eCollections – Choose from over 30 subject eCollections, including:

Archaeology	Language Learning
Architecture	Law
Asian Studies	Literature
Business & Management	Media & Communication
Classical Studies	Middle East Studies
Construction	Music
Creative & Media Arts	Philosophy
Criminology & Criminal Justice	Planning
Economics	Politics
Education	Psychology & Mental Health
Energy	Religion
Engineering	Security
English Language & Linguistics	Social Work
Environment & Sustainability	Sociology
Geography	Sport
Health Studies	Theatre & Performance
History	Tourism, Hospitality & Events

For more information, pricing enquiries or to order a free trial, please contact your local sales team: www.tandfebooks.com/page/sales